THE COMIC INQUISITION

Conversations with Great Comedians

by John Hind

VIRGIN

First published in Great Britain in 1991 by
Virgin Books
26 Grand Union Centre
338 Ladbroke Grove
London W10 5AH

ISBN 0 86369 352 0

Typeset by Medcalf Type Ltd, Bicester, Oxon
Printed and bound in Great Britain by
Biddles Ltd, Guildford and King's Lynn

This book is dedicated to:

Roberta Valensi-Hind (who did the shopping)
Dorothy Hulme (who once asked if I had a sense of humour)
and Stan Laurel (who was born about 100 years ago)

Thanks to:

David Boszormenyi, John Cleese, Jo Foster, John Gamble, Stephen Gordon, Alan Hind, Gillian Hind, Jacquie Hind, Cat Ledger, Natalia G. Levkoeva, Stephen Mosco, Judith Murray, Marcus Osborne, Gerry Sadowitz, Sonia Serafin, Irene Simpson, Maureen Thannet, Jane Wright

Special thanks to all those humorists who lent their time and roots

CONTENTS

THE AUTHOR

John Hind has written for many publications, amongst them *Blitz, Punch,* the *Listener,* the *Sunday Correspondent,* the *Face, Punch,* the *Truth, i-D, New Society & New Statesman.* He was co-editor of *Ego* magazine. His previous books were *Dominance & Submission* with Irene Simpson and *Rebel Radio* with Stephen Mosco. John Hind is a self-confessed humorologist. In his spare time he collects damp flannels.

FOREWORD

Excuse my husband's sledgehammer wit, Mr Johnson.
– Cybil Fawlty

In this book I have set out to explore the world of the humorist, to create a mass comic biography, of sorts.

In the introductory chapter I succumb to laughter and I aim to celebrate humour's glorious existence, but at the same time to ponder the strange forces creating it. Great Humorists, meanwhile, are those people who need comedy and laughter the most, who want to comede and set about doing it with a vengeance, and who produce great laughter in us as a result. For that reason it seems fitting to concentrate on great humorists for the purpose of comic celebration and inquiry. The introductory chapter to this book contains both my musings on laughter and comic theory, plus short immersions in the comic and private worlds of various humorists who are sadly no longer alive. Plus Woody Allen, who – as it happens – still is, although he daily 'ponders' suicide.

In the following fourteen chapters I consider, and make contact with, fourteen living humorists of great interest. Aside from my composed interludes (taking in numerous minor points and quotes), the chapters contain, most importantly, question and answer sessions, or rather *conversations*. I met and spoke to each of the fourteen humorists at least once, more usually twice or more. Several of the interviews initially came about through magazine-writing assignments I arranged, the bulk through making businesslike or casual contact concerning this book. To Victoria Wood, for instance, I sent a large picture of Margaret Rutherford with her mouth open, plus a note requesting we converse 'over a piping hot flagon of coffee'. To most of the humorists I sent a letter which began by pronouncing them each 'a wit, a philosopher, a scholar and a gentle(wo)man', before double-crossing, and thereafter attacking them *momentarily* with less kind words.

We met at various different places, sometimes at their homes. Some of the photographs are mine, others were taken by associates and acquaintances. After I had conversed in earnest with the humorists I asked some of them, if the circumstances seemed right, whether I could borrow a photograph of themselves at 'a younger age'. Where forthcoming they are enclosed.

The one unusual case of interview circumstances contained in this book is that with Steve Martin. Whereas I met all the other humorists in 'repose', as it were, I only conversed with Steve Martin (at a slight distance) by, *as much as possible*, dominating a small press conference I attended. When I got home and transcribed the responses I had on tape from this event I decided that my material on the 'shy' but 'diplomatic' Martin was still interesting enough in itself to warrant inclusion in this book, despite no really close contact with him being made.

All the humorists covered in this book are, in my opinion, *great* humorists. They too are *all* highly engaging characters off stage. There were, of course, assorted other people I would have liked to include; Richard Pryor, Robin Williams, Spike Milligan, Sam Kinison, P. J. O'Rourke and Sarah Bernhardt amongst them. Of them, 'Another time I hope'.

My greatest regret, however, is over Max Wall, who agreed through his agent to talk to me, only for the agent to cancel the arrangement when Wall became ill/disturbed. He later died, in mid-1990, in his council flat.

I hope readers will not mind my interest in childhood and formative roots in the lives of humorists. I also hope I will not be admonished *too* severely for the no small part Laurel and Hardy play in this book (reasons for this should become apparent also in the book), and for the scarcity of women herein. Generally the book's flavours are *rather male*. In my defence I would say that there are undoubtedly fewer female than male professional comics, and that I nevertheless tried in earnest to organise meetings with several fine female comics other than Victoria Wood (all as it happens, Americans) but in the end they did not surface. Furthermore, as a male, I find it easier to understand (by reflecting within my male self) 'humour' produced by males. I would quickly add that Margaret Rutherford is portrayed in the introductory chapter as the true muse of comedy, and that my conversations with Victoria Wood played an important part in this book. I believe that further inquiry into 'female' humorists is well in order, but will leave *you* to ponder where Wood fits in here.

Of the fourteen humorists analysed *and* interviewed here, for what it's worth: seven of them have dressed up as women; only one does *not* appear 'in person' in his humour (Mike Leigh, who nevertheless composes it personally and stringently); one is Australian (or Anglo-Australian); four are American (another was born in America); five are of Jewish descent; their ages range from the 20s to the 60s; eleven of them have performed as 'comic actors'; nine are (or have been) 'stand-ups'; five or more have been 'artists' or collect art; most of them have worked in several mediums; and – most importantly – all of them have a *large* degree of control over their own comedy, thus making it a reflection of *their* minds and intents. All of them, in the main, steer clear of script-writers.

There are 997 questions to ask of great humorists. Six of them are: How *do* they do it? *Why* do they do it? Where does it *come* from? How does it *feel* while they're doing it? How does it feel the *rest* of the time? and, Do you know any good jokes?

The responses contained within this book will, I hope, work on numerous levels. Sometimes they are serious, sometimes humorous, sometimes humorous when intended seriously and sometimes serious when intended humorously. And more besides.

I would like to admit, here and now, that it *is* slightly perverse to want to chase important comedians to ground for two years and to want to make their acquaintance and grill them. In order to explain this I can only offer my long-time amusement and bemusement at the contradictions in humorists' lives and works, and add that – many years ago – a very interesting single sentence was dropped in my ear by Alison Jones, the wife of Monty Python catalyst Terry Jones: 'They're not very nice people, you know – comedians.' (I must add that she seemed to make this remark seriously but was *not* including her husband in the picture.)

Not nice people? Certainly I found them all charming, if occasionally bewildering, to converse with, and I would like to thank them all for letting me riffle through their comic drawers, so to speak.

As for *drawers* of an even more personal kind, perhaps I should end this foreword with recollections of a moment spent in the company of John Cleese, a 'silent-comedy scenario' not mentioned in the Cleese chapter herein. (I warrant you won't be able to guess at which point it occurred during the dialogue.) While in mid-conversation in a film-company charabanc Mr Cleese decided to change clothes while in my company. Stripped down to nothing but his red Y-fronts, pacing the floor, all the while eagerly expatiating on one great topic or other, Cleese gave me 'a look' in that moment which just *dared* me even to *consider* laughing.

I have to admit I didn't.

John Hind, November 1990.

AN INTRODUCTION

Nothing betrays people's characters
more than what they laugh at.
– Goethe

Creation

Eugène Ionesco, the French absurdist playwright, who was devoted to pinpointing the arbitrary nature of the world, once said – *slightly* contradicting his atheism – 'I imagine that the world was *created* as *One Big Joke.*' The only animal that this thought would concern is, of course, humankind – the only creature to develop laughter as a reflex, and laughter-making as a reflex or skill. It is interesting (but perhaps futile) to consider that at some monumental point in time the creature known as *Homo sapiens* first 'laughed'. Zoologist Konrad Lorenz, for instance, imagined, in his book *Man Meets Dog,* a band of prehistoric hunters crossing the bush, shaken by their recent encounter with a sabre-toothed tiger, then suddenly startled by a sound which turns out to be only a harmless antelope. 'Their fear is then replaced with relieved and excited chatter,' followed by hilarious laughter. But this theory suggests, wrongly I feel, that laughter 'began' in adulthood.

Babies, of course, cry from birth. Parents respond instinctively to the shape of a baby's face, which provokes feelings of protectiveness. Crying is a direct human 'alarm' call which, nevertheless, parents can find irritating. At first babies gurgle when they are contented and not crying. Soon they acquire a propensity to smile and, later, laugh; some argue that the latter is a natural progression from the former. There are those who believe, however, that laughter grows directly out of crying rather than smiling. One only has to console or tickle or furthermore *tease* a crying youngster to see this switch occur in an instant. Thus the gurgle and cry are combined into nervous giggles, and the link between the two seems strong indeed: to wit, the phrase, 'I laughed until I cried' (and vice versa); and of course Stan Laurel's glorious comic ability to flick back and forth between smiling and sulking/crying when he was in a confusing predicament. As Samuel Richardson once wrote, 'I struggle and struggle, and try to buffet down my cruel reflections as they rise, and when I cannot, I am forced to try to make myself laugh that I may not cry, for one or other I must do.'

Birth, in effect, is both painful and an immediate let-down for all humans. One has been quite comfortable and secure in the womb, thank you. Nevertheless the relocation to 'the outside world' is made easier by a period which, aside from unpleasant (crying) times, involves varying amounts of blind (one cannot really see for many weeks) and narcissistic union with the mother's body. (For humorists' thoughts on mothers sample George Formby's song 'Oh Dear Mother' and Oliver Hardy reading out the self-composed greeting-card message – 'Happy Birthday Mother, Happy Birthday Ma, Hi Mommy Mommy, And a Hot-Cha-Cha'). The mother's protection is instinctual and the baby has instincts to remain with the mother, to feel the warmth and hear the noise (heart-beat) of her body, and to find the breast (the source of food and also a great security symbol post-birth). The mother, when *she* is happy, additionally offers noise to the child which has no meaning other than to console and show affection – and youngsters presumably take 'moods' rather than real meaning from these sounds. Her words glide into each other, they exist in themselves and float.

This early mother-child union is, some believe, the source of a lost totality that all (adult) utopians later dream of rediscovering, or somehow re-creating. It is likely that, at the back of their minds, all humans, especially males (females often shift their strongest attachment from mother to father for a time) never really want or wanted to escape that bond, a bond which – early on – involved no laughter and thus suggests there was no early *cause* for laughter. But, of course, this is impossible, absurd – either to remain in union or return properly later. The mother is not always in tune with the child and not always in its presence; other humans surface and have to be taken on board (the father, other relatives) before the child's opening eyes. As children's laughter begins at the point they can first focus on and differentiate their mother unquestionably from others (after a few months of life) it is reasonable to suggest, therefore, that a sense of humour throughout life – in each small moment of laughter – may help to re-create the narcissistic feeling of 'early life'. Just a theory . . . Whatever, by seven-months-old the mother is completely imprinted on the child as the primal source of all things, and smiles and laughter secure that bond tighter, hopefully. But importantly laughter also plays a large part in a growing child's energetic play. For children almost anything that is new, and not completely threatening, can be cause for amusement.

Childhood, in essence, revolves around simple symbols and tasks. 'Toilet training' is an important and (as months pass by) increasingly more demanding part of life. It involves 'performance', with reward and punishment. Toilet training is the second, and most forceful, parental request or *demand* placed on a youngster (if we count 'Please Shut Up' as the first). There are those, indeed, who believe that toilet-training is wound up inextricably with money matters, neuroses, rebellion/conformity and the arranging of 'Art', from orderliness ('a very well-drawn picture' or the 'tidying of a room'), to Jackson Pollock's explosive paint-splashing. As for laughter – and comedy surely is 'an art' – there seems nothing in the world, at any given time, more likely to raise a laugh than a 'fart' noise. This simple sound creates an almost universal release, given the right circumstances. It is not unknown for babies to release their very first laugh while having their nappy changed. There is meanwhile the sadistic nature to the bowels which belies, or contradicts, their role as gift-giver. Hitler, a true sadist if ever there was one, is known (there are several sources) to have farted frequently when he was making speeches. It was almost as if in those moments – howling the odious but heart-felt words he did – he felt anally relieved; in effect his bowel movements meant 'I don't *care*' or '*Now I'm really in control*.' Hitler was, of course, a 'failed' artist, also a man daily beaten by his father as a youngster, and that he did not remain an artist or – indeed – develop a more humorous approach to life (and become a comedian perhaps) the world can only now regret. As for more pedestrian cruelty, children indeed learn early that, as well as having fun with laughter, they can also be cruel – belittling and distancing someone by laughing at them. But few, I hope, would suggest that this is as unpleasant as destroying them. Thomas Carlyle once proposed that 'No man who has once heartily and wholly laughed can be altogether irreclaimably bad.'

Laughter, after all, *feels* good and doesn't really do the laugher any harm. Well, perhaps it does *a little*. People have actually *died laughing* (what a way to go). They've also laughed *at* death. But let's ponder for a while the fine and noble nature of this 'respiratory convulsion'. Comedy certainly came close to being universal during 'silent' days when speech was displaced or refined into pure body language. And certainly laughter is understood, as a sound, the world over. It can be health-giving or health-enhancing, and the latter at least has been scientifically proved. Saliva tests, administered to large groups of people before and after they had seen, on the one hand a comedy film, and on the other a realistic, slightly downbeat documentary showed that the humour watchers came out afterwards possessing more antibodies to resist illness. Laughter, too, can create or preserve great bonds; one's laugh can draw a laugh from another person in return. Laughter – as a form of nervous release – can calm us about forthcoming, unsettling events (our own – unspoken – death being the big one). Laughter can console us and make up for disappointments. Uncontrollable laughter, meanwhile, often occurs a while after a disaster of some kind, from relief that something awful that has happened is now not *so* bad in retrospect, but also when the situation is really as bad as it seemed. This 'excessive' reflex is most associated with women (thus 'hysterical', resulting from *hustera*, the Greek word for womb), but it is far from unknown in men. Hysterical laughter is the necessary, but overly pendulous, swing back from misery. And if, indeed, sex is the central purpose of life (if only to create more life), laughter is almost an ideal way of relieving tension connected with it. Youth is a *very* funny time. Certainly during teenage days, when sexuality is awoken (or re-awoken), people become most involved in sexual humour, and they begin to distance themselves from their parents. Furthermore the teenage years are ones in which budding humorists begin to emerge and to set about fine-tuning and contemplating more seriously their humour. But, as Jean Cocteau once claimed (or hoped), 'True youth is a quality only acquired *through age*.'

Is laughter really pure and decent? Let me contradict myself. Laughter gives pleasure but it is ultimately hostile; it seems to grow into (or from) sadistic intent. We are all animals after all. Certainly humour can be very calm and adult and sophisticated, but to be sophisticated something must have begun in 'baser' form. Children can be incredibly cruel in their 'wit'; they may laugh at the sight of a deformed person or (I have heard it!) can suggest with great amusement, 'Let's go out and piss/shit on someone.' Laughter is induced by the misfortune of others: slip on a banana-skin and the world laughs at you. It's 'heart-warming' to see someone fall flat on their buttocks, but it is 'heart-stopping' or 'life-threatening' to take a fall yourself. 'Not by wrath does one kill,' said Neitzsche, 'but by laughter.' Similarly he proposed that in laughter 'all that is evil comes together, but is *pronounced* holy and absolved by its own bliss.' 'No, I was only joking,' meanwhile, is the ultimate comic get-out; it certainly saves on the apologies. Laughter *is* rather nasty. People are often vaguely disturbed by hearing over-raucous laughter from others, almost as if the 'intent' behind the laughter is too exposed. Jokes appear to de-construct, or destroy, far more than they construct.

However, on a more positive note, the famous 'custard-pie in the face' is aggressive, but hardly dangerous. The great satire of (deadly) Voltaire and (tragic) Jonathan Swift was condemning and angry and embittered, but at its centre these men were certainly proposing or pining for a *better* world. Does it all lead to a better world though? William Hazlitt, analysing comedy, commented, 'Comedy naturally wears itself out – destroys the very food on which it lives; and – by constantly and successfully exposing the follies and weaknesses of mankind to ridicule, in the end leaves itself nothing worth laughing at.' One has to decide whether Hazlitt was making this point with a positive or negative feeling! Sigmund Freud, meanwhile, the most obsessive human-theorist and comic-theorist of them all, related humour intrinsically to the Big Three – sexuality, aggression/superiority *and* ambiguity. Genuinely assumed to be a dry analytical old stick, I will quote only one actual sentence of Freud's words directly here. They surfaced when he was forced to sign documents by the Nazis before his escape from Vienna in 1938. At the bottom of the document he chose to scribble a P.S. which went, 'I can *wholeheartedly* recommend the Gestapo to anyone'; a piece of clever, sublime, contradictory, ingratiating and aggressive wit for which he should not go unnoticed.

Laughter is animalistic but also totally human – something only *we* have. Humour has thus formed a thread through humanity's history, more often than not as a subversive force. The very first dramas were performed not as entertainment but as rituals intended to gain the benevolence of forces of nature or Gods. It is known that elements of foolery and caricature were allowed to enter these serious rituals, with certain participants, in essence, ridiculing what was otherwise being performed or espoused. The very earliest forms of folk theatre in Ancient Greece quickly incorporated comic characters, wearing happy and sad masks. In Roman times burlesques of the legends of the Gods were allowed into straight-faced theatre. From the fourteenth century onwards, and possibly before, the custom grew up of keeping a 'tame fool' or jester at royal courts – some of them were simply idiots (whatever that means), but in medieval society these 'lunatics' were regarded with some awe as being 'possessed by God' (not by the devil). Out of this custom grew 'professional' court jesters carrying a mock sceptre and wearing a hood with ass's ears and peak. Meanwhile, in French cathedrals, minor (younger) clerics took over ceremonies on one day of each year, dressed as bishops and completely burlesqued the orthodoxy of the institutions' other 364 days. Jewish tradition includes a similar festival called *Purim*.

The original Anglo-Saxon meaning of the word 'gag' was 'interpolation' – the process of improvising or adding something, to conceal memory-loss or unforeseen occurrence. 'Ha-ha' sounds remarkably like 'A-ha!', which is either the sound of surprise or realisation, *or* a statement of one's superiority. Comedy involves versatility and play with codes, conventions and meanings. It challenges, or at least tests, categories. It exercises a concept's hinges so to speak; or rather it throws an idea up in the air for at least a moment. Good jokes begin by offering an expectation but shifting from it. There is surprise and then release, and thus coherence. Contradictions exist in humour and they are resolved through laughter. There is a palpable tension in humour, as there is in the synapse that exists between comedian and audience; there is a push and pull between recognition of the familiar and the *possibility* of the casting aside of convention, of authority. The message seems to be: 'RESIST NORMALITY'. In a humorous situation one person has to cause chaos and one has to experience it, although a single person can actually take on both roles. Most jokes seem to settle for a compromise, of sorts, between affirmation and subversion. There is caring and hope there, amidst the aggression. All these factors point to the suggestion that humorists ultimately desire *reconciliation* of some kind.

George Bernard Shaw said that, 'My way of joking is to tell the truth. It's the funniest joke in the world.' George Orwell proposed that, 'The aim of a joke is not to degrade the human being but to remind him that he is *already* degraded.'

'Don't tell anyone, but you're looking at the new King of Comedy' announced Rupert Pupkin (actor Robert De Niro) in Paul D. Zimmerman's story and Martin Scorsese's film. *The King of Comedy* is perhaps the most telling, and funny, film made about the quest for comic fame. Pupkin's hero is the witty chat-show host, Jerry

Langford (Jerry Lewis). Pupkin wants to be his friend, to share his lifestyle and also succeed him as Comic King. Langford, 'a professional' who enjoys golfing in his free time and seems to live alone, has little time for Pupkin, but *Pup-kin* (meaning 'little offspring') refuses to realise this. Pupkin, aged 34, who has not even performed on stage, is desperate for fast comic fame – he believes success (becoming 'the comedy find of the year') arrives through sudden recognition. At home he jests with cardboard cut-outs of celebrities and records fake stand-up tapes of himself for his hero. Meanwhile his mother, with whom he lives and who is ever present (although never visible to us), interrupts his ramblings by calling out things like, 'Rupert, what are you doing so late down there?' (There is, meanwhile, neither sight nor the vaguest reference in the film to an actual father.) Pupkin is either masochistic or blind to the indifference of those around him from whom he wants recognition of his talents. The only messages he receives are in the order of: 'There are ground rules, you've got to start at the bottom. What looks so simple . . . it takes years and years of honing that and working that.' Pupkin lives in a dream world. He imagines audiences roaring with laughter at his material and dreams of his hero pouring great respect on his skills, asking him, 'How do you do it, you son of a bitch?' (Answer: 'I look at my life, see the awful terrible things in my life, and turn it into something funny.') And he is arrogant (or romantic) enough to want a girl he meets to become his non-comic partner instantly ('Every King needs a Queen'). He imagines himself married 'live' on television, the ceremony administered by George Kapp, his principal from high-school days who is now a justice of the peace. Kapp says to him in that dream show, 'Tonight, before the whole nation, we'd like to apologise to you personally and beg your forgiveness for all the things we did to you, and to thank you personally, all of us, for the meaning you've given our lives.' Dreams and humour and sexuality are linked strongly throughout the story. Ultimately though, in 'real life', after Langford has called him a moron (for invading his premises), Pupkin vows, 'I'm going to try 50 times harder than you and be 50 times more famous than you!' Then, in partnership with a female fan who loves and pesters Langford, he kidnaps the star and gets to perform his comedy on television as ransom-payment, with the kidnappee taped to a chair so that he is forced to watch the spectacle.

The director Scorsese ends the film in the ambiguous and contradictory fashion he is well-known for. Pupkin is imprisoned but then eventually released to continue (very successfully) his comic fame. Yet, is this simply another dream sequence . . . or is it absolutely for real? Only Scorsese knows. Is 'the comic' a good guy or a bad guy? Certainly he doesn't seem to be an excessively unpleasant person, despite the great irritation he has rather diplomatically created. And one last question is left up in the air: As a determined individual, subversive and comic (although we never really hear his jokes), is Pupkin someone who would actually be loved by the great general public, for all his faults?

'The test of a real comedian,' said George Jean Nathan, 'is whether you laugh at him before he opens his mouth.' But who really wants to be laughed at before they even open their traps? Well, most comedians presumably. Whereas almost everybody laughs and creates laughter within their lives, there is obviously something exceptional about comedians – people who wish to create and sell laughter for a living, even for *life*. They need to be humorous for its, and their, own sake but they also want *others* to experience that humour. For them comedy becomes a profession, something that has to be exercised, maintained and improved upon (if only to remain standing still in laughers' eyes). Yet every time comedians walk on stage they become gamblers.

Professional humour seems intrinsically related to a search for fame; comedians need attention, appreciation and respect, or perhaps they would not perform. Comedians keep on doing it because they are good at it, but also because each piece of attention they receive is merely momentary and transient. It is only after all *laughter*. A burst of laughter is the only *real* proof for a joker that a joke has hit its mark. 'All that the comedian has to show for his years of work and aggravation' concluded Fred Allen, 'is the *echo* of laughter.' In the 20th century this is not altogether true, as the successful comedian now at least has a book or video of their work on a shelf in the living room (and *other* peoples' living rooms), but Allen's point is taken. Comedians probably need more and more laughter to feel satisfied, and probably desire other substances (monetary or otherwise) to *prove* their worth. Does that make them any different from the rest of us?

'What you have to understand about comedians,' Alexei Sayle once said, 'is that they are *the* most egotistical, sly, cunning, self-centred individuals in the entertainment business, which is saying something.' From this overly harsh summation Sayle was presumably not excluding himself. Even if he was excluding himself (he didn't say so) his comment suggests that he has these strong forces in him – he is, after all, beating down all other comedians (his rivals) by saying such things.

Certainly professional comedians are driven by degrees of obsessiveness, high energy, anxiety and desperation. Mel Brooks summed it up thus; 'I don't think in terms of results at all. I think – what next insanity can I shock the world with? What can I say to, or for, my fellow citizens of the world? How crazy shall I be? I've got to get this stuff out of my system.' Comedians are creative people (they have created their comedy even if their comedy 'destroys') and, to quote Schopenhauer now, 'In the creative individual the sensitive system and the activity of insight remain preponderant in an abnormal way throughout his life.' Comedians are out of the ordinary, and funny and successful, one presumes, largely by dint of their *hyper*sensitivity. Great humorists are those who are the most obsessive about their humour, who have the greatest thirst and drive for it, but who also *hone* their talent like a scalpel. Whereas laughter feels, or is meant to feel, 'spontaneous', the task of creating humour is very far from spontaneous – comedians are wrapped up in its technicalities and its refinement. Comedy, a funny thing, is 'a serious job'.

Humour is, at once, childlike and adult. We should therefore take both these elements on board when considering the nature and character of comedians. While they are adults now, at least off stage, they were once children. When we look back over the roots of many great comedians of bygone years we see both adult and childlike flavours in abundance – dark and light moods, serious professional concerns, a perception and love of the profoundly silly, and – in their early roots – often a confused and uncomfortable childhood.

Before we go in search of great humorists of our time, it may be fruitful to consider, and warm to, the backgrounds and natures of some great humorists of the past.

BUSTER KEATON, for the length of his career, deliberately did not smile or laugh in his films; he remained persistently gloomy throughout. While he didn't laugh with us, the audience, he nonetheless *wanted* to be laughed at very much. He perfected for us the image of a great bungler who, at the same time, had great saving skills. Contradictions abounded in Keaton's work. Perversely he combined extremes of *good* luck and *bad* luck. He had a strange, accident-ridden, dangerous childhood, at one point being carried out of his bedroom by a cyclone. At the age of three he was co-opted into the touring 'medicine show' act of his parents – adoring mother Myra, who played musical instruments, and father Joseph, a comic monologist. 'The Keaton Two' became 'The Keaton Three'. Buster had been christened after his father; furthermore, he was dressed for the stage as a child-replica of his father. 'The Keaton Three' moved into vaudeville and Joseph Junior was then literally used as a 'prop', being thrown back and forth across the stage and between the arms of his parents. This inevitably involved taking many falls and his father taught him how to – indeed insisted that he – take them. Finally, after many years of this, and aggrieved by his father's moods and alcoholism (something the son adopted in later days), Buster departed – with his mother – to start life anew and his career proper.

CHARLIE CHAPLIN (the other founding father of 20th-century comedy), like Keaton, had a respected but *feared* male parent. Volumes and volumes have been written about Chaplin's life and works but perhaps it is worth reiterating various points here. He had a gruesome childhood of Dickensian flavour. His father, a great philanderer who punished Charlie often during the times he spent in his son's company, died of alcoholism; Charlie's strong mother became 'insane' when he was fourteen and he personally had to institutionalise her and then survive alone on the streets. Twelve years later he was a world-famous comic millionaire, a Hollywood 'stud' with a taste for teenage girls whom he desired to adore him, to 'train' in his films and, generally to treat him as a father figure. In his films he, the Tramp, reflected the pain and anguish of the poor but nevertheless stood somewhat apart from them. In real life he was a very rich man, making films about deprivation. He brought both sadness and joy to audiences in equal measure; a rare, clever and bizarre achievement. He both claimed and denied he was Jewish throughout his public life, and desired both order and chaos in his private life. As a child, he had a 'terrific inferiority complex' – on film he was an overly sentimental, even vaguely effeminate creature but on and off set he was often a tyrant. He either attracted unstable people into his private world or had a damaging affect on them personally; his first wife died from alcoholism; his second wife suffered from alcoholism and mental breakdowns; after his break-up with Edna Purvience (his most noted co-star) she was obsessively influenced by his memory to old age; his last young girlfriend (Joan Barry) became a full-blown schizophrenic after their break-up, institutionalised till her death; Chaplin is said to have threatened lovers with guns; and his second son died from alcoholism. A friend of his, Nancy Pickford, called him 'that obstinate, suspicious, egocentric, maddening and lovable genius of a problem child.' Towards the end of his own life, no longer making films, Chaplin indeed seems to have turned his attention more directly to childhood memories, taking numerous private chaffeured journeys around the streets of his desperate London childhood. 'The truth is I went into the movie business for *money*,' he once said. 'Art just sort of grew out of it.' He died crippled with gout, leaving a legacy of both human wreckage and a score of classic warm-hearted comedies.

JOSEPH GRIMALDI is reckoned to have been the funniest and most celebrated British stage pantomimist in history, the man who – in the nineteenth century – essentially created and defined the 'English Clown' (partly combining the French character 'Pierrot' with the English 'Booby'). While he, in his private life, was apparently a considerate, faithful husband and a pleasant, if rather nervous, child-rearer, his father was a deeply paranoid and tyrannical man. The father was domineering, morbid, superstitious and a notorious womaniser who maltreated his wife. He beat his son, making him stay in corners for seeming days on end under fear of death, many times holding off, and setting dates and times for, severe punishment (thus compounding their mental effect). Joseph, a performer who is said to have literally saved British pantomime, was nervous, petulant and had a morbid – but unviolent – temperament, yet once on stage he said *all* his fears dissolved in seconds.

CHARLIE RIVEL, classic clown of the late nineteenth and early twentieth century, had these words to say about his profession and professional acquaintances:

> 'The clown, the bungler, the rag-doll, is always regarded as the lowest of the low. Yet nevertheless he must be more intelligent, more human and more *sensitive* than all the others . . . I have known many clowns in my life and with very few exceptions their lives *ended* in want and misery. Once I knew a clown (and) he dearly loved a young girl. She was in love with him too, but she soon tired of him because he was a clown, a fool, a jester, whom

everyone laughed at. So she left him and he finally took his own life. I knew a clown who was well on the way to becoming famous all over the world. He already saw himself as the greatest of all clowns. But one day the audience didn't laugh at him quite so loudly and he became unsure of himself. The moment a clown starts drinking it is all up with his clowning. A few years later he was a human wreck . . .' Rivel's listings went on in a similar vein.

W. C. FIELDS (who had 300 bank accounts) stands as cinema's great *abusive* humorist. Misanthropic, misogynous and much more besides, at his 'best' he encapsulated and exaggerated what were largely his own character traits and domestic environment. His films display his arrogance and crudity, his intolerance, his silly and threatening names (Filthy McNasty, T. Fotherington Bellows *et al.*), his excessive drinking (he was a gin-fiend), his mal-shaped and mal-coloured nose, his malice and trouble-causing (the only people shown to love him, and love him deeply, in his films were fictional daughters). Was he parodying himself, satirising himself, sending himself up when acting this way? Do audiences laugh *at* him (the misery-guts) or *with* him (the anti-bureaucrat and anti-conventionalist)? Can we, the laughers, like someone who exclaimed to friends that he was currently helping a charity, the F.E.B.F., adding later that these letters stood for 'Fuck Everyone But Fields'? Fields (his real name was William Claude Dukenfield) made great play of the fact that he/his characters (he wrote the scripts under pseudonyms like Mahatma Kane Jeeves and Otis J. Criblecoblis) loathed animals and, especially, children. 'Later,' he said to a child, 'I'll take you outside and let you ride piggy-back on a buzz-saw.' 'I *never* met a kid I liked' he exclaimed . . . to him they were brats, sheer mental midgets. When his wife Harriet gave birth to a son, W. C. Fields Junior, the comedian, aged 24, left home and kept travelling alone (thereafter husband and wife kept up a correspondence mainly to argue over money). Nevertheless, Fields certainly didn't avoid putting children in his films, thus sharing their company on set, and – once – was obviously a child himself. (And when he died he left $1 million to an orphanage.) As for William's own childhood, he had an extremely strong, protective mother (Kate) who packed sandwiches for him and walked him to the road-corner when Fields left home at nineteen. His father, meanwhile, was moody and distant – in William's sister's words, 'very strict'. As children, noted the sister, William (who taught himself to juggle and conjure at an early age) and brother Walter would needle their father mercilessly 'to get his goat . . . *all for fun*', and presumably receive a lot of stick in response. William, so his later stories claimed, ran away from home many times, soon working in vaudeville – the one thing in life his father talked highly of. All evidence points to the suggestion that it was from his father's personality that Fields junior evolved his moody comic character.

MARGARET RUTHERFORD, she of the plump – almost shapeless – body, assorted wobbling chins and face like 'an English muffin',

A stern and shocked, but soothing, MARGARET RUTHERFORD
Photograph courtesy of the National Film Archive

she of the shocked expressions ('Sirrrr!'), the feather boas, tweed caps, delicate and vibrant hand flourishes, the exquisite talk, walk and prowl, was an *extraordinary* comic actress. She was an actress in part only because, although she never wrote the roles she played in theatre and on film, she nevertheless personalised and improvised around them with an eccentricity which was all her own. She personified the heroic nature of the comic, playing un-deflatable determined organisers, slightly bossy English ladies who were also (to old and young audiences) lovable, kind and extremely human. 'This is no time for sartorial tittle-tattle' she would opine, offering no time for 'shilly-shallying' except for occasional cups of tea before leaping 'into the fray, like lions refreshed'. She played, fittingly, a perpetual spinster who, seemingly, had guarded her honour but was by no means an innocent; yet at the same time she oozed motherly charm and understood that 'the infant animal needs space to breath and bloooow'. There has perhaps never been a female humorist quite like Rutherford – the mould was broken when she died in 1972 (childless). The sensitive lady did not begin performing professionally until she was in her 30s and yet almost instantly perfected a theatrical comic power and charm which stayed with her until she was 80. Most of her life she claimed bafflement at how funny people found her to be; indeed she never played for laughs, rather teased them out through her characters' natural, but eccentric, reactions to a new day, a new event, a new crisis.

It would seem that her own upbringing had much to do with the sensitive and warm portrayal of her characters. But where did she come from and how did she live her own days? Rutherford was born into a Victorian world of a mother who – when her child was just three years old – committed suicide. She did not pass into the care of her father but to her mother's sister, Aunt Bessie, a woman who gave her warmth, protection and a love of theatre. Margaret believed her father (whose real name at birth was William Benn) had died in India, sometime after her mother. Aunt Bessie, a serious believer in the occult, frequently advised Margaret that dead people's spirits floated around live relatives, watching over them and aiding them in times of trouble. On the cusp of puberty though, at the age of thirteen, Margaret discovered after all those years that her father – a manic depressive schizophrenic, a man of great mood swings – was not actually dead but incarcerated in a prison for the mentally disturbed. Thereafter she spent her life dealing with private depression. Her shock was compounded by the further disclosure that her father – long before her birth – had killed *his* father, Reverend Julius Benn, by battering in his skull, and that he had spent many years incarcerated for patricide, before lucky release and fatherhood. Such were Margaret Rutherford's roots – *The Happiest Days of Your Life*, indeed. Consequently she spent her life showing a sincere and steadfast face but nevertheless dealing with severe bouts of melancholia, the fear of 'going insane' herself, often having nightmares and nocturnal screaming fits concerning her father. It was her belief in floating dead spirits which lent her such warmth and character–sympathy towards the medium she played in *Blithe Spirit*, the droll comic masterpiece performed on stage and screen. She did not undertake acting proper until after the death of her replacement mother, Aunt Bessie (the third loss in her life). The characters she then went on to play, with such apparent ease, encapsulated all her innocence, charm, perseverance, respectability and bizarrerie but, ultimately, little of her inner sorrow. She was, in all effects, a romantic, a glorious combination of maturity and the childlike. She looked like a sexless aunt, while 'adoring' cucumber sandwiches, the great nonsense poet Edward Lear and her cuddly toys (her favourite being Minnie the stuffed mouse).

Asked about the ultimate meaning behind her work, Rutherford would first say that she liked 'to be sympathetic' then add that her pure aim in life was to make audiences 'laugh and forget their worries'. This was her simple philosophy, her release, her love . . . her selfish *and* selfless quest.

Hurt me – the pain stops when they laugh,
and they don't laugh unless you really stamp on it.
– Tony Hancock (who once said that comedy started from the feet and travelled upwards) talking about his right foot.

TONY HANCOCK, at the peak of his success, was watched and enjoyed by over fifteen million people. His full real name was Anthony John Hancock, his full fictional name Anthony Aloysius St John Hancock, the extraordinarily complex grand old small-man of 23 Railway Cuttings, East Cheam. That the latter – pompous, vulnerable, irritable, arrogant, conservative, reactionary, philosophical, mournful and determined – was named after the real man is highly relevant. He was, essentially, an extension and elaboration of the real man – composed by his wonderfully fluent comic writers (who met in a psychiatric home) but based much on their observations of Hancock off set. Hancock was the offspring of a domineering mother, who encouraged him professionally until he was close to success and *then* began criticising, and of a distant small-time theatrical father who died suddenly when his son was eleven (giving the son many father-nightmares in later life). At school Tony said he felt ugly and laughed-at (later on stage he beat himself and shouted 'I'm so ugly! I'm so ugly!'). He had little regular security in his early home-life, thus spent much time in the cinema. After his father's death he developed a forceful but highly nervous desire for comic success. His older brother died fighting in the war. In his early stage work, as a stand-up, Hancock included numerous impressions, all of them of long-dead people. It is noteworthy that he was also much more aggressive in his early stage-work, yet – during National Service – he didn't fight shy of singing the twee song 'I'm a Hero to My Mum' to Royal Air Force theatre audiences. A man with a huge ability to laugh at comedy (the sound he made he called 'The Family Chuckle') and to create laughter, he meanwhile was a profoundly – and increasingly – sad character internally.

In real-life and on stage Hancock had highly schizophrenic

thoughts, desires and values: from hour to hour, even minute to minute, he both disliked and felt attracted to mess and squalor around him (at home or in theatrical digs); he was an atheist who often said he would like to 'find' religion; he was not Jewish but often said he would have liked to have been; he disliked rest and the idea of 'family-life' (which made him depressed or edgy) but had craved this as a youngster; he was self-pitying and yet abhorred comic pathos ('it's too easy'); he did not repay small debts but often gave large gifts; he desired 'reason' and 'logic' in all things but had many superstitions; he most enjoyed the nocturnal world but wanted to express the flavours of the waking day and world; he felt hostility to audiences but wanted their love; and his laughter-making was life-giving yet he was highly self-destructive. Hancock was a great procrastinator yet also a workaholic; a gambler but a man logical enough to realise that in gambling the odds are forever stacked against you. He actually liked children but did not want to have any of his own. He was interested in 'all that life means' but was blaringly, *too* blaringly, aware that life led to death. His comic hero, Sid Field, he knew regrettably to have died as a result of alcohol, and yet Hancock took to the bottle excessively himself. He was variously romantic, moody and violent with his two wives, women who very much played mother-figures in his life.

Hancock was an anxious and masochistic practical humorist (from the 'self' he based his humour on, to the way he thought he could *never* perform well enough from one day to the next), and he was an obsessive, tormented theoretical humorist. As Hancock's life unfolded he desired his comedy to become more and more 'real', more and more universal, more and more simple yet poignant. It was an extremely delicate and potentially disastrous quest, taking apart every line of a script, reworking it and re-performing it until it was bone-dry (contradictorily, he did not like long theatrical runs). In real life he was never sure whether he wanted to be very famous and noted or stay rooted in, and keep an image of, the *pedestrian*.

With both these aims in mind he (along with brother Roger) visited Stan Laurel in Hollywood to pick the retired comic's brain, but did not realise that Laurel's success lay in his relationship with Hardy. Hancock wanted to hone and hone his comedy, bringing the camera ever *closer* to his face; indeed he was a master of faces and apparently was acutely sensitive to the reactions of all those in his company off stage. He wanted, for whatever reasons, to get rid of comic performers around him (on the same stage or set) and thus centre on 'One Man' in all his glory and misery. This led increasingly to his performances being almost schizophrenic conversations with himself (set, now, in a lonesome Earl's Court bedsit with confusing philosophy books on his table). 'Comedy' noted the comic actor, is 'frustration, misery, boredom, worry'.

During the later part of his life, drinking excessively (ultimately during work), and more and more wrapped up in the great imponderables – Where do we come from?, Where are we going?, What's it all about? – Hancock went over the edge. His great, but unobtainable, desire was to make a comedy about life 'from the first plip to the final plop'. His plop came early. In his early days on stage he had told a joke about a comic writing a suicide note, the idea being that a comic's death leaves 'One less feed to feed', yet in private he told people he thought the idea of suicide ridiculous, selfish, chicken. Ultimately though, at the age of 44, with his international cinematic dreams unfulfilled, his health and facial expressions flagging and his career and private life on a down-swing, he did take his own life, thus completely destroying the image of moody but dogged *resilience* his comic character had offered up in 150 'Hancock' shows.

He wrote his two suicide notes on a script he was soon to perform in Australia. Then he died in a drink and drugs blur (like, indeed, his mother's second husband). His notes referenced both a psychic medium and his mother. They did not contain any jokes. Which was – in itself – the biggest joke, the ultimate, ironic non-punchline. Meanwhile, we can still remember and relish the line he often ended his live performances with: 'Sanctuary!' he would cry, nay *howl*, 'Sanctuary! Sanctuary! . . . Sanctuvery-much!'

Bryan? This is Peter . . . Look, I want
to marry Nanette [*his happily-married wife*].
Is that all right with you?

PETER SELLERS was a chameleon-like actor who could, and did, wrap himself in scores of unique comic roles. At one point, taking his ability to ludicrous excess, he played seven different characters in one film alone (*Soft Beds and Hard Battles*). Sellers could play villainous, erudite, simple-minded, pompous, respectable, manic, low-key, male, female, straight and surreal, and much more besides. His career dominated his life and made him so stressed and anxious that he had little 'normal' off-screen life and was often racked with depression and schizophrenic moods. Indeed it seems to be his in-built schizophrenia which fuelled his ability to take on, and conquer, the performances he was so rightly praised for.

His parents had been vaudevillian troupers: his father a Protestant with work-ethic to boot, and his mother a Jew with an obsessive cloying personality who expected him to become famous (dressing him for it at three-years-old) and who once said, 'My son doesn't have to think for himself – I do it for him.' Ironically he was sent to a strict Roman Catholic school. After his mother died (after his father) Sellers 'kept in touch' with her through a medium. After his mould-breaking performances in the *Goon Show* he desired international film fame – something we can only be thankful for because many great actors consider that Sellers became the greatest all-round film actor of all time (although he never really received that fame because he never stuck to one recognisable role).

Yet in his private off-screen life he was deeply unsettled, had a ferocious temper and never escaped for long from uncontrollable paranoid schizophrenic tendencies. He was obsessed with himself or rather his self-centred craft (posing and rehearsing in front of mirrors). He had a strong fetish for gadgets, watches and cars, and he would give expensive jewellery as presents, then take it back. He desired to mix frequently with the respectable for its own sake, he would buy his children toys so that he could play with them himself, he had a frenzied temper, he destroyed inanimate objects, he buried and burnt things and he had four wives but never settled. The times he seemed most comfortable, indeed, were in the company of Spike Milligan, his fellow Goon and Goon-writer; he enjoyed both talking melancholically about life with Milligan *and* being extraordinarily silly and amusing with him.

Sellers' first wife said she came to know her husband as two people – the Actor and the Person. Unfortunately for her and his other wives and family-members, he spent increasingly less time in the Person mould. His son Michael once wrote, in his book *P.S. I Love You* (see Bibliography, p. 196), that Sellers could, in good times, be kind and gentle, caring and considerate, funny and joyous. 'But when the horizons clouded, and the horrific black depressive moods descended abruptly upon him,' Michael said, 'he could snarl like a tortured animal, haunted by suspicion and trapped by persecution mania, convinced that the world, and his family, were set against him . . .' He had very few memories of rational periods in his father's life.

'I'm just a big fat jolly boy' Sellers Senior once told a wife; but he was a non-returnable *man* highly nostalgic for boyhood, if not perhaps quite for his own, at least for one he dreamt of. Sellers' last film-role proper, perhaps his finest and most subtly portrayed, was in *Being There*. It is the film of a story he long pestered Hollywood to let him make, about a gentle, unassuming, innocent, childlike, sexless, totally unparanoid man, with few thoughts in his head except television images, who goes on, thanks to his personality and a few simple mistakes, to become the toast of Washington, the 'assured' benevolent graceful father-figure of the nation, and ultimately President of America. (And possibly God.) Intended presumably as a joke at the expense of politics, the media and the public, Sellers imbued this character (named Chance) with such appeal and sympathy that it seemed almost as if he was saying that was the way he would've liked to have been personally.

Sellers spent the last months of his life, aged 55, sapped of energy and humour, washing himself frequently, and at one point tossing his CBE into a dustbin. Prior to his last fatal heart-attack, and while promoting *Being There,* he phoned Spike Milligan and proposed (years after the last show): 'Let's write another *Goon Show. I want to laugh again*.'

Peter Sellers' favourite humorists were Stan Laurel, who he once went on a pilgrimage to meet and based his ambivalent Chance character on, and Laurel's perpetual partner, Oliver Hardy.

*

I was present at the cremation, and at his son's request brought the marshmallows, but few of us could think of anything but our pain.
– Woody Allen in his book *Side Effects*

WOODY ALLEN, who – of course – is still very much with us, making films almost perpetually, produced with *Stardust Memories* a grand statement on where comic philosophy and comic fame could lead. Coming after two grand New York film romances which had evolved his comedy to more graceful tones (*Annie Hall*, previously titled *Anhedonia*, and the black and white but ultimately youth-desiring *Manhattan*), as well as a humourless argumentative family drama (*Interiors*), *Stardust Memories* saw Allen portray a comedian lost between personal relationships and torn between humour and sorrow. Attacking, or rather showing up the irritations of, critics, fans, agents, film companies and assorted other pressures, the film was set around a film-festival weekend in which 'the comedian' contemplated his career and life. An elaborately and painfully crafted outing, it is one of his best works and his personal favourite, and includes the pungent line, 'If he's such a genius, why can't he make funny films anymore?' This is a film about confusion and desperation, about *paralysis*, about a comedian who wants to 'get out'. Allen gets himself, or rather 'Sandy Bates, the great comedian', to say 'I don't want to make funny movies anymore . . . I don't *feel* funny. I look around the world and all I see is suffering.' In a dream sequence within the film Allen has an extra-terrestrial creature visiting Earth and telling him, trying to convince him, that he's not the missionary type: 'If you want to help the world, tell funnier jokes!'

Since then Allen has gone on to make both funny and decidedly 'serious Art' films, both and all to be applauded, but it is worth dipping into the complexities of the man and his thoughts on the value of comedy, to understand where he stands in his 50s. 'Of the next ten' he said of his outings, several years ago, '*half* of them I'd like to be quite serious films', which of course seems perfectly fair and balanced. The point is though that all his films, serious or comic, cover serious themes (watch *Love and Death et al.*), although often he seems to be denying this. He frets that he has not made *any* great films yet and cites *The Bicycle Thief* and *La Grande Illusion* as the latter. The point is that, funny or non-funny, he will probably never make any film he is satisfied with, that being the reason he goes on making them. 'If people knew how much better my ideas were than the finished results they would not like me,' he once noted.

Meanwhile, he has down-graded comedy on various occasions. 'I like the dramas of Shakespeare and I don't like the comedies of Shakespeare very much,' he offers as support of non-comedy, adding that, 'In comedy what you want is fast-paced cutting . . . bright lights . . . you don't want the camera drifting around in a lethargic way

. . . that's not enough to wallow in when you're making a film.' He exclaims that he does not 'rank it as serious work – it doesn't confront the issues'; that comedy may deal with serious things on the way, but it's limited. 'It doesn't see the big background picture.' By this he means the 'horrible' background picture – the awful world, or rather uncontrollable life. The bottom line is that when making 'funny' or overly 'funny' films he feels as if he is somehow lying to, or fooling, the audience and himself. There is a perpetual self-hating guilt there which seems born of, or rather developed on from, rebellion from the father. His parents, a domineering Yiddisha mama (much like the mother in *Oedipus Wrecks*) and a more remote, uptight father, both frequently argued over money while he was a child. Concurrently they tried to raise him very religiously (it was, he says, 'forced on me'). The latter leaves him with seemingly ever-present confusion towards meanings and values ('My rabbi . . . used to say, "We're all guilty in the eyes of God" '/ '*Do you believe in God!*'/ 'No, no – but I'm still guilty about it.') His parents, meanwhile, are still alive today (indeed his father cleans his Oscar awards, which Allen passed on to him) and it is worth considering that it must be very hard indeed for a humorist to retain the rebellious nature needed for comedy when he has become very much an adult himself, and indeed – fairly recently – also a parent. Asked, when his wife was first pregnant by him, whether he hoped the child would be 'a chip off the old Woody', he replied, 'I very much hope it will be a *girl* – that's *very* important to me.' Nevertheless he now has male offspring. Possibly he copes with the male comedian's 'anti-son' dilemma partly by living separately, but close, to his wife . . . almost as if his work would not survive such a family environment. Similarly he says of his 'serious' films that he is marginalising his own appearances (or not appearing at all) because he 'can't get too emotional on film' as an actor. Nevertheless, he wants very much, ever more, to have his family of actors play very real emotional roles. Allen in all senses grows ever more paradoxical. He is a truly introspective personality ('I don't get an enormous input from the rest of the world') living in the most bustling city, which he loves, in the Western world. He sometimes says that the characters in his films are not really him or reflections of him – that he merely draws on his own experiences, such as his 'type of profession', to give his work 'a sense of verisimilitude'. At other times he says the films are about him and that 'I try to be *completely* honest in my films'. Certainly he is confused, saying – off screen and in apparent seriousness – that there is not a day he does not consider suicide, at least as 'an option'. When he feels old he says things like 'The concentration camp is a metaphor for life.'

It is worth looking at *Hannah and Her Sisters*, for instance, to see the various different sides of Allen. In that film he personally played (one must say, far too briefly) a suicidal humorist who says, 'The only thing that stopped me [killing himself] was my parents. They would have been devastated. I would have had to kill them first . . .

Then I have an aunt and uncle . . . I would have had to kill them too. It would have been a blood-bath.' This is one side of Allen. He has said, also, that the other two central male characters in that same film are based on parts of him and that he could have played *all* of them . . . the hypochondriac-humorist-turned-God-seeker, the confused romantic and the moody anally-obsessed artist. This is a man who also really likes, or likes to call on, the company of women, lots of them, on screen and off.

Career-wise, Allen has been a consummate (if extremely nervous) stand-up comic (in the early 1960s), a surrealist comic writer, and – in film – a bizarre dialogue and action comic, a romantic comic, a serious chamber-piece dramatist, a melancholic comic, plus much else uncategorisable. It is reasonable, therefore, to hope that he never seriously considers suicide, that he relishes fatherhood, that he accepts moderately the demise of his parents (if that occurs in his lifetime), that he continues to toy with *all* his psychological elements, and that he goes on making *exactly* the type of films he wants to.

One extra point. In 1973 Allen said, quite categorically, 'Oh, I *never* found Laurel and Hardy funny.'

This slightly confuses things. I think we should return to Laurel and Hardy, seemingly still the most popular humorists, among other humorists as well as the general public of the world, at the end of this book.

Meanwhile, numerous great – and living – comedians beckon. All very much individuals, in life and on stage, it will nevertheless be interesting to see if they reflect, or have opinions on, the flavours of humour – happy, sad, adult, childlike, parental, social, philosophical, sexual, rebellious, aggressive, monetary, toilet-ary, religious and so on – detected in this Introduction.

The Inquisition embarks. Bon Voyage!

BARRY HUMPHRIES, 1987: '*It's strange for me, looking out from behind Edna's spectacles . . .*'
Photograph by Steve Double
(Inset) An early snap of EDNA EVERAGE, Moonee Ponds, 1961
Photograph courtesy of House of Edna PLC

BARRY HUMPHRIES

Mother's Touch

Dame Edna is now at the height of her powers. Never has she been more incisive, pivotal, compassionate and seminal.

Exactly what kind of a man goes on television dressed as a self-inspired female celebrity ('Interrupting her busy schedule to be with us tonight') and small-talks, 'You know, the other day my gynaecologist, he looked up at me and he said, ''Edna . . . how do you give and take so much love?''' Barry Humphries' falsetto Dame Edna Everage, of course, is unintentionally crude; she is at heart an *outgoing* prude. But this does not stop – indeed, within fluctuating censorship rules, positively encourages – Humphries using her to plant many subtle and howling obscenities into the television system. 'This is my little spunky number' says Edna, ' . . . I wouldn't mind the biggest organ [skin] on your body pressed against the biggest organ on my body . . . My husband is into oral socks, viewers . . . I have my drives and juices . . . I'm not a hologram. If you don't believe it, stick a finger in me . . . ' Her sexual references are never 'deliberate' ('Trust my audience to misinterpret *everything* I say'). Humphries' sexual and subversive intentions are pumping away, but they are coded by the Edna mask. The mask of suburban gentility, and 'suffocating niceness'.

The mask of Edna, Humphries' most popular and ebullient Australian comic creation, was originated during a 'party turn' way back in 1955, as a playful satire on Melbourne suburban sponge-cake gentility, as witnessed in the behaviour of his childhood nanny (actually called Edna), his proper mother and his aunts. 'Mostly she represents the aunt-types that would peer into my bassinet (cradle) or playpen,' he says. But the male centre remains, however much we believe the feminine guise, and it is most glaringly symbolised by Edna's favourite flowers – those being 'the fresh pink gladioli phallically flapping in the wind'. The gladioli are, it seems, his Australian penis substitute, and a weapon (like the court jester's pig's-bladder-on-a-stick) which reminds us that he/she is out for fun, *and* trouble.

*

When the check-besuited, suave, *real* Barry Humphries walks into the breakfast room of a favourite neo-colonial hotel, in a gentle mood, somewhat tired from dance rehearsals (in high heels) the previous evening, I remind him of the spate of 'gynaecological jokes' offered during an appearance on someone else's 'family television' chat-show. On the occasion of this chat-show Humphries first excelled himself by having Edna broach the details of her offspring's shoplifting. Holding back a very slight tear Edna explained how her daughter, Valmai ('now married to Merv Gittis'), went into supermarkets and stuffed frozen chickens down her 'panti-hose'. Unfortunately for Valmai, the store detective smelt the barbecued chickens as she left. 'She's a human microwave is Valmai.' Then on to the gynaecologist, an 'old gynaecologist with a bit of a tremor, actually' said the Dame, shaking one of her (or rather, Humphries') subversive hands, '. . . but I think they're the best kind, don't you?' *Then*, just as the presenter began introducing the next guest, Humphries could just be heard off screen mumbling, '. . . *Uuuumm, I can feel him now*.'

When I remind the mysterious, enigmatic Humphries of this perfectly timed line, he laughs for eighteen seconds, looking rather happy.

What do people imagine Barry Humphries, behind the masks, to be like? Larger than life but a third as cheerful?

'A lot of people, for reasons I don't understand, are puzzled by two things they discover about me,' he offers, licking his very strange lips. 'One, that I wasn't an only child; that I have a sister and two brothers. And secondly that I drive a motor car. So outwardly I must give the impression of solitariness and also irresponsibility, or extreme, almost professorial vagueness. In reality I have actually driven a car since I was eighteen, and I have never had an accident . . . or been wheel-clamped. Meanwhile, my sister is a school-teacher and a housewife. One of my brothers is a librarian and historian, and the other an architect. They are both slightly younger than me.'

Were you a dirty, or rather crude, youngster?

'No, certainly not.'

Really?

'Well, no more than I think of myself as a *dirty man* . . . But it is great fun to see what you can get away with on stage or television. To see where you can take it. Innuendo is a great release, you know.'

Is part and parcel of what you do on stage turning the audience into children?

'Yes, I think that's probably true. I feel Edna controls an audience, even her guests, like they were children. She certainly thinks of herself as a good mother. She's very clean.'

What kind of a youngster were you then?

'Rather serious, I'm afraid, with a poster-size photo of myself on the wall. Not an outdoor type. Magic I took seriously, and drawing and painting. I was mostly interested in arty things. I read a lot. But I remember dressing up a great deal. It was quite a pastime. I had all these outfits . . . cowboy and red indian costumes, and sailor uniforms. Most kids do that, though, I suppose. My son Oscar really likes dressing up, I've noticed. Children understand the *business* and *value* of play-acting.'

Does your son easily equate Edna with you, the father?

'Oh, coming backstage and seeing me getting made up doesn't puzzle *him* in the least, I think. I'm sure it must be far more mystifying for those children who see their father leave the house and vanish with a Samsonite briefcase. They probably couldn't begin to explain what father does at the office – other than speak on the phone all day to people he doesn't know, have lunch with people he doesn't like, and sit at a desk looking at a wall.' Humphries looks slightly loathing now. 'How can you explain *that* as a lifestyle? Whereas *my* children can see me turn up at a theatre, don a number of funny disguises, prance on stage and make a crowd of people laugh – hopefully. And at the end of it all they see me throw a whole lot of *very* expensive flowers over the audience.'

Naming a son Oscar – is this a giveaway, as to your intentions of making him into 'a wag' too, like yourself . . . and Oscar Wilde? You once said Wilde was a hero.

(A snortle.) 'Honestly, that name was chosen *more* because it was an unfashionable name with a good ring to it. Oscar Humphries, you see. My other son's name is Rupert. And I hope very much he doesn't go into publishing . . . or become a bear.'

What I'm really trying to get at is why, or how, *you* ended up as this grown man purveying – rather wittily admittedly – a large dose of crude innuendo under a female – and rather motherly – guise?

'Oh, goodness knows! I've had no luck psychoanalysing it. I can't psychoanalyse Edna, never mind myself. I just can't get to grips with it.'

Well, what does your mother think of your stage personae?

'I could tell you a story. Some time ago I took Oscar to Melbourne, so that she could see him for the first time, and when we arrived at the house she ignored him because she was so deeply involved in listening to the radio. You see, in Australia, which I call a *Disc-Jock*ocracy, the radio DJs become gurus . . . And my mother was sitting there in the sun-lounge of her comfortable suburban house listening to a radio phone-in about *me*. The DJ had started by saying, "I haven't seen Barry Humphries' new film but I hear it's a real disgrace," and this had become the topic of the morning. So my mother sternly nodded at these housewives' angry comments, turned to me and said, "*This is what they think of you Barry, this is what they think of you!*" I couldn't believe it. So I went into another room and phoned the radio show in Edna's voice. When I got on the air I said, "Hello Brian, I'd just like to say that, even though I haven't seen any of his shows, I agree *whole-heartedly* with what everyone has been saying about Barry Humphries . . . and furthermore I happen to know Barry's mother agrees too.'' So my mother is in the next room listening to a radio show in which her son is . . . God, I can't explain the intricacies of it all. It was pretty *knotty*. But it was the only possible way of getting through to her.'

Did it work?

'Well, she changed the subject and switched her attention to her grandson.'

Has your mother ever seen you perform as Sir Les Patterson – drool, tobacco, vomit, alcohol stains and all?

'No no, she hasn't. She never arrived at the theatre for that. She pretends Les just doesn't exist.'

You were brought up prudishly?

'Yes, I'd have to say both my parents were prudes. They banned me from going to Melbourne's only music-hall when I was a young man. And I can certainly see there's a bit of old risqué music-hall in *me*. Max Miller, I think, was marvellous. *He* used to wear check suits, by the way.'

Sometime before our meeting in person in London, I made a telephone call to Humphries at his agent's office in Melbourne, while he was visiting his old 'sun-bronzed homeland', with a view to posing 20 questions about the nature of the Real Barry, the man behind the vaudevillian masks. Only it wasn't Barry who replied – it was his salivating protégé, Australian cultural attaché Sir Lesley Colin Patterson, the most uncouth character in his repertoire and one requiring the use of a false penis and hair-whitener. For 35 minutes Humphries maintained this oral act without a falter, seemingly dribbling whisky into the telephone and unleashing an inspired response to each and every serious query. There were Les's stories of teenage 'rod-walloping in the bushes', and of 'drool transfusions and phlegm banks'. He spoke of alcoholism ('the late Oliver Reed, and the late George Best . . . gentlemen who could hold their liquor'), of plans for 'another speech at the United Nations', secrets on how to get a vibrator through customs, and of Pattersonian intentions towards certain TV researchers of his recent acquaintance. 'I'd fill her up with liquor, check out some doubtful videos, and then – whilst she's sleeping it off – I'd put in a loving phonecall to Lady Patterson.' Most of all, though, Humphries (Les) improvised on the topic of 'those pieces of hardened dairy product', cheese. 'I got into cheese a few years ago' he said. 'Really, when it comes down to it, cheese is just milk that's gone bad and smells a bit off . . . So I started to attend a few cheese-sniffing parties, and at these events you get to meet a lot of sheilas who work for cookery magazines and publish books about cuisine. You meet a lot of *spare* at sniffings. And, of course, sheilas get turned on by a ripe old piece of camembert. There again, I've always been loved by women – I truly have an indefinable ''something''.'

The 'real' Mr Humphries, as he sits sniffing, pondering, nibbling and picking over a bowl of morning muesli, definitely has an indefinable something. But this is no Edna or Les. Today he sports 'my only checked suit', which is in pristine condition and which he says is 'to let the television company know I'm in the office.' It lends him both a youthful and a traditional elegance. Offsetting these checks is a sharp, blood red tie, and a hair-parting which suggests his fringe may at any moment droop to conceal his eyes (although it never does, except while he marches in and out of the room). By his chair he places an ageing but stylish briefcase. (He's taking a briefcase to the office!)

His laugh falls somewhere between a croak and a hefty emission of air. His mouth makes all kinds of unique shapes as he speaks, as he eats and as he explores and reacts to the 'nooks, crannies' and layers of meaning in conversation. These are the same bottom-heavy lips which droop to one side as Edna's face registers confusion or mild distaste towards an audience's sexual sniggers, or towards an uninteresting guest on *The Dame Edna Experience*, the British (London Weekend Television) TV show in which Humphries inflates and deflates celebrity and small-talk. These same lips also unleash an incessant, and increasingly dramatic, spray of saliva and alcohol, under the guise of Sir Les Patterson, the persona which – with Falstaffian lack of glamour – most offends his old homeland. Decostumed, though, Humphries' voice is more University Australian, and his posture and pacing is English Respectable, almost Edwardian Toff, topped up with a multitude of sardonic asides. 'Without wanting to sound pretentious' he begins a sentence, '. . . although inevitably I will.' Today, the comic looks as if he could fit in at a Freemasons' dinner, in Executive Class, in church ('. . . I'm more interested in going now, as I approach death' he says), at the Athenaeum Club (and other clubs of which he is a member), at Selfridges (where he shops for Edna's shoes), and at Sotheby's (as a connoisseur bidding for the furnishings and art – French and Belgian symbolist paintings – which bedeck his immaculate London home). And perhaps even in the company of British royalty. 'The Royals always seem to come to my shows' he says. 'They never tell you in advance, of course. You just hear they've arrived in the theatre, and then they come backstage at intermission to say hello.'

Funnily enough, one of Humphries' most effective performances of the garish Les Patterson – at a Royal Variety Performance in the mid 1980s – was particularly effective due to the upset it was bound to cause viewers believing such behaviour in front of Royals to be beyond the bounds of etiquette. Slobbering, stained and near catatonic, he was the perfect antidote to the mildness and showbiz platitudes found elsewhere in the show. 'You British are very protective of your royals, aren't you?' he remarks. 'But the problem with such shows is that all these old-timers are desperate to run respectfully through their three long songs. They like to really hog it, don't they? . . . So that was just me going on *quick* and giving them three moist minutes of Les.'

It was at the St George's League Club in Sidney in 1974 that Humphries first introduced his drunken Les personality to the repertoire (taking ingredients from his coarse 1960s comic-strip 'Barry MacKenzie' – 'Drain the dragon, syphon the python . . .'), honing Les thereafter during two years of cabaret he performed in Hong Kong in front of businessmen and the rather respectable. 'I'm as full as a seaside shithouse on Boxing Day,' Les would intone to these professional gents. For Humphries the initial inspiration came simply because Les 'seemed a useful disguise for me to adopt when confronted by a threatening audience.' Years later, in 1987, his 7½-million-dollars film *Les Patterson Saves the World* explored the Sydney-derived caricature so gutturally and scatologically that his 'parochial and rather philistine' mother-country, and mother, took ultimate offence. Not least at the early scene in which Patterson created an international incident by releasing anal gases and thus setting fire to an Arab delegate smoking a cigarette, at the United Nations General Assembly.

'It received the worst notices of anything I've ever done' says Humphries, with only slight bitterness. 'People were absolutely horrified to see Les close-up on the wide screen. The film was branded as *treacherous*. There were people exclaiming in public, in print – and in parliament – that Les was undoing "all the good publicity work that *Crocodile Dundee* and Paul Hogan have done". I returned to England just in time to escape the lynching parties. Even *friends* wrote to say how disappointed they were . . . But I've always tried to make Australia seem as inhospitable as possible.' He smiles now. 'I've been known to exaggerate on occasions, but honestly if you heard just five minutes of the real Australian Minister for Tourism he would make Lesley seem like a pale innocuous shadow by comparison. You see, "the yobbo" is still on the throne in Australia.' (Having earlier assaulted antipodean niceness, he is now decrying its machismo.)

You give cultural 'honours' to some of your characters. Despite the excessiveness of those characters, are you really rather respectable underneath?

'Well! *No* comedian – as you should well know – can ever be *truly* respectable.'

But is a desire to be respectable reflected in your off-stage manner, your clothing?

'Mmm. Ever since I had to start meeting bank-managers, I thought it just as well to look like one. There's certainly a bit of that in there. But I see myself as a bit of a dilettante; a man of *some* taste.'

Do you consider yourself perhaps rather an *English* gent now?

'Ummm. No, not really. That is my advantage, you see – being and feeling an outsider . . . But yes, having been raised in Melbourne suburbia, I am ultimately certainly a bit of a middle-class smart-arse.'

Born in 1934 in 'the Roman Catholic Melbourne suburb of Kew', Humphries was a book-ish youngster and youth who disliked sport and 'too much outdoors', objected to 'everything having to be new' but – presumably – exercised a great thirst for words, exquisite minor detail and donning outfits. His great love of the nuances of language, painting and of re-inventing his own character presumably derive from those early days in all people's lives when they discover the nervousness, freedom and humour of self-expression. Humphries' father was a well-off, busy construction manager who expected his son to follow in his footsteps – or at least become a 'businessman' – but Barry 'never wanted a career'. In his bones he 'hankered for moister landscape'. Spurred on by the conservatism of his family, meanwhile he became a poseur and a part-time trickster; once he got friends to enter the carriage of a buffetless train and pompously serve him an elaborate meal in front of bemused passengers. (Later he developed the *Chain Chunder*, a neat communal trick at 10,000 feet which began by eating mixed vegetable soup, from an in-flight sick-bag, in front of fellow passengers.) A clever lad, at Melbourne Grammar School he was, in his own words, 'infinitely better read than the masters'. In 1952 he entered the University of Melbourne to study Law, Philosophy and Fine Art, where he was noted for irrelevance or irreverence in essays and examinations. There he began appearing in revues, his early characters being 'Dadaist, insane, menacing, baleful creations'. He impersonated Hitler, played 'a crazy scientist in mascara called Dr Humphries', and – off stage – mounted an exhibition of Dada-like art-works. The latter included 'meat pies, with tomato sauce, nailed to a canvas', plus a pair of wellington boots with custard contained therein and entitled *Pus in Boots*. This rebelliousness seems erratically at odds with his private hobbies in middle age of collecting distinguished late nineteenth and twentieth-century art and of – himself – painting 'nice, non-pretentious landscapes in peaceful places'. Seriously, now, he tells me 'I always wanted to be a painter . . . that's what I thought was for me. It's lonesome but soothing, I find, when it's going well.'

Certainly there is much evidence to suggest that Humphries is a very *anally* confused character, if the theory is to be believed that an artistic bent derives from toilet-training, the early important years in which there is pressure on each child to perform and arrange matters in a manner satisfactory to those training them. That Humphries life covers the range from serious art appreciation and acquisition to 'sore prostate' jokes and 'major urological explosions' makes his centre most elusive. Perhaps at the crunch, though, Humphries is almost polymorphously perverse. Certainly he had an assortment of women around him physically as a child. He is an obsessive concerned with the pleasures and pitfalls of *all* the senses – visual, oral, anal, aural, genital and especially nasal (Humphries on stage frequently tilts his head backwards to draw in a *huge* breath of air). And, for such sensual excesses, humour proved the most cathartic release, one that saw him (or rather, Edna), during a grand theatre finale, being joyfully, egotistically projected – sniffling and dropping small tears of pleasure and obscenity – 30 feet above his/her theatre audience along an extendable crane.

'I merely stumbled into comedy', he offers, 'because I found acting in student revues more entertaining than studying law. I failed examinations and began devoting more and more time to amateur theatrics. I wrote my own material. Edna surfaced as a party-turn back then, and was played much like a pantomime dame. Her name and some characteristics were inspired by a nanny I had for a while. Everage came from Average; she was to have an average suburban flavour. It was me, vaguely dressed up to look like a Melbourne housewife, talking in a falsetto . . . entertaining party-goers. She was rather nervous and genteel. Then she appeared in a sketch in which she almost became the hostess for a foreign athlete visiting Australia for the Olympics. Always though, like all my characters, she spent all her time expecting to talk about *herself*, her possessions, her relatives, her gladioli-arranging and sponge-fingers. Despite her increased glamour, Edna has always appeared to be like someone who has just stumbled on to the stage.'

Was your idea always to write and present your own material?

(Sniffle.) 'Well, I was at one stage offered a position in a newly formed repertory company touring Shakespeare in Australia, where I earned a precarious living whilst I slowly developed my own act. Along with a gentleman called Peter O'Shaughnessy, I was involved in putting on the first Australian performances of Beckett and Eugène Ionesco. But I also nervously tried out my own material at a place called the Philip Street Theatre.'

The characters which Humphries evolved alone were distinctly Australian folk presented in heightened realist style largely through monologues, people truly obsessed by their attitudes, enjoyments and possessions. Humphries jokes that they were 'accurately based on real people who never lived', by which he probably means they blend part of his own personality with those of family-members and others he grew up witnessing. His growing repertoire included Buster Thomson (a loutish ex-public school boy based on folk at Melbourne Grammar School, where he felt 'a bit of a loner'), Neil Singleton (a leftish intellectual), Morrie O'Connor (a salesman of 'used pictures'), Lance Boyle (a class-conscious trade-unionist), Colin Cartwright (a hard-pressed businessman father who, like Barry's father, had a daughter and three sons), Graeme Polkington (identified only through letters from his mother) and Sandy Stone (a Samuel Beckett-like study in immobility and fading 'nostalgia'). Many of these characters reflect the male textures of Humphries' childhood and 1950s youth – all of them pinpoint his ever-shifting search for identity.

Humphries' parents 'never encouraged or accepted acting as something I should seriously turn my hand to.' Thus the opportunity to reinvent his world and person properly came when Humphries 'determinedly, but rather guiltily' boarded the ship *Toscana* in 1959, bound for Venice, and went on for the first time to London. He arrived while there was still a smog in London '. . . it had a very funny *smell*.' He then felt he wanted to settle in and become a serious actor, '. . . if indeed any play or actor can be serious'. He appeared in musicals, for some time as the undertaker in *Oliver*. 'Meanwhile, I was drinking at the Salisbury, the actor's pub, taking lunch at Jimmy's, a drinking hole, for 2s 6d and exploring Soho, where there were still quite a few literary and legendary figures stumbling from bar to bar.' (Humphries' bouts with alcohol – first explored at that point – are somewhat legendary, if not so much as his supposed past bouts of melancholy.)

He had rediscovered the supposed 'cultivated' roots of his Anglo-Australian history; what Humphries now craved was to feel settled in London, to become a resident, perhaps of Hampstead amidst the wall-plaques denoting the previous existence of writers he respected. He was both a serious and a comedic Londoner. At parties he often took on the guise of a self-imagined conversationalist called Des; and his comic drives finally found fruition on the stage of Peter Cook's Establishment Club. He was received very badly: 'I was put on there one night when Lenny Bruce was too drunk, or drugged . . . or dead, to appear,' he says, very cuttingly. He finally got out of his musical theatre contract (*Oliver*), so that he could mount a one-man-show, after an elaborate accident on a cliff while visiting Cornwall. (He is prone to relate the tale of this accident in almost prophetic or mystical terms; he was winched 'off a tiny ledge [after five hours] and onto the cover of the *Guardian*'.) Since that point he has resided ('been based') most of each year in Britain and somehow managed increasingly to sell, espouse, deflate, criticise and glorify distinctly Australian culture to, and for, both Britons *and* Australians.

He is particularly proud of pieces of early material he recorded for British television, around 1968. 'All of them have now been wiped,' he winces, 'They were rather experimental and involved Edna travelling to places as a tourist in London and *nattering* to camera. It developed on from slide shows I had put on for friends during early return visits to Australia. Unbeknownst to them I'd project photographs, taken by my then wife, of British tourist-sights – photographs in which Edna would crop up in the corner. It was all part of a process of taking the theatrical figures and introducing them seemingly into real life. To create a real presence.'

This ongoing process has progressed so well over the decades, feels Humphries, that celebrities and notables like 'Charlton Heston now talk respectfully to Edna, they clamour to come on her show, and she can say to Larry Hagman, "You're used to being interviewed by ordinary, uninteresting people . . . What's it like to be interviewed by your peer?" I must say it's strange indeed for me, looking out through Edna's spectacles and seeing people looking at "this woman", who was originally conceived as shy, smartly-dressed but certainly not glamorous, and them deciding to tell her things they haven't even told Johnny Carson. It's rather bizarre, don't you think?' Mostly, though, within performances, Humphries likes his characters (Edna most effectively) to talk about themselves, and for ever more important and celebrated folk to attentively listen. Indeed, not only listen but to be completely dominated; to be laid bare and sucked dry under Humphries' huge egis. Similarly, in 'real life', it has been reported that Humphries' second wife, painter Dianne Millstead, has claimed or joked, 'The only person Barry is in love with is himself.' If this is true it is a schizophrenic self-love – given the great number of personalities, within his character, that Humphries explores – and a self-love full of contradictions. One such contradiction can be seen in the fact that Humphries is currently considering the creation of a 'brother character for Les' who 'would be an evangelist perhaps' for the stage, while at the same time he is 'more interested in traditional religious beliefs than I used to be' off-stage. Furthermore he took Les Patterson's drunkenness to new humorous extremes around or after the time he attempted to banish alcohol from his own life. Also he says that he '*never* wanted a career' and yet he runs remorselessly, with ever more speed and tenacity, along the 'gorgeous' show-business path.

When you walked on to a particular chat-show in 1987, which I've just watched again, it really did seem that you were *delighted* with yourself as Edna. Bedecked in diamanté and to the sound of 'Jesus Christ Superstar', you seemed very much on a high as you giggled, '*Don't I look ab-so-lutely gor-geous?*' Does Edna's personality truly take hold of you?

Humphries sniffles and giggles at the memory. 'Well, that's acting, I suppose,' he underplays. 'It's the difference between acting and drag or pantomime. King Lear or Edna – the audience has to believe, so *I* have to believe. I become Edna.'

But you're obviously not a woman. Gilbert and George, the artists, once said that the creative forces of the male come from the head, the body and the cock. There's a different driving force there in at least one out of three respects.

'Gilbert and George, of course, I must say, are Edna's favourite artists.' (He snortles.) 'Whereas *I personally* lag a little behind on these things . . . so in response to that question *I* certainly won't be paraphrasing Gilbert and George.' (He is teasing now.) 'Obviously I have to *imagine* some of Edna's whims and drives. But it's more a matter of keying into her preoccupations. I just have to think what she would be thinking about. And Edna's central concern is her family, which of course she stands at the centre of and thinks she controls. Indeed it must be rather bewildering for her guests to have to listen to all her family small-talk.'

So can you conjure up imaginary family members?

'Yes, son Bruce who's married to Joylene, who Edna doesn't like; daughter Valmai, who's a bit disturbed . . . And there's son Kenny, who is rather gay – something the audience is aware of but Edna is not. So I have to come up with new ways for a parent not to notice or accept their children's nature. Thinking up new ways of not seeing what's in the house is an interesting exercise.'

Is the most important thing about Edna the fact that she's a mother?

'Haa. She likes to mother – she is rather motherly, don't you think? She once won a "Lovely Mother Contest".'

Do you think Edna, at the bottom line, is a nice dame?

'Well, this a very interesting question. Whatever she says to, or at, people they seem to *forgive* her. They always seem to believe she *means* well, but personally I'm not so sure she does. I must say I try to incorporate in her, perhaps more so than all my other characters, *all* the paradoxes of my old homeland. The sentimentality, the harsh extremes, the galloping cultural paranoia, the leaping at the second-hand and taking it to excess, the transcendental vulgarity . . .'

Is it not true though that most of your audience now miss the original satiric intentions concerning Australia which she grew out of?

'Well, yes, her original audience were people in beards and sandals laughing at suburbia, 1950s-Melbourne style. Now she is a great artifact, an ever-changing phenomenon, a very *real* housewife megastar loved by young and old. Haaa. So it's all been a rather strange evolvement. I, of course, have guided her. The cultural elements are my own *memories*.'

You've been quoted as saying that you now 'forgive Australia'; would you ever consider moving back there permanently?

'Wellll . . . perhaps Tasmania. I'm currently considering buying a large expanse of it. . . . *Otherwise* perhaps I would quite like to fade away in Europe and work as an assistant at a small, quiet museum or gallery in Belgium, or somewhere like Leamington Spa. Or maybe the one in Bournemouth, on the cliffs, which has only two paintings worth looking at, but rather good ones. Hardly anyone goes there, and if they do, they always think it's something else and walk out again.'

The thought of philosophical Barry ('The only person you can change is yourself') as a quiet museum attendant is, for now, romantic but preposterous. Humphries is a workaholic, relentlessly building and immortalising his characters, mainly mother Edna ('I seem to get younger, don't I possums?'), through – in two years truly non-stop – a major television series, a record album, a theatre tour, a Christmas TV special, a lengthy run on stage in London, another tour, a return to the London stage, the writing of another book (a ludicrous but 'gorgeous' Edna 'autobiography' which begins with 'Jewish roots' and ends with a visit to husband Norman's grave), an Australian tour and then another TV series. He degrades Patterson ever more, continues to bring sad, reflective old man Sandy Stone back to the theatre stage even though the character is actually deceased, and takes Edna from superstardom to 'megastardom' and beyond.

And if Edna is perhaps Humphries' mother and mother-figures rolled into one, who else can Edna's husband Norman possibly be but a father? There has long been, it must be remembered, profound confusion over the mortal existence of Edna's husband Norm, a character noted – when living – for immense problems with his prostate.

'*Norm* . . . ' says Humphries, 'He keeps coming back to life again. It's difficult to know whether he's alive or dead sometimes. As we speak, as far as the Australians are concerned he's dead. For the English I decided to bring him back so I could kill him off once more. So Norm (Norman Stoddart Everage) passes into periods of extended coma . . . his prostate, of course, has been hanging over Edna for years.'

You've been around for quite a while now . . . What in essence gets you back on the boards?

'Oh, nice people who say, "We did enjoy you. When are you coming again?" ' Humphries answers gently. '. . . But ultimately one has to admit it's *selfish*. Because once I get up there and the nerves are gone I really enjoy it enormously. Indeed, I enjoy it *so* much that the audience pick up on it. I honestly think that half the time they don't hear what I'm saying at all . . . they're just enjoying my enjoying it. It's to do with fun and *confidence*.'

Do you ever get on stage and just 'go through the motions'?

'I hope not, because I like the audience to think it's being made up on the spot. That it's a one-off. And, given a certain amount of pre-thought, it most often is.'

Do you ever have humorous night-dreams?

'Oh, certainly. Sometimes I wake myself up laughing, thinking of lines for a character. I will then be asked the tricky question "What's the matter dear?" and have to explain that I've amused myself so much that I've woken myself up. So often my work must be going through the night.'

Can I ask you who you think the *classic* comedians might be?

'For me it may be Laurel and Hardy, who were way above Chaplin in my opinion. They were immensely clever but far more human and likeable.'

Humour is very much your world. Where's the serious, 'straight', actor in you now?

'Oh, friends like Germaine Greer still occasionally taunt me by saying. "When are you going to get down to it and do the right thing?" as if somehow I've let the side down by making people laugh.'

What is your reply?

'I couldn't think of one, and anyway – it's embarrassing trying to justify yourself. Of course, I'm inclined to feel guilty over *anything*. I've always felt like that about what I've done. And if I run out of my own guilt I'll borrow yours for the moment. So consequently I'm inclined to agree with them. Am I taking the easy path, I wonder? . . .' (A pause.) 'On the other hand, not so many people can do what I do, *the way* that I do it. And anyway – it gives me great pleasure. At least once I get going . . . when I'm in character, on stage and in control. It's just all that worry and agonizing pre-production. When I drive past the theatre and see a queue I think to myself, "They're buying tickets for something that doesn't even exist in my mind yet . . . So *I really mustn't let them down*" '

Humphries a man racked with worry and guilt? There is, however, a coda.

> '. . . Or else I see the queue and worry that this time around they'll all find out I'm a fraud . . . that I'm really doing it purely for pleasure. That pleasure actually being mine, *not* theirs.'

The centre of his comic prism momentarily unleashed, Humphries sets off 'to work' in his chauffeured car, which he detours briefly to his favourite Soho record shop to select, like a connoisseur, and relish 'something classical and Swedish'. *En route* he uses the car-phone to set about eagerly communicating ideas and instructions for a Christmas Edna television special in which to impose his personalities on other celebrities.

'Forget Olivia (de Havilland)' he says, moistening his lips now, straightening his tie and flicking back his hair, 'Eddie Grant? . . . Ummmm, yes, yes. Does he have dreadlocks? Oh *very good*.'

Earlier that morning, well over a year ago, Humphries had told me he was shortly intending 'to make a change' to spend 'more time just relaxing with the family. I've made that mistake before and I don't want to again.' A divorce (his wife 'got' the children) and a new marriage aside, he has barely paused from working since.

STEVE MARTIN: '*Comedy . . . comedy . . . comedy . . . and drama!*'
Photograph by John Hind

STEVE MARTIN

Movements of a Jerk

Comedy is the ability to make people laugh without making them puke.

'I was born in a place called Waco, Texas, 14 August 1945. I had what I think of as a very normal American family life – WASP (White Anglo-Saxon Protestant), conservative, middle-class . . .'

A warm happy family?

'Just typical. Two children – me and my older sister. Not a robust family, hugging and emotional . . . but there were no beatings, nothing bizarre . . . totally typical.'

Religious?

'My parents were concerned to bring us up as decent baptists. But I was more concerned with riding bikes and *having fun*.'

How else would you describe your parents?

'My mother was a generous mother, my father hard-working. He was a real-estate broker, but he also was involved in some amateur acting.'

It's reported that you remember once seeing him perform.

'I was about four at the time. He gave it up soon after. It's the only time I remember seeing him on stage.'

How did you feel?

'I didn't understand. I didn't understand what he was wearing. I didn't understand what he was doing, or saying. I just didn't understand it.'

Were you impressed? Were other people impressed?

'Well . . . I remember that it was hardly a full house.'

Were you a bright child at school? Did you get good grades?

'At early ones reasonable, at high school very mixed, at college very high.'

What were you aiming to be when you grew up?

'An electrician. No, really – a comedian, a performer, a comic actor. It's all I ever dreamt of.'

Steve Martin has a rarely-seen stage routine, a piece of ludicrous silent comedy, which he performs without vocals but with illustrious aid of his trouser-zip, a beautiful woman and a score of unpredictable props. Dressed in the suave attire of a self-imagined magician called

'Flydini', Martin somehow achieves – in this seven-minute routine – an explanation of the link between magic and comedy and indeed an encapsulation of the penis's role in magic and comedy. Flydini produces from his trousers, with a flourish, first a rabbit, then some eggs, then a ringing telephone. Flydini's attention is then distracted by a woman crossing the stage, and – with the grace and charm of a professional and a show-off – draws both a bunch of flowers and a glass of champagne from his open fly, presenting them romantically to the lady. For several glorious moments he reigns supreme as both a magician and a lover. Then, suddenly, she is gone. He pines, then is grief-stricken. Ultimately, as a symbol of his feelings, he plucks, from his trousers, a small doll of the opera-singer Pavarotti who stages a rendition of 'Vesti La Giubba' from *I Pagliacci*.

This short performance says much about Martin's character and comedy. There is the startling range of emotions, from shy to confident, from blasé to enthralled, from independent to yearning, from innocent to cognisant, from funny to sad . . . central to his performance are his manhood and his ego, which lead him to turn his attention to a woman when she arrives on the scene. There is a sense that romance is *the* goal; that it can hopefully be acquired through a combination of self-confidence and ludicrous attention-grabbing activity. Martin beguiles the woman, but there is the ever present threat, or reality, of separation, like a mother leaving her son. As tools in the job of getting, and retrieving, that attention and any other attention he may acquire, Martin has personally developed a zestful wrist for a banjo, a face that can be read on the other side of a stadium, a juggler's spirit, a body capable of epileptic pantomime, and a magician's playful but scholarly belief in surprise. Martin has put it on record, several times, that the reason he joined 'the world of show-business' was, quite simply, '. . . to get the attention of women', '. . . to meet girls', '. . . to meet lots of women'.

To find 'Woman' – is attempting to be sexually appealing truly at the heart of an illusionist pulling a rabbit from a hat, of a joke snatched from a moment of boyishness or tense embarrassment?

When Martin was five years old his family moved states, west to California, settling five years later in Garden Grove just close to the massive 'fun park', Disneyland. It was the mid-1950s, and Disneyland – over-blown, garish, ultra-clean, hilarious, artificial and mesmerising – became the centre of Martin's world. He first became a guide-book seller at the park; a child barely in double digits, he dressed in the trappings of affluent fun and games. He wore a straw-boater hat, sleeve garters, a bow-tie, and one day he sold – he claims – '625 books at two cents per book profit'. After a brief spell dressed as a cowboy while clowning and selling (later revisited in his film *Three Amigos*), and other tourist-land jobs during the summer and weekends, he was employed at 'Merlin's Magic Shop' within 'Fantasyland'. Magic had been an eager interest since his uncle had bought him a trick when he was six or seven, after which he had combed libraries for magic books and had begun entertaining parents, sister and household visitors with his know-how. Within the magic shop, he relished the plethora of fake and sleight-of-hand gadgets and amusing and bemusing tricks. He became academically enthralled, writing out and storing away a file of 'gags' on pieces of card, then – at fifteen or sixteen when he began performing magic shows – jotting elaborate notes on the technique and success ratings of specific tricks. Meanwhile he learnt to juggle, with the aid and enthusiasm of Disneyland's court jester. Much of his work since then has retained the excitement, cockiness, vulnerability, subtlety, unsubtlety and dedication of those times . . . the sheer gall and exuberance. We still see the excited child stumbling over 'a trick', the same child swooping into raucousness and self-assertion, the same entertainment ethic . . . only Martin's situation *has* changed. He is now a film-star – a comic celebrity who got what he wanted – but also a privacy-seeking middle-aged man. Now his best chance of anonymity is to take 'a two-week driving holiday in Ireland' or simply sit among his vast art collection in a house with few visitors. Matured, channelled and rich, *is he having fun?*

Steve Martin, aged 44, dresses cleanly and crisply in expensive casuals, soft pastel colours and a shirt buttoned up to the neck. He has dark eyebrows and eyelashes, a white helmet of hair, a rubber face seemingly without blood-colouring, a large nose, and yet he retains a certain rugged Southern handsomeness. He appears in the room, unassuming, purposeful, polite, fending off questions with a self-effacing grace, giving every appearance of being embarrassed by celebrity, 'the media' and of appearing 'straight'.

Who were your comic heroes as a child?

'When I was a child I loved Laurel and Hardy. I went to the cinema all the time. I'd see funny guys like them and think "Wow, wouldn't that be fun to do." I *never* thought of the business side. I just thought about being funny. Laurel and Hardy meant a great deal to me. They're always considered as slapstick merchants, but you only have to look at the detail. And Jerry Lewis, too, was a great influence; I enjoyed the stupidity and the athletics, the commotion. I didn't think of them as *actors* then – I thought it was really *them*.'

What are your happiest childhood memories?

'. . . Dying of laughter with friends.'

What are the checks and balances of acquiring comic celebrity?

'One of the good points is being able to get tables in restaurants. One of the bad points is being video-taped while you're eating.'

What is celebrity?

'Being interviewed on television and being presented to someone at a banquet . . . much of it superfluous. Celebrities can rarely be themselves. Everyone is watching you and you even end up watching yourself, which is the worst part.'

But you craved being in show-business?

'It just seemed the best of all possible worlds. I knew it was for me from a very early age.'

What would ultimately satisfy you?

'I want to look back on my career and feel I've made five really funny films . . . which perhaps have also said something fairly truthful about the human condition.'

Do you think your audience have specific expectations of you?

'No one wants to see me stretch. I've done a few things just to show I can act, be serious.'

When was the last time you were depressed?

'Now.'

Do you criticise yourself a lot?

'All the time.'

Do you ever have self-doubts?

'All the time. You know you're only as good as your last joke. But you just keep going along.'

Are these short answers shyness, or are you being humble?

'I still can't really believe it's all happened. Yesterday I was having lunch with Paul McCartney. I never thought I'd have lunch with Paul McCartney and I never thought I'd be starring in a movie with Michael Caine. It's all slightly bemusing.'

What characteristic is most responsible for where you are now?

'Determination. I was just nuts enough to keep plugging away. There were two real career decisions I made, probably the only calculated decisions I've ever made. One was to start headlining clubs, therefore not to be the warm-up act for rock groups, but to be my own man and to control the takings on the door. The other was to move into movies . . . and not look back.'

What is the most important technical discovery you made as a stand-up?

'It's just that when I started there was a very set comedy style which involved telling jokes about other people. I always incorporated myself into the scenario. I wanted to make it a personal performance, about one guy in a crazy world. But I was never political. When I started working, every stand-up was political. It was just the easiest thing to do. All you had to do was say "Richard Nixon" and . . .' (he lets out an absurd highly sarcastic laugh) '. . . "Oh-ha-ha!" . . . everybody would fall about. So I'm non-political, which I consider is really quite a political statement. The world of politics to me seems ineffectual.'

Can comedy change the world?

'It can certainly make it laugh for a while. But I *suppose* it is dealing with pretty lightweight issues. I don't know if I can make any claims over changing the world. There are two great goals in movie-making; one is to make art, the other to make entertainment. The latter is the level I keep it on. I try to hang on to that definition.'

You have said many times that you will never tour as a live performer again. Why is it so final?

'I simply have no desire to go back there. They were hard times, very hard times. And stand-up comics have it even harder now – it's so competitive. I don't want to be competitive that way any more. It's the hardest material to write, the hardest to develop and it comes with a lifestyle which I find very hard to adapt to. I'm too old for that.'

You didn't relish the attention it brought?

'Well, one night after a show I'd feel great, and the next night I'd go home or to a hotel and feel very depressed. It took me ten years to realise that that's show-business. I thought the depressions were probably arbitrary . . . Making *Planes, Trains and Automobiles* was fun, in a way, because it brought back all my memories of when I was touring. When you see me bawling and cursing at the airport check-in woman, there's a lot of heart-felt aggression there. It's my revenge for having been "on the road" . . . but I feel, I hope, too, that I'm shouting and crying for the audience out there. Haaa!'

There is a short trailer film, produced to advertise Martin's first film in 1979, which selects performers in movie history who have been immortalised by the roles that they have played – the Vamp, the Champ and the Tramp. 'And now,' announces Martin's voice in the trailer, 'the most perfect casting of all . . . Steve Martin, the Jerk.' The comic was equally blunt, arrogant, honest *and* self-deprecating in the trailer to *Dead Men Don't Wear Plaid* (1982) which included, amidst sprightly editing, the exclamations: '. . . No pain is too great, no joke too disgusting', adding that, 'He'll do *ANYTHING* in his quest for the elusive Academy Award . . . Comedy . . . Comedy . . . Comedy . . . Comedy . . . and drama!'

To have become a comedian, he was confessing, means sinking to new heights, rising to new depths, over-acting monstrously, ridiculing oneself, ridiculing a few others, adopting the epileptic movements of a village idiot, an over-excited party-goer or a psychopath, and acquiring a ridiculous name (Dr Hfuhruhrr, or Navin R. Johnson of 235 1/8 Elm Street). Martin the Comic is one who flits between moods and realisations in order that the audience is always on the edge of their seats, always oscillating between surprise and release. He plays romantically outraged ('Into the mud, Scum Queen!'), perverted (canoodling with the wax lips attached to a jar of formaldehyde containing a brain), sexually aroused ('Mam-ahh!!'), ashamed ('Oh no!'), barely apologetic ('Well, excuuuuse me!'), coy ('I want to do the M word'), desperately alone ('And could you turn the spotlight off me please'), and even more desperately alone (kissing and wooing a pillow, almost embarrassingly, in *The Lonely Guy*). He sprints exuberantly, grins manically so that creases appear all down his cheeks, he jigs, strums, falls to the floor, stands agasp and then recovers in the face of death. He adopts 'Happy Feet', juggles (badly *and* well), tap-dances, beats his head against a microphone and fights off assailants with a tennis racket. He wears an eight-inch nose, rabbit-ears, or beer – unknowingly – on his top lip. He leaps through a door, wears a hat on his penis, fights, rides a horse with gusto, climbs out of lifts and schemes and struggles to get glamorous women into bed. It's a living.

This is what it takes to be a mobile comedian. In *The Man with Two Brains* there is a joke approximately every eight seconds. When, earlier, Martin moved from small clubs to concert theatres and stadiums where he opened for rock groups, his contortions and absurdities had had to become ever more ludicrous, ever more readable, like the larger-than-life characters of his Disney childhood. Bound up in this excess, indeed, must have been a strong desire to hold masses of people in his grasp, a thirst to be truly – as he once joked – 'The World's Funniest White Man'. What this meant was a thirst for celebrity, notoriety, attention, money and ever greater laughs. To appear as host on *Saturday Night Live*, the New York TV comedy programme, as he first did in 1976 (since then, returning ten times), must have felt like he was on the very nub of the nation's funny bone. And when a comic can sell out the Universal Amphitheater (as Martin did in 1979) to an ecstatic Californian audience (20,000), for nine nights, at $9.75 a ticket, he must be a very determined, powerful and professional man. The effect of his act, of course, was largely to ridicule and tease over-confidence, pomposity and celebrity – his live show became a huge *parody* of his own supposed fame. But it is also obvious that these very forces created and evolved Martin's presence in show-business. You don't entertain and get money from perpetual punters at 'Disneyland' without a perfectionist's face and a body full of gall; you don't get an audience to follow you out of a club and literally into a swimming-pool (as Martin once did, Pied Piper-like, in North Carolina) without a perverse belief in yourself. In amongst the pantomime and the clowning pratfalls of Martin's later stage-shows (post-Vietnam children's parties) were innumerable confirmations – or rather declarations – that he really *was* in control, that he desired to be respected. *I can't juggle . . . Oh yes I can,* he seemed to be saying, *This is over-the-shoulder juggling, this is under-the-leg juggling . . . Look, I may have just done that ridiculous walk – but hear how well I play the banjo . . . I'm a virgin; oh no I'm not . . . You at the back paid a lot of money and you can barely see me . . . Ha! Ha! . . .* On stage at the Universal Amphitheater Martin knew that, even with a bad joke, he just couldn't go wrong.

When Steve Martin moved into celluloid, which was after all his original childhood dream, he made many comic shifts. He placed himself in something approximating a real world; the whole surroundings became his props. He could now technically control his comedy (perfectly spicing the 1½-second period between set-up and punchline) – he could become 'a comic actor' rather than 'a comedian'. At the same time the immediate audience reaction vanished, his daily tool became a typewriter or word-processor rather than a microphone, and elaborate creative and business concerns unfolded. At the same time as he moved a medium away from the audience (from stage to screen), he, perhaps coincidentally, perhaps not, acquired the fictional company of beautiful women – the foils, angels, femme fatales and pieces of double-crossing sexual apparatus in his full-length stories. Arousal, control, wooing, care and loss of these women became the fabric around which almost all his comic tales have since been woven. He almost seems to be saying that there is an unbreakable bond between romance, or sex, and comedy; all comic paths lead – eventually – to exquisite conquest. Conquest being, for instance, the local angel (*Roxanne*), a plump mother figure (*The Man with Two Brains*), or domestic security (*Planes, Trains and Automobiles*).

Most of Martin's films are awash with schizophrenia, and it is something in lighter form which pervades the flavour of his personality. Within his films he has variously been split between two loves, two brains; his right side has taken on the guise of a (martyred but brash) woman while the left has remained male; he has been stuck in choice between a female mind and a female body; he has leapt back and forth between control and desperation, between extraordinary grinning and intense childlike weeping. Sometimes his character can cope, sometimes it can't ('Well excuuuuse me . . . But I'm watching my entire career go right down the toilet because I've got a dead woman inside me!'). He talks to a dog, talks to a mirror, talks to the dead, talks to the air; he has no shame and then he is ashamed. One minute he is calm, the next psychopathic. In *The Jerk* Martin plays a white man raised by black parents, in *All Of Me* a man split between music and law careers. The great talent in Steve Martin, the performer, is indeed that basic schizophrenia, whereby the audience cannot anticipate from one eight seconds to the next what mood he will feel, what elastic face he will pull, what excuses he will make, what absurd or poignant stance he will assume in the midst of each comic set-up. From a brain-surgeon to brainless, and back again.

From jerk to millionaire, the life of being a professional celebrity comic involves similar 'schizophrenia'. Martin studied philosophy for four years at Long Beach University and yet here he is on screen, playing fools and idiots of sorts. He plays 'the class clown' yet at the same time he is a philosopher, a gentleman and an art connoisseur. He is split between the professional and the amateur spirits, between inspiration and control, between childhood and adulthood. He is desperately split between wanting to be a much loved comic and yet an anonymous person, between being a star and 'a regular guy'. Almost every member of the public he meets will hope or expect him to be 'a wild and crazy guy', although this is the furthest thing from his desire during off-hours. He is shy and claims to be lonely, yet his face is perennially 30 foot or more high on cinema screens . . . something he *also* wants. All his films are about resisting normality, yet he undoubtedly relishes a dose of the opposite.

Steve Martin, the Private Man, lives in a house containing the material fruits of his career ('my biggest hobby'), which are an apparently *exceptional* collection of nineteenth-and twentieth-century

American art. His house, and this might say more about his off-screen life than anything, has absolutely no windows facing the front outside-world.

Off-screen Martin once defined himself as 'a lonely guy, who is alone even with people'. With this he fails to mention his wife, an English beauty, whose company he obviously relishes. *She* has said, succinctly, that he is 'very interesting to live with' and 'amusing'. Outside their house, though, he seems to feel larger than life and thus half as cheerful. 'Sometimes' he smiles nervously, 'I'm able to disappear into the woodwork. I really just wish I could do that *all* the time.'

How did the style of your stage work pass over into film?

'Well, all the movements and fancy mime and the excess, which was sort of rock-and-roll-in spirit, was suddenly placed within a large rectangle. I think I've toned down that mime. On a big screen I tend to feel now it's the very small details, rather than the broad sweeps, that get the laughs. They're blown up 30 foot in the sky anyway. The small pieces are certainly what I find funniest.'

After *The Man with Two Brains* were you shocked or surprised by the relative failure of your next few films?

'That was a low period. A *very* low period. I don't know how to explain it. The simplest way to look at it would be that the movies just weren't good enough, with the exception of *Pennies from Heaven*. But I tend to take these things personally. I felt very strongly that people didn't like *me*.'

Do you think moving from cinema removed you from your audience, to a large extent?

'It makes it harder to know what is right and what is not. Going into a cinema and watching your own film is the only way to really check the response.'

Sitting amongst your own audience?

'Yes. I do that. But just to check they *are* laughing. I try and arrive last, I sneak in, dressed in disguise.' (He is suddenly in a joking mood.) '. . . I wear a dress. Sometimes I go as Michael Jackson. Just so as not to be noticed.'

Was it easy to return to the stage, albeit for a play (Beckett's *Waiting for Godot*, with Robin Williams)?

'When I was eighteen I did a melodrama in California – *four times a day*. Sometimes we did it *five* times a day. To do that, physically it brings you to a very low ebb. But, technically and professionally, you lose all your fear. It only feels like work, after all. And that confidence all came back for *Godot*. Once I'd got all the lines in place I really didn't have any opening night fears at all.'

What appealed to you in *Godot*?

'It's about the fundamental problem, the existential dilemma, that confronts 20th-century man. It's about loneliness and how people can't get close to others . . . But it's also obviously a comedy, and that's how we played it. We concentrated on laughs and let the existentialism take care of itself.'

It didn't do very well critically.

'Reviews were mixed. It didn't get many laughs. And I took it personally again.'

Do you ever re-watch your old films?

'Sometimes. But only if I'm alone. I think *Roxanne* is still my favourite. It was very personal to me because it was the first feature I wrote entirely by myself [from an adaptation of *Cyrano de Bergerac*]; there were 20 or 25 drafts along the way there. The character is certainly my favourite guy. I look on him as a kind of ordinary man. When it boils down to it only his nose really sets him apart.'

Is it fair to ask which film character is most like you?

'That's very difficult. I like to think of myself as the character in *Roxanne*, but maybe I'm fooling myself and I'm really just, ummm . . . the guy in *The Man with Two Brains*?'

What do you think would sum up what's at the heart of most or all of the characters you portray?

'[Director] Carl Reiner once described me as a guy who saw Fred Astaire and said "Oh, *I can do that*!" Stupidity with confidence is just a great mood to play. It's sort of all I did in my stage act, and a lot of that remains. There's sadism there too, but I'm not a sadist, really. Haa. It's just great fun to play tough.'

Do your characters realise deep down that they're 'jerks'?

'Freddy in *Dirty Rotten Scoundrels* certainly doesn't seem to. He's not offended by people's hints; he's so self-confident that he just bounces off a bad feeling and moves on without a pause or reflection. I find that resilience rather appealing.'

Do you do any sport?

'Err . . . I have an exercise bike. Is that a sport?'

Much of your comedy is bodily. Is it something you take great pleasure in – moving?

'It is a great pleasure, certainly. And it's a style which fits in with what I've just said about self-confidence. My characters usually can't control their bodies very well. But they're doing their very best to make it *seem* like they can.'

Are you pleased with the progress of your career, and your life?

'I am, yes. I'm *pretty* happy right now. The last three or four films have been just delightful to make. I'm happy in my private life. But it's very hard to be what the public want, at the moment. It's very hard.' (He forces a smile.)

The ancient question: What's harder to do, straight acting or comedy?

'I've done both and I still believe comedy is harder.'

What do you do to unwind, to switch off from comedy, from work?

'I'm switched off now – completely. No one is a maniac all the time, it's that simple. You can't be a maniac around home or with friends. They'll all get up and leave. I can't, and won't, do material all day.'

Who do you consider the most 'normal' character you've ever played on film?

'I think I've played increasingly straight roles more recently, around which there is comedy. The guys in *Roxanne* and *Planes, Trains and Automobiles* are pretty straight. But the most normal guy was in *Parenthood*, undoubtedly. I'd say it was the first *real* character I've played. It's just a film about the realities of raising kids.'

You took to fatherly matters with zest and calamity in *Parenthood*. As you've had no children yourself, are they something you have specifically chosen to leave aside, or would you like to become a parent?

'That's a very personal question which I won't answer.'

OK, who's your favourite philosopher?

'Ludwig Wittgenstein!' (Wittgenstein proposed, for one, that words are not strong enough to convey a thought.)

Why do you collect art?

'Because I want . . . Because I enjoy having beautiful things around the place, all around me.'

If perchance there was a fire in your house, and you had to leap for one painting amidst your apparently hefty collection, which would it be?

'What an *awful* thought.' (Martin is not amused.) 'I think . . . I think . . . I think the first thing I would leap for is the insurance policy papers. Definitely.'

ALEXEI SAYLE

The Fat Kid

It's a funny game, Comedy.
Isn't it?

The plump, bald/shaven/baby-headed comedian donned a white three-piece suit and top-hat for the very last moments, of the final show, of his first series of star-billed BBC television programmes, *Alexei Sayle's STUFF*. Waving a cane, tap-dancing briefly and spiritedly attempting the rudimentary movements of a glittering song and dance man, with a gleeful grin across his face, he unfolded his lyrical conclusions on 'all life and science'. 'The only conclusion I have come to', he pronounced, with all manner of seriousness, mock-seriousness, defeatism, optimism, humour and (fake?) show-biz campery, 'is that . . . *it's a funny old world*.' 'It's funny, it's weird, it's strange, it's odd,' he cheerfully opined. 'It's curious, it's wry, it's risible and bizarre – it's weird, it's sardonic, sarcastical, it's mad . . . It's comical . . . It *really* is quite a-mus-ing . . .! *It's a funny old world!*'

During the song Sayle interspersed, or rather tucked, short segments in which, dressed still as the show-man and trouper, he accosted supposed staff-members in the corridors and garden of the BBC's headquarters – a tea-lady, a receptionist, a gardener, a door-man. He would project at them a wise old comment, statistic or fact concerning 'the real world' – about the disproportionate ownership of wealth, the charity status of public education, or that 'Through the actions of mankind one plant or animal species is becoming extinct *every half an hour*'. He would thereafter note, 'It's a funny old w-o-r-rld', and he and the recipient of each 'joke line' would laugh brusquely, uproariously.

In the very final moment of the programme, Sayle, now dressed (supposedly as 'the real Mr Sayle') in jeans and jacket, shrugged – with half-hearted acceptance – and tugged at a light switch, calling it a day.

Sayle rides to meet me on a bicycle, wearing thick-lensed glasses. He carries a 20 pence note-book of comic ideas and a pen, he wears a jacket and black jeans, he sports a dark beard and he sits down to drink sparkling water and smoke small cigars (he is on a health binge). Sayle is known for his loud stage personality and great

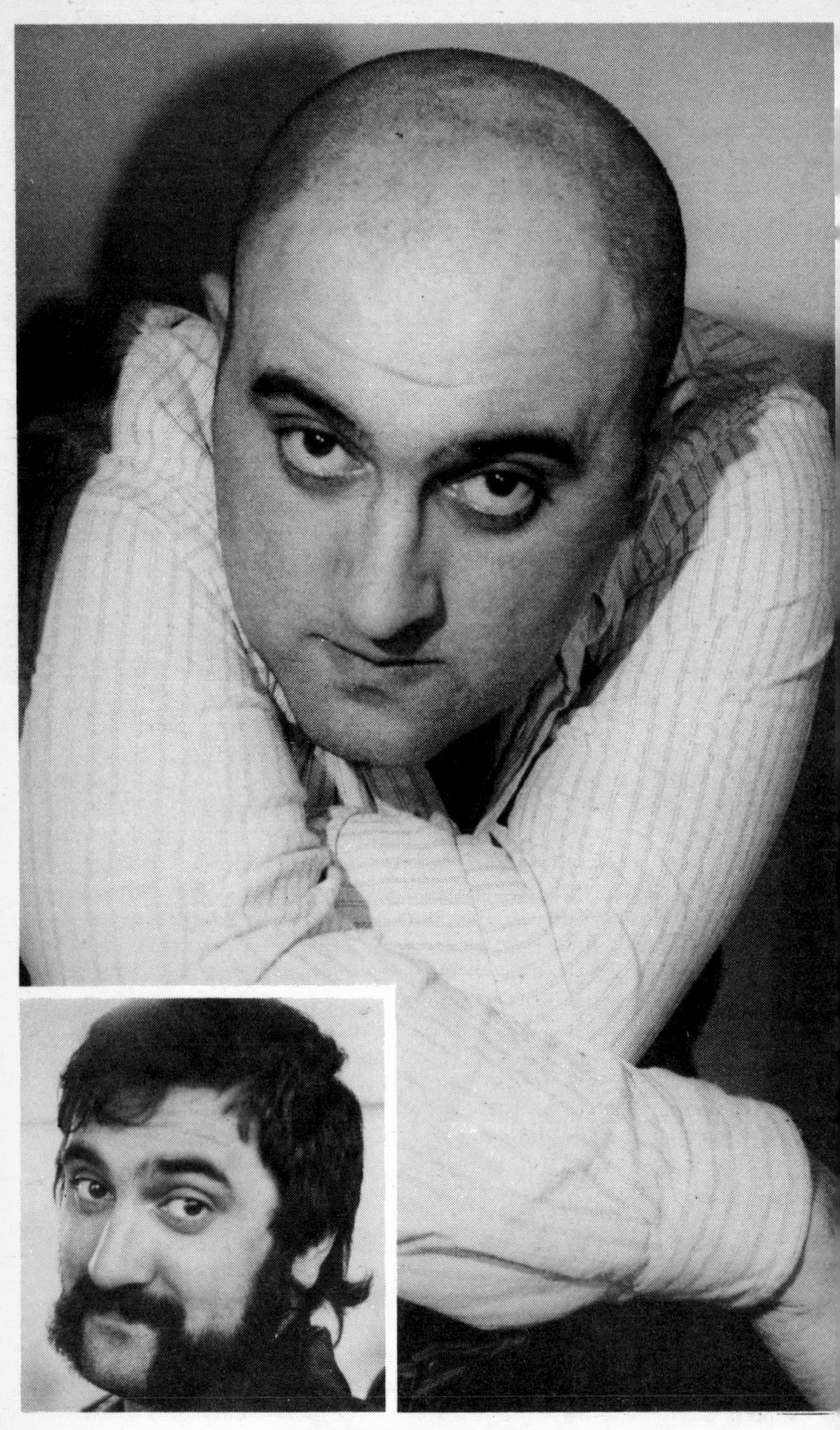

ALEXEI SAYLE, in need of a shave, 1984
Photograph by John Gamble Jr
(Inset) ALEXEI, at about 20 years old
Photograph by Deidre Sayle

self-belief; he first made his name abusing, amusing and bemusing audiences, and other comedians, as the curt compère of the London stand-up club 'The Comedy Store'. But in person Sayle talks softly, almost whispers unenergetically, increasing the decibels (a great deal) only to laugh. A self-confessed 'working-class' Liverpudlian born in 1952 of lapsed-Jewish, communist parents, Alexei is to many the most important British comic to evolve out of the late 1970s. He is one to which politics and the bizarre appear to have had equal influence and import, and it is in this clash – which often produces an amalgamation, but not always – that there seems to be the key to his comic roots and psychological drives.

'I think there's something in everyone that leads them to their "talent",' he says quietly, unwrapping then sniffing a cigar. 'Presumably a person inclined towards carpentry, if they saw a piece of wood, would think of what they could make with it. Well, when I was taken to the theatre by my parents, I wanted to get up on stage. I *knew* I could do it. It seemed easy and obvious to me . . . I was always a bit of a show-off.'

Did you grow up self-conscious of your appearance?

'No.' (He is rather adamant.)

You've many times called yourself 'Mr Fat Bastard'.

'It never really bothered me. The reason I'm trying to slim a little now is *purely* for health reasons. I'm getting on a bit, age-wise.'

It's generally assumed that a main ingredient of your on-stage, and even off-stage, personality seems to be a desire *not* to be loved.

'I haven't got the desire to be loved. But most comedians have. I'd honestly say that I think most comedians are psychologically disturbed in that way.' (He laughs now.) 'They are . . . They're not well. But the desire for love and applause is not in *my* make-up. For a start, I'm not remotely show-bizzy – *I hope*. The impression I try to give is "I don't like *you*, you don't like *me*, I'm just here to make you laugh." '

Is that not a contradiction, though – to want to perform and gain attention, but not be loved?

'That's because, well . . . I don't perform from a *lack* of confidence. *Quite the reverse* – I have an excess of confidence. Arrogance, really. I was a very spoilt only-child; that's why I'm a show-off, I suppose. Indeed my mother always convinced me I had, well – *a unique vision to give to the world*.' Sayle says this without the mildest grin or guffaw. But he has a coda. 'There's millions of people like that. *I* just happened to be great.'

So you are a result of your own thirst rather than your mother's?

'Well, she could have been wrong! But . . .' Sayle takes up an academic and somewhat contradictory posture now, '. . . It's here we come to the political crux of it all. If people are encouraged or receive high expectations, they *will* achieve, I think. That is the difference between public-school and working-class education really. In the latter you're told over and over again that you're stupid, that you shouldn't expect too much, or much at all. But as for the Jewish-mother thing, certainly my mother is an archetype, even though she's a communist. I got a great emotional, or genetic, emphasis on achievement from her.'

When you write or perform, *who* do you feel you are doing it for?

(He laughs.) 'The BBC, I suppose – if they're giving me the money.'

(Fair enough.) Was your father equally supportive?

'Umm . . . *Fairly* adoring, I would say. He died quite a few years ago, a while after I'd started in comedy. He had Alzheimer's Disease. He worked on the railways as a guard, even while he was ill, and retired when I was about fourteen. After he retired he was sort of "around the house". When he was well he was friendly and genial. I mean, neither of my parents were too outgoing or witty. My mother is pretty po-faced! She has the sort of sense of humour women at Greenham Common have.'

Can you elaborate?

'Plodding, fairly humourless, a sort of Polish sense of humour, like you see in a cabaret in Prague.' (He laughs.)

Did your mother work?

'She was a pools-clerk.'

What did they both want of you, given that you were their only child? You escorted them on assorted Marxist-Leninist activities in Liverpool – did they want you to be a professional politico?

'I don't really know. My mother did, perhaps. I did find myself spouting politically, in her manner. My father, meanwhile, worked very hard, and got nowhere really, and was bitter about it. My parents put their faith in socialism; they were of a generation who believed whole-heartedly that the world was changing for the better, and thus were devastated when it didn't. A lot of people I mixed with in my youth were very badly done over, like my father, and embittered. So I resolved never to put too much faith in anything, but at least get a secure base and some money and succeed on my own terms.'

Have your political ideas altered much over the years?

'I still *believe* in Marxism, in the sense that I think it's the most accurate science for analysing the way things are. The people that make everything get the least reward and are always crapped on. No power and no dignity, really. That's really what I *like* to think is at the core of what I do, comically; that it has a bedrock of political belief. But whether or not it is and does is another matter.'

Did it affect your sensibility or sense of humour when your father died?

'If I think about it there's certainly a gap there. Although it didn't really affect me strongly, on the surface, when he died. But certainly I reckon death is at the centre of a lot of art, if not *all* art . . .'

Can I ask what your mother thinks about your comic material?

'I don't know. No idea.'

Surely you must have *some* idea?

'No!' (Alexei laughs heartily – a loud bearlike, bass guffaw.) 'No; I've no idea.'

But given that she was the one who thought you, 'my son', had this 'great vision' to propagate . . .

'Well, I don't think she expected me to be a comedian. But I feel she's proud of my achievements. Although I don't think she's understood most of it, really . . . As for my father,' (he laughs again), 'he wouldn't understand it either.'

Do you think your anti-authority attitude is at all born out of feelings towards them?

'I don't really feel it. My attitudes, my feelings come mainly through politics.'

It's worth bearing in mind that in Sayle's book *Great Bus Journeys of the World* (see Bibliography) he proposed a philosophy blending Marxism with Sportism and Humorism, and suggested that 'If when Lenin uttered the chilling words, *Liberty is precious – so precious that it must be rationed*, everybody present had burst into hysterical laughter, made farty noises and wiggled their ears, then the history of the Soviet Union would have been very different.' With this joke he seems to be rebelling against, but also paying credence to, the straightforward dogma he grew up on. The theme is further explored elsewhere in the same book, in Sayle's short-story 'The Odd Dream of I.N. Skytyvkar'. This story involves the central character being unknowingly tested as to his 'Marxist-Leninist teaching' by a Soviet Commissar, a 'test' which requires actual *matricide*.

You say you don't want love but you obviously want success. Where does money fit into the equation?

'I think I decided I wanted to be financially secure because of how I saw my father work for so many years without really getting any of it.'

What sort of people did you mix with as a teenager?

'Obviously a lot of communists, at meetings. I always used to go out with girls older than me. At school I usually hung around with blokes who were older than me, one of whom was the son of a friend of my mother's in the Communist Party. We used to get blind drunk. Occasionally he used to encourage me to sing, dance and tell jokes. But the thing about Liverpool, anyway, is that there's a great *lingua franca* between people to begin with – an exchange and a drama about *everything*.'

Did that lay the foundation of the raucousness in your stage performance?

'It was all about making trouble. The basis of my humour is making trouble, certainly. I irritated teachers, I carried on in pubs, I did routines, little skits. To attract attention. Ha-h-ha.'

Attention?

'Yes, not love – *just* attention.'

In 1971, at nineteen years of age (he was born on 7 August 1952),

Sayle made the break from Liverpool to London, 'setting up shop' there and studying painting (and 'making lots of little home movies') at Chelsea School of Art. 'I stayed clear of the Hall of Residence' he notes, 'I moved into a flat with some Palestinian friends, and two French au pair girls. Which was sort of riotous.' He never had any doubts that all his Merseyside friends would relocate as he had done, but found the capital city 'very lonely . . . especially as my girlfriend was back in Liverpool'. He remembers feeling at art school that he did not want to articulate his paintings, and of this attitude he jokes 'I can just draw 'orses out me 'ead!', although this is slightly at odds with his return (several years later) to lecture on General Studies at Chelsea. In the meanwhile, post-college, he worked variously as 'an occasional free-lance illustrator', a clerk in the social services (the then DHSS), and a dish-washer. He says this left him with an abiding love of 'the comedy and sophisticated, highly technical interplay of the work-place, of work-mates . . . canteen comedy'. He felt at the time that 'there should be a way of making that performable'; and remembers 'one guy I worked for who used to say I was the only bloke in the country who could be a *genuinely working-class* comedian'. At this point, in 1976, his old friend Cliff Cocker asked Alexei, who was noted for a vague physical similarity to the East European intellectual Bertolt Brecht, to play a part in his Brechtian cabaret troupe. The troupe toured, rehearsed, argued, recited poetry and songs for a year, and then 'after a huge row' various members left, leaving Cocker directing and only Alexei and one other to perform. They resolved to create a new style and repertoire, and took to humour as 'a fruitful area'. The group performed 'anywhere we could get a booking – colleges, old people's homes, Communist Party gatherings'. Their very first 'performance', indeed, was at a Communist Party *party* in somebody's house, and Alexei remembers improvising and developing material about 'yuppies, then upcoming, and my hatred of subsidised theatre and the patronising element of the welfare state . . . things I *despise*'.

Despite his political affiliations, which remain in concept the same to this day (Sayle says that, as a 'self-employed petit bourgeois' he has a choice of cultural affiliations, and chooses the working-class as his, although 'I don't mix too much with them now'), he has never felt obliged to 'confirm the prejudices' of his audience. 'Even performing for the Communist Party I was always *challenging* them' he declares, 'taking the piss, laughing at the 8,000 unsold copies of the *Morning Star* under their bed'. Indeed he became disillusioned with the Left in London, and 'their mind games', compared to the more down-to-earth, social nature of his Marxist folk back home. Sayle and company played elaborate hoaxes on their politico audiences, engaged them in contretemps and often received semi-violent reactions. Indeed, he says, 'I've always felt an antagonism towards *every* audience'; although this seemed to be less the case when – after his beginnings in theatre – he organised productions, lectures and workshops during his spell of teaching at Chelsea. He disliked signing the contract to work there, and he did not enjoy the responsibilities of educating. 'I found kids actually like you to be bossy and firm' he remembers, 'But it's something I *hated* doing. I occasionally said things like "You make me *so* cross!", when actually I wasn't at all. Generally lessons would fall apart, I'd send the students away. . . . which was obviously quite dangerous – legally – if they'd got *mown down* by a truck or something.'

Between 1979 and 1981 Sayle both taught, during the day, and then performed, abused audiences and gonged off other jesters at The Comedy Store, where he ventured and was chosen as compère after his wife saw an advert in *Private Eye* magazine. From that club came a new generation of comics and a rebirth of cabaret in England, Sayle's contribution being a dynamic aggressive style of stand-up blending a shaved head ('the only style too ugly for the ruling classes to appropriate'), confrontation, politics, the (four letter) language of the street and surrealism.

How did you fit in at The Comedy Store? Did you feel a member of a team or an outsider, a loner?

'Well, I was the compère, I got the best exposure. I was fairly rude to the others, who were mostly younger than me, but they had to be nice to me or I'd put them on last. And I know I was one of the best, if not *the* best. And I had gained a pushy, healthy equilibrium from knowing I *was* the best.'

How did your on-stage style evolve?

'I just got up and it was there. But you only really create a stage persona by the fact that it – or various ingredients – work; that you produce reaction. I learnt how to deal with all types of heckling, and my work took on those ingredients. On another level, when you get into show-business, you get to remake or *reinvent* yourself, anyway. And indeed I partly, or mostly, invented that whole new style of stand-up comedy. Although, to be fair, I'd say I was very much a post-punk creation, attitude-wise, inspired partly by John Cooper Clarke (the Mancunian stage poet), Ian Dury (the distinctly London working-class singer) . . . and from another direction, Monty Python.'

How serious were the 'non-sexist, non-racist' declarations of The Comedy Store club and the jokes of its new generation of stand-ups?

'I think it was fairly heart-felt. I've personally never wanted to make fun of the underdog. But certainly it became and was used as a gimmick, a counterpoint to the kind of stand-up that previously prevailed. But where the new generation often went wrong was in becoming preachy and self-satisfied.'

What audience did Sayle acquire? Despite his desire for genuine 'working-class' appeal, the bulk of his audiences – at least in his club and tour days – were students, all-round liberals and social-worker types, paying to hear abuse and be abused. At one point he claims he gained an '80% working-class audience', but this seems debatable. And yet, abandoning the live stage, he can be seen to have achieved a broader, more mystical (and further removed) audience with his subsequent moves into TV performances and column-writing, albeit with much restraint over the harsher tones of his language. And although he has now moved from the small tower-block council flat he occupied in the days of his barn-stomping performances in *The Young Ones* and his early cinema outings, Sayle remains at least in theory and spirit aligned with his roots . . . although he certainly has joked a lot about being 'very famous in America now' (a serious desire?). There are suggestions that in the 1990s he may want to become 'a serious actor'.

From 1979 until 1985 you honed and developed your stage material, playing assorted venues and taking on large-scale tours. Did it feel like play, or hard work?

'Bits of both. ''Oh well, another gig.'' I did as many as seven appearances a night, sometimes – one audience would be cold, the next warm, then one luke-warm, then another cold, then a really hot one . . . In a technical sense it's *fantastic* training. You adopt a comedian's mentality. I've been in the situation where I've had appalling flu, been put in a taxi shivering, covered in sweat, barely able to walk and raced to a club to perform. But, however I felt, as soon as I got on stage it just clicked, and I felt I could stay on for two hours. Because that's the way my body works. And you pay a price for that, which is probably why comedians drink a lot. You pay a price in all kinds of ways for that energy, but it's always there. You switch on, go full steam, and your ailments always feel considerably worse afterwards. So you can't keep drawing on that bank-account for ever, and that's why I tapered off the live work and finally stopped.'

Did you always feel rough after a show?

'Surely, yes. Absolutely knackered. And there's a certain kind of strangeness in the sense that after you've been entertaining 600 to 1,000 people, or whatever, then there's just you and a couple of others in a car, poodling down the motorway. It's peculiar. I think if you do it too much it could send you crackers.'

Were there moments in which you felt you were going over the edge?

'I got to a point where I was seriously drinking. Then I got to a point where I couldn't be bothered to cope anymore.'

You've often done material based on the bizarre comments and eccentric, unnerving behaviour of drunks.

'I'm just interested generally in madness, really. In bizarre word-play, dreams, alcohol – it's all there. I've always been interested in reading about madness; if only for the humour of it. My line ''Eh, didn't you kill my brother?'' was actually brought to me by David Stafford (Sayle's occasional co-writer), who seems to have a magnetic attraction to nut-cases. He sends out vibrations of some kind to the insane. Someone asked him, on one occasion, ''Does this tube-train go to Oxford Street?'' David replied ''No, you have to change at . . . , and then the guy chipped in with *''Didn't you kill my brother?''* ' (Early Comedy Store comedian Keith Allen claims the line was inspired by his own, 'Didn't you kill my mother?')

You also have an obsession with East European characters.

'I travelled there with my parents a lot, as a youngster, because my father got free travel on railways. We went on NUR delegations to ball-bearing factories in Eastern Europe. That's before many people were travelling there, or even having foreign holidays. And I was intrigued and also amused by what I saw – the complete lack of advertising, the one brand of toothpaste, the strange design of the cars which looked like something from *Dan Dare*, and the belated trappings of Western culture reaching its cities.'

Perhaps what's rather important is that your work seems to contain a distinct push and pull between what is 'working-class' and what is 'intellectual'. As just one example, you used to adopt a Cockney strain and opine 'We fucking hate Jean-Paul Sartre 'round our way . . . You know why? 'Cos he knows fuck-all about the Cortina!'

'That's about several things, really. It's partly a gimmick, but for me it's always been an assertion. A reaction against the public-school nature of most of show-business, but mainly an assertion that you can be working-class, have a working-class accent and yet hopefully be open to intellectual notions. Or rather, I'm very anti-intellectual, but *pro*-intelligence. And I feel that working-class ideal, that self-assertion, has been lost, in a way. It's known as *the auto-didact*.' (Sayle draws out the phrase with all manner of serious, humorous and phonetic enjoyment, and unwraps another small cigar.)

When did you first sample and recognise that intellectual and working-class ideal?

'My parents were always fairly literate, but in my teens I came across all these people in Marxist groups who were dockers, coal-miners and hard-cases and yet nevertheless read *Tess of the D'Urbervilles*. They appeared very interesting and fruitful to me; it just seemed to make perfect sense. They would even have fist-fights over, for example the meaning of, well, *auto-didact*.'

You admired that?

'Yes.' (He chortles sharply.) '*In a way*. But I tended to be less ebullient then, in older company. I sat there, watching, observing. I took it all in, quite liked it and yet didn't know what to do with it.'

Did you have a sense of it being amusing?

'*Potentially* funny. But although I found them admirable, I never wanted to be like them.'

Further to the 'working-class' and 'intellectual' clash, very often your jokes revolve around first referencing an intellectual or a revolutionary idea, 'the proletarian struggle' or whatever, and then deflating or exploding it with a punchline about dolphins or eels.

'Haa-ha. Well, that's because I'm a comedy writer! It *has* to be like that! That's because it's my *job*.'

Like the Surrealist Movement of the Parisian 1920s onwards, from which he derives the shape and flavour of his material, Sayle's work, his humour, is born out of all manner of seeming contradictions. André Breton and his fellow proponents of 'surrealist revolution' conceived and evolved their intellectual and artistic ideas during years of debate and pamphleteering over (what amounted to) the two contrasting principles of *Reality* and *Pleasure* . . . They craved, fretted over and pined for an elusive middle-ground – a middle-ground nevertheless extreme – between individuality and collectivism, consciousness and unconsciousness, free-form and structure, irresponsibility and responsibility, liberation and repression, logic and illogic, love and anger, the political and the apolitical, and even the Proletariat and the Bourgeoisie.

Whether in the stand-up mould or on screen, much of Sayle's humour is markedly surrealist in vein, tunnelled through varying degrees of aggression and delight. In his comic mind, human paranoia produced by worrying about mortgage payments can be filtered and recycled to heat one's lounge. If you do evil but 'it's for a spina bifida charity', he snaps sarcastically, '. . . then that's all right then!' Spiralling off, as is his wont, he is both amused by and spiteful towards do-it-yourselfers who make 'a dustbin full of Pernod for four pence', of music-hall acts like 'Ken Platt and His Talking Pond'. He sincerely quotes the words of German philosopher Hegel and then changes sides, snarling 'What a load of crap!', before trailing off into another bizarre notion . . . 'Auction my scrotum for Oxfam!' A serious comment is often denounced with a boyish, embarrassed or dismissive 'Naaaaah!' (No). Within his comedy exists both the boy interested only in play (the pleasure principle) and the adult faced with social and political facts (the reality principle). Sometimes it seems as if he is saying that childlike imagination, or *humour*, offers a higher plain of thought than adult politics; at other times it seems that Alexei the free-spirit is brought down to earth by adult responsibility, parental wants and political reality. It is in the schizophrenic slips and slides between these two forces that his comedy arrives. It was all perhaps succinctly summed up in a particulary sharp twist in political discourse pontificated dramatically in his 'Comic Strip' film *Didn't You Kill My Brother?* Seized with revolutionary vigour, Sayle's character (or rather the nobler half of his twins 'double act') put into words his dream of international co-operation, trust and decency derived from 'schools and factories and community-centres'. Filled with spirit he spoke of a new single socialist economy, of a great new vision, then paused quixotically before announcing 'Then suddenly my dream changed . . .', thereafter recording the vision of himself in a swimming-pool full of puppies, one of the puppies – who has the facial features of Lord Palmerston – begging him the imponderable question: 'Where's the spoons, where's the spoons, WHERE'S THE BLOODY SPOONS?!'

There is a childlike side to all surrealism.

> 'Yes, and I'm a big kid really. The thing is, I've *never* had a totally mature attitude, I've *never* held down a proper job. I've *never* had the full dose of adult concerns, and I'm stubborn like a child.'

How does your material evolve, and how does that blend of social comment and nonsense come about?

'It's unconscious and also *perhaps* rather mechanical at times. They're both things that interest me, so when I come to putting sketches and pieces together, I often think "This piece is fairly heavy-duty, so I'll put this mad bit next, then something semi-political". The thing about surrealism and writing is that you have to be fairly systematic anyway, however free-form it's to seem. You have to develop a method of taking notes while allowing ideas and traces to collide. You sit down alone and fantasise; I hate writing with someone else. One of the greatest problems for me is simply getting the pen and paper in place. So I get a lot of ideas whilst walking; I like to get a lot of exercise . . . Comedy writing is a fairly nebulous business. It depends on a central idea that takes a second to think up. It's often pointless to rack your brains because that idea will come in the bath, or on the bus. So a lot of the time you spend ostensibly doing virtually nothing. Which is actually *a bit wearing*.'

What happens when the pressure's on? You apparently wrote the bulk of five TV shows in almost as many weeks.

'That was freaky. Two songs and 80 or so minutes material, although others wrote the rest. What I find interesting is the way your body metabolism changes, the way your functions contort themselves to fit that demand. So I'd work all day, fall asleep, wake up again and move *straight* to the typewriter.'

Whether it's work or pleasure, are you fairly self-critical?

'Very. I'm not totally pleased with most things I do . . . I *want* to do it, but I don't know if it gives me much pleasure, except in the moments I make myself laugh . . . Although I do sometimes enjoy the dress-rehearsals, the prancing around in costumes.'

Can we make it clear whether you think politics in humour works, or whether you think it better to be an absurdist, totally off-the-wall?

'Well, politics is central to people's lives in the rawest, broadest sense. The purpose of art, I suppose, is to reflect people's lives. But I don't carry on from that and conclude that it can change the political situation. I don't think as a comedian you can do an *enormous* amount about changing people's attitudes. But if you mention Marx or Thomas Hardy there's at least the *possibility* of people picking up on it. And certainly humour can operate as a code and expression of friendship and love between individuals. Indeed, I feel rather sorry for people without a sense of humour.'

What sort of fan-mail do you attract?

'I don't get much, thankfully. It's a bit like getting an obscene phone-call, y'know? "Dear Alexei, I think you're great", "How do you feel?" or "Why don't you fuck off back to Russia, you fat bastard!" I don't like people being obsessed with any performer. I get quite a few letters from unmarried mothers who think I'm nice and want to marry me . . . which I suppose is *quite* good. And I had a lot of funny stuff from readers when I used to write a column for the *Daily Mirror*, which was good. I had a long correspondence about cake-shops and why they always put the cakes away at 3.30pm, and a lot of mail concerning lobsters, which I incorporated into the column. But I don't like people getting obsessed by any performer.'

Where do you think comedians can go wrong as their careers progress?

'Well, you have to bear in mind that show-business is specifically designed to send you round the bend anyway, and most succumb to that. It's not constructive; it exacerbates any personality problems that already exist. And sycophants propel those problems onwards.'

What attitudes does your wife bring to you; what part does she play in your comedy?

'She plays a very central part, despite not being visible. She has a very good over-view of what I do – she restrains my worst moments and appreciates the best. From the first time I met her she saw through me, took the piss out of my cockiness, my pretensions, bringing me down-to-earth. She's very good at *taking the piss*.'

Is she a replacement for your mother, too?

'Haaaaa.' (Sayle makes a long loud laugh which fills the room. But he does not answer.)

Do you think all comedians need that kind of close relationship?

'It would be a good idea if they had someone like that, certainly. But most of them very deliberately get rid of anyone they know who is close to them and down-to-earth. I think that's one of the first signs you see of when big-headedness and madness and celebrity have taken hold . . . when they get rid of friends, the people who know they can be fools. That's a very common thing. Comedians, revolutionaries . . . they *all* get rid of their old buddies! Most comedians have an inflated sense of themselves anyway. So they can't handle having the piss taken out of them, even though they can do it to others and even to themselves.'

'I enjoyed that . . . I like talking about myself, I really do,' said Alexei, prior to departure. When we left, he paused at the top of the steps to the building, looking – momentarily – for all the world like Benito Mussolini. Then he stepped down, unlocked his bicycle from a lamp-post, tucked his trousers into his socks, donned his thick-lensed black National Health spectacles and cycled off with his head to the wind. Tucked amidst the traffic he looked almost unnoticeable now, save for a great, eccentric unfashionability, akin to an East European office-clerk peddling to work, probably with a diary full of alienation in his inside breast pocket.

STEPHEN FRY

Pretty Well-Balanced

People, I think, can be divided into two groups.
Those who divide people into two groups . . . and those who don't.

Stephen Fry sits at a large oak table in the lounge of his London home. On the table rest two packets of cigarettes, a bank-holiday-sized cryptic newspaper crossword (shortly to be completed, even though it arrived just earlier this morning), plus a large bowl of internationally selected fruit received as a house-warming present from his parents. He toys – like a nervous or simply playful youngster – with pieces of fruit as he talks, punctuating the conversation with occasional wide-eyed *and* poetic comments on the exotic nature and variety of the fruit.

The uncrowded woody room says several things about him. It is a games-player's room and it looks to the future and the past. A modern painting of Oscar Wilde hangs on one wall, a stool bearing an ashtray full of stubbed cigarettes stands in front of a game of televised cricket ('My kind of comedy is the cricketing kind – comedy of the Shires'). A glossy white electric piano stands against one wall, this turning out to be a device which moves its own keys to the orders of a digitalised computer disc, but on which (his sister tells me) Fry has also been known to offer the odd private rendition of 'Send In the Clowns'. A scholar's collection of bound books fills a few high shelves. Hanging on a wooden coat-stand are assorted tweedy clothes and a motor-bike helmet.

A slightly stocky man in his early 30s, with dozy eyes, a nose which veers off towards his left cheek half-way down the nostrils (and then veers back again), and a curved fringe of hair constantly in danger of covering his eyes, Fry speaks in a patrician accent but with great joy for tone, language and life. With little prompting he is keen to ponder on his comic actor heroes and heroine.

'I adore Margaret Rutherford, Alistair Sim and Mark Madison,' he says. 'They had a lot in common in many respects. They performed as character actors without any trace of preachiness, but it's obvious they were people of great social conscience. They were at once funny and caring. Take Alistair Sim. I've seen a recording of an address he once gave, as Rector of St Leonard's University, and it was one of the most brilliant speeches ever made by anyone. Much better

A successful STEPHEN FRY ponders whether he slept last night
Photograph courtesy of Noel Gay
(Inset) FRY tones down his Wildean ways for a graduation photograph. Photograph by Mrs Fry

than any *political* speech I've heard. It's also *fantastically* funny. He tells them how to be students, how to be young, what to look forward to, what perhaps to be wary of . . . it's quite superb. You only have to look at him. The way he wears clothes, the way the hair grows out of the side of his head, *his eyes* . . . You can tell he *loves* people. He gives so much resonance to everything he says. In the J. B. Priestley film *Let the People Sing* (1942) there's a scene in which he arrives to stop industrialists closing down a Northern music-hall. The industrialists say "What the workers do in their spare time is entirely their own affair." And Sim replies, with all manner of wonderful expression – "*Gentlemen, gentlemen, gentlemen* . . . There's no spare time – *only time*." It's both very funny and immensely true. You can just tell the idea of being shackled was abhorrent to Sim, and Rutherford. They loved life and people, and that's why their performances – even when they were just cameos – were so staggeringly human . . . People who are strong oaks apparently, but they reveal in fact that they're wonderfully hysterical little saplings blowing in a frenzied howling breeze of chaos that comes from without.'

I show Fry a photograph of Laurel and Hardy pondering over a jigsaw puzzle (see at the end of this book). He looks at it long and hard. 'Oh yes' he smiles, flicking back his fringe now, 'It's absolutely perfect, isn't it?'

Perhaps, I offer, Oliver Hardy and Margaret Rutherford were rather similar, linked in physique, manner and resilience despite their sex (they had in common facial expressions, optimism and lightness on their feet, for example).

'It's all to do with dignity,' Fry responds, ' . . . A gentleman and a gentlewoman. Tidy, immaculately dressed, kind, soft, motherly, resourceful, relentless . . . larger than life and yet graceful. They both refused to perform for jokes, per se, and they never played to elicit pathos. They were quite wonderful. They were *angels*.'

All you've said connects great humour with warmth and love and sincerity and a generous nature. Is it not surprising, then, that Laurel and Hardy, for instance, were adored by dictators like Mussolini and Stalin, who collected their films and watched them avidly and yet were cruel people elsewhere in their lives?

'Oh, well . . . that may be true. But laughter is an uncontrollable force. You cannot laugh at something directed specifically at your thought processes, so to speak, only what can be observed. Comedy is abstract, just as music is abstract. Hitler adored Wagner and Beethoven but that's not to say that they were fascist. Beethoven, indeed, was anti-imperialist. And it's a great mistake to assume that people like Stalin were just humourless fools. I'm not surprised that Laurel and Hardy touched people like Stalin – who was, now I think of it, rather Oliver Hardy-like . . . in some ways. "Charming" was often a word used about Hitler too. Stalin was a jovial figure, with a big sense of humour and a large wry moustache. But that, in the background, or foreground, he was responsible for millions of people dying is something we all have to come to terms with. You can say of Jews, "If you prick us do we not bleed, if you tickle us do we not laugh?", but one can *also* say that of the dictators.'

The question being, despite the gentle warm images you connect with comedy, is it not also connected strongly with aggression?

'Laughter is like violence, in one sense,' he agrees. He moves on at unnerving speed. 'It is also like *sex*. A metaphor I often use is "pornography and erotic writing." The point is that comedy provokes an absolute physical reaction which is uncontrollable. Comedy makes people produce involuntary noises, shake their bodies and even shed tears. These are all things that they cannot control. And that's also true of one's reaction to pornography *and* erotic writing. The metaphor is the Stiffy – the erection. In Hollywood people read scripts and say "This script just doesn't give me a hard-on." What they mean is they haven't laughed.'

But are you implying that there is base laughter and also *artistic* laughter – the latter being of true quality, like supposed erotic writing in comparison with pornography?

'Yes, there's cheap comedy, just as there is pornography which gives a physical reflex whether you like it or not. If one is in a certain kind of mood one can find oneself watching all kinds of very bad comedy; thinking "This is terrible! Why am I smiling?" And I think there is good quality comedy just as there is erotic writing. There are people who work in comedy and say "Well, it got a laugh, didn't it?" and that's enough for them. And then there are those who say, "Well yes, but it was really the *wrong* laugh." '

(Fry goes on fondling various pieces of fruit. He keeps a reasonable distance from both the table and me. I feel, with his hair now slipped over his eyes again, he is somehow avoiding the gist of what I am suggesting. I quiz him again.)

But do you, whether to good, bad or no effect whatsoever – think people like Stalin connected mentally with humorists like Laurel and Hardy because they, like the comics, had an aggression and a misery tucked behind their charm?

'Umm . . . Quite why people laugh or create laughter remains a mystery to me'

Ahhh. Freud said that humorists, the makers of humour, were disunited personalities predisposed to neurotic disorders.

'He may also have said, though, that *human beings* are neurotic and disunited personalities. In fact, most of his life Freud did say that. He proved that a person's *id, ego* and *super-ego* are rarely in balance. I don't know if comedians are any *more* guilty of that unbalance, although certainly they exploit that human characteristic more than others. If it's true they're predisposed, I think it's very unfortunate for them.'

The theory is that not only do they have stronger neuroses but that the neuroses fuel the comedy and the comedy releases the force of them.

'But psychologists will tell you that almost anything anyone does outside the humdrum, and even *including* the humdrum, they do as a solace or in order to avoid neurotic disorder. From sucking a pencil to eating sweets to smoking . . . it's almost obvious. We know that we do things to feel pleasure, and part of that pleasure is avoiding dis-pleasure. Comedians do comedy to stop being unhappy . . . but they also do it to be happy. I'm not sure where I fall on the graph. But, in my experience of meeting others, I would say comedians seem reasonably well balanced to me. I don't know of many who are prone to absolute melancholia, at least that I'm aware of. Obviously in someone like Tony Hancock's case it became clinical and pathological, but maybe he would have had just the same symptoms if he'd been a musician or a straight actor. In fact I would estimate that far less comedians have committed suicide or drugged themselves to death than actors or musicians.'

So comedians, in general, are well-balanced personalities?

'Well . . . Let's say, perhaps *pretty* well-balanced.'

The humour of Stephen Fry, at its best, is at once phonetically eloquent, linguistically playful, pompous, anti-pompous and conceptually perverse. As reference briefly, a look at three of his television sketches with partner Hugh Laurie may suffice. In the first, they – as two stern grumpy gentlemen – discuss how once decent words have become indecent; how 'gay used to be such a lovely word' and 'homosexual', 'pouffy' and 'arse-bandit' once could be used in their 'proper context', to wit; 'Ah, Jane, the garden's looking very homosexual today . . . Landlord, I'll have two foaming pints of your most homosexual beer please!' In a second sketch, Fry, as a dishevelled prisoner-of-war, recovers consciousness tied to a chair in a Nazi's office. After a few moments, Fry's character takes his first look at the stern Nazi and falls in love. 'You're so *beautiful*,' he says: 'That it should happen *here* and *now*, of all places.' 'Maybe you are playing on me some of your English senses of humour', says the Nazi (Laurie). As Laurie turns and walks across the room, Fry hollers, 'Get that arse!' A third sketch, titled and credited on television (for reasons of humour and offence), 'Bitch-Mother Come Light My Bottom, by Sir William (Now Lord) Rees-Mogg', showed Fry grafting an eloquent, linguistically playful dialogue on to a prim and proper barber who is untrained and in essence doo-lally. 'Which of the manifold hairs upon sir's crisp and twinkling headage would sir like to place in my professional care for the purpose of securing an encutment?' begs Fry, wielding scissors and nine barber's cloaks. Despite the small world the barber inhabits, and despite – or because of – his madness, he is a romantic at heart relishing ' . . . the desire that we should both of us embark upon this journey [the cutting of hair] together as innocents – as wide-eyed travellers to a distant land, unknowing of our fate, careless of our destination . . . to embark, some day, somewhere, bruised, sad, a little wiser perhaps . . . but ultimately, and joyously, *alive*.' The twist, or at least the camply overplayed punchline to this wordy sketch, was Fry leaving the barber's shop at the decisive, hair-cutting moment, and returning wielding a chain-saw.

'I love games' Fry explains, 'I see Man as essentially a games player. I'm very good at Scrabble. Way, way back, I've always had a facility for words, been very speedy with anagrams, crosswords, puns, words spelt backwards, word sequence quizzes, finding rhymes. It's a sensual joy, really. I love the sound of language being uttered – the hitting of the tongue on the palette. And I relish great prose writing which comes alive on the page.'

You had a great fondness for P. G. Wodehouse in your youth.

'And still do. Since I was twelve years old I've found him absolutely peerless as a funny writer. I wrote him when I was fourteen and got back a signed photograph which I treasure to this day. His quality was to do with two things – the language *and* the good nature. I've always responded very adversely to cruelty, even cruelty *against* cruelty. So even if I read a book with a minor character who is shat upon . . . I just get very *upset*. I can't *bear* cruelty. But Bertie Wooster in Jeeves' stories was a man of such good taste . . . And as for the prose, it was of such fanatical or fantastic quality that you wished it were made of a thick viscous fluid so you could submerge yourself in it.'

In a sense then you've created that environment for yourself in adulthood.

'Well, I've certainly retained and developed a thirst for language. It's a facility on one hand and a love on the other. The spoken word means a great deal to me . . . I love the wireless, for instance. I found myself to be pretty insomniac as a youngster, so I spent many many nights in bed listening enthusiastically to the BBC World Service.'

Is this linguistic pleasure to do with structure or freedom?

'It *is* about structure – because we all yearn for structure. But words can also fly off and send us on a journey.'

You're a great admirer of Oscar Wilde, who relished turning assumptions on their heads.

'Because, in a way, that is the key to everything. You can find that almost anything, when turned on its head, is equally true. Wilde took the phrase "Drink is the curse of the working-classes", rotated it by 180 degrees, and made "Work is the curse of the drinking-classes". Which is a very witty epigram, and also a sharp social and political comment.'

How personal is Trefulsis, the philologist character whom you evolved for radio?

'He is, incidentally, the central character of a novel I am writing . . . which appears to be becoming rather autobiographical. Trefulsis is a historian of language, of words' origins and development. *He* did a year or so of segments on Radio 4. He did various *impassioned* "Wireless Essays" on assorted subjects. I found that, as he was an old man, I could be extremely satirical and vicious without any complaints. One week I said of Norman Tebbit, ''Well, we can't be doing with this maniac, this baaastard running our affairs – it's too impertinent.'' If I'd said it in my own voice the BBC switchboard would have been jammed. So a voice is very useful to hide behind. Whereas the urban working-class comic is direct, the provincial middle-class comic is far more likely to hide behind a character – it's because they're more frightened of people.'

But why do you think some people develop more propensity for and love of (humorous) language than others? Is it self-protection?

'I don't know whether all reflexes and taboos develop because they need to. Perhaps it's dangerous to go completely along the path where you say everything we do is in order to survive. Not all things function for that reason, surely? I mean, there is no reason *I* know of why men have nipples. But we have them, don't we?'

The first sound a 'normal' baby makes is a primal instinctual life-giving scream, remaining its main form of expression for the first four weeks after its departure from the womb to the nipple (breast or bottle). Soon it is prattling – nonsense sounds. It can distinguish and react to its mother's voice (and indeed breasts and heart-beat) for quite some time before it can see her face. In its relaxed moments it is seemingly in narcissistic union with its mother – a semi-womb-like omnipotence. Usually crying frequently from birth, a baby begins smiling at around five weeks. As we noted in the introductory chapter, the baby frequently shifts – almost in an instant – from crying to smiling, smiling to crying. Laughter generally begins during the fourth or fifth month, at almost exactly the same time the baby can visually recognise its mother and then, more nervously, its father or male 'father' figure if one exists (which presumably leads to the saying 'It is a wise child that knows its own father, but it is a laughing child that knows its own mother'). At around 28 weeks a child offers its first recognisable words, usually 'Ma' . . . and then 'Da' or 'Da-da'. By 40 weeks it will on average have begun reacting to its own name, as well as to positive and negative sounds. By the end of its first year it is usually repeating words it hears and also remembers some, and it begins to show signs of obeying orders. By eighteen months, numerous direct words may be replacing gestures. By two years it may be reflecting on language, repeating words to itself, often before falling asleep. At around two-and-a-half years old a child usually becomes rebellious or two-sided in its nature, switching back and forth between vocal desires, acting both inquisitively and uncertainly, generally showing rather schizophrenic tendencies. From three years onwards it is usually 'keen to classify, identify and compare', and by its fourth birthday it is actively proffering 'How' and 'Why' questions. Soon it begins commenting on meaning and form, and quite often corrects other speaker's language. From around its sixth birthday onwards a child can be both aggressive and boastful in its use of language. Subsequently it will offer illogical and/or bizarre answers, with a straight face, to illogical questions. By seven-years-old it is often posing riddles and plays-on-words, in the male's case most regularly to its father. It appears to be thoroughly relishing now the twisting of words and the manipulative powers that language brings. And by now, surely, the great humorist is on its way.

Stephen Fry was born, on 24 August 1957, into a provincial middle-class home in Norfolk. He had an elder brother and several years later received a sister.

I propose to Fry that most male comedians appear to have experienced a dominant but 'warm' mother, and a fairly distant father who nevertheless had a strong sense of humour.

'That's certainly true of me on both counts,' he offers, 'that's exactly my background. Woody Allen once said the two key elements of his upbringing were guilt and indigestion. My mother's Jewish with roots in rural Hungary and also the intelligentsia of Vienna around the turn of the century. Apart from the religion, which is minimal or non-existent, she is very much "a Jewish mother". She's been a historian, a company secretary and a J.P., but always very much a mother. As for my father – he has been, or has felt, distant – certainly. But he had a sense of humour, hugely so – he still has. He's a very funny man. But in a different way.'

From *you,* you mean?

'Yes. It's hard to explain. His humour is dry and slightly Fawlty-esque. My father assumed the world was against him. In a car, for instance, he would say angry things like "Oh right, I'm late, so *he's* going to park and block me . . . yes, fine!" I found him rather forbidding; we all did, really. He seemed so tall, dark and saturnine. He was an immensely intelligent man, an inventor. He was witty, he played the piano perfectly and worked an enormous amount . . . at first the technical officer at Hoover, he then set up laboratories at home, in converted stables, working away on control systems, a calibrated ruler and all manner of things. His brain was so overpowering that I felt tremendously inferior anyway. In that sense I was very *awed* by him – he was an awesome presence. And I found myself very silent or stammery whenever I was in the room with him.'

What pressures or expectations did your parents put on you?

'Well, one could turn it on its head and say that *I* brought an enormous amount of pressure to bear on *them*. Not necessarily by asking them to do things . . . but by being an extremely difficult child. Immensely naughty when young, and – indeed – quite perverse when old.' (He laughs now.) 'I was very difficult to handle over schools and things. So it was always a matter of them having to find a new school for me. I pressurised them. At about ten, I remember deciding categorically I wanted to become an actor. And my mother replied "Well, why don't you be a barrister

– that's *like* an actor.'' So I conjured up the thought of a wig and thought ''Umm, not bad.'' I used to tell people I'd be a barrister when I grew up. I was both shy *and* precocious.'

You've often been quoted as saying you dislike the concept of 'the family'.

'I've got nothing against families, *per se*. But as for ''the family'' being something that exists to be enshrined, it's ridiculous! Families can be very pleasant, but they can also be very dictating. The fact is that 90% of all murders, 95% of all child abuse, and 100% of incest are committed within families. Families, and the values of love, decency and care, don't necessarily go hand in hand.' (Fry sounds rather cross now.) 'One might also refer to servility, tyranny, over-obedience, violence, distrust, hatred, anger . . . madness. All are just as much family values. So, really, at the crunch, people can only depend on themselves.'

But do not *all* those elements within a family create the characters we are? To refute them would be to refute what as an adult one has become.

'Exactly. That is the great irony . . . And the proof of the pudding, of course, is always *in the eating*.'

Would you like to have children yourself?

'In a way . . . yes.'

Educationally rather advanced, but uncomfortable (he was 'sent away' to school at seven), Fry found himself expelled from two or three public (private) schools for truancy. 'I took O-levels early at thirteen and fourteen,' he ponders. 'The academic part of my brain was advanced but I don't think the rest was. I wanted to slow down . . . I wanted . . . I really don't know.' When at fifteen Fry was expected by masters to take his O-levels for a second time he felt 'very restless', but he and 'a humorous school friend' wrote to and then met an 'open-air' TV programme's producer with the idea of making comedy. Realising the programme had to be serious, they then proposed to make a programme about 'Where is comedy going . . . Where can it possibly go?'; about how comedy had perhaps abstracted itself into nothing and would therefore have to go backwards to be renourished. The programme was never made, and shortly afterwards Fry absconded again from school. His next stop was sixth-form college, to spend two years acquiring A-levels. Prone to bouts of kleptomania, Fry found himself 'taking lots of things that I had no business or need for, going into ironmongers and pocketing spanners and all sorts of things.' He laughs at the thought. 'I think it was a way of drawing attention to myself.' (Later his parents sent him to a psychiatrist, who announced Fry had all the symptoms of a diplomat's child, 'of someone whose father or family move around a lot'.) Shortly before his A-level examinations he disappeared to become 'a runaway, of sorts' in London. One day he went into a public house, stole a coat from a rack ('because it was cold') and 'later' discovered credit-cards in the pocket. Consequently he went 'ape-shit, on a spree' for a month or more, staying in expensive hotels.

Just turned eighteen, he was arrested by police at the Wiltshire Hotel in Swindon, and sent to short-term prison. Visiting him there he says his parents were 'angelic', his mother bringing along a hefty wad of crosswords she'd collected for him going back three months. Receiving them through the visiting hatch, he remembers thinking 'That's a mother', and relates the feeling to 'a mother hen folding its wings around you'. 'It was,' he says, 'the worst moment, and in some ways the best.'

What did you get up to in prison?

'I read a lot. I taught someone to read. I played the piano in chapel on Sundays. I had quite a merry time. But, as a con, one also has to work. I had to brush plastic soldiers with enamel paint, and then I was moved on to the considerably more glamorous job of polishing the corridors.'

What were your reflective thoughts while inside?

'I felt a fair amount of guilt concerning my parents – wondering "*Are we still friends?*" And I decided it was my last chance, really. I think I was determined that this was the last time I was going to muck about, to a certain extent. I realised I'd got about as low as I could and it was time to climb out. And I decided I wanted to go to university. So when I got out I obviously still had no A-levels so went to Norwich City College for a year, where I felt rather older than the students and quite independent. Then I went on to teach for a year, a time I remember fondly . . . kindling enthusiasm. I can still imagine myself returning to teaching at some stage in my life.'

After teaching you studied English at Queen's College, Cambridge.

'Yes, where most of the students started by going wild, because most of them had just previously been good boys at public schools. I did my fair share of drinking, but I was altogether rather bored of having a wild time. So I immediately took to acting in a big way; it was like work to me. In one eight-week term I appeared in *six* plays, serious and comedy. I was studying days and writing or performing every night. I thought of myself as a rather literary show-bizzy figure. I became very driven. *I never wanted to stop*. And in the third year I was introduced, as a potential writer, to Hugh (Laurie), who was President of the Footlights at the time. We both, it turned out, felt very nervous of each other, but we began writing together almost instantly, and everything else clicked.'

Since university you've worked almost constantly . . . remorselessly.

'Well, I *have* to.'

Alone, and in partnership with Hugh and others, you've written and performed in theatre and countless radio and television shows, written for books and magazines, acquired your own series, voiced and appeared in abundant commercials . . . (Fry has two houses, seven cars and assorted home technology).

'Yes – it's all work, I'm afraid.'

Are you in truth a workaholic?

'I just think I'm a generally addictive person, full stop. I don't think it's simply greed. It just all sounds so appealing, so I'm addicted to it. Similarly, I get addicted to not working if I'm not working. After two or three days not working it takes the same amount of time just to summon up the energy, the will. It involves heaps of coffee and hours wasted gazing out of the window before you even pick up the pen. So I like to keep working – so I *can* keep working. I'm just plain addictive really. At the same time I am fearful of dependencies and any loss of self-control.'

It's well-known that you are sexually celibate.

'I am, but I first announced it simply because I was asked to write an article for a magazine which happened to be about "Things I Don't Do" and the only thing I could think of which I don't do is sex. I wrote this article about the fact that sex was extremely unpleasant, about how "the damp tufted areas of the human body" had to be avoided. It happens to be true that I'm celibate, but it's also true that I don't eat chewing-gum.'

Was it something you specifically decided not to engage in?

'Yes, like someone deciding not to eat chewing-gum. Because you don't particularly like it.'

You think sex *is* disagreeable?

'I had a rather sexually active youth, which was largely homosexual. I had a good innings. But for the last five or six years I've been celibate. I'm just not particularly interested anymore. And that of course is self-perpetuating. I'm *perfectly* happy with the fact that *other* people have sex – it's a jolly merry thing for them to do . . . But personally, I stick with, and am rather partial to, self-abuse.'

Do you think the energy you avoid in sexual relationships is diverted and sublimated into your work?

'Possibly, yes. It's very hard to say exactly. It certainly leaves me clear of commitments which might effect me continuing to be *absolutely* committed to what I do. On a day to day basis I don't really have to consider anything else except myself and my work.'

How self-critical are you about your 'job'?

'It's rather intense. I rarely like what I do – I always think "It will be better next time." '

Does it feel like work now? Is there still the childlike enjoyment of comedy within you?

'Oh, Hugh and I often become like adolescents. We can be very embarrassing in a BBC lift. We giggle, we play stupid games, we stare at people. We can't help it. Being funny is a compulsion, really. [Fry was previously questioning this assumption.] The comic will always shout out from the back of the classroom, even if he gets into trouble and even if everyone else is fed up with hearing his funny responses. It's like a batsman – the ball's up there in the air, and you can't but hit it. It's a genuine compulsion. And obviously show-business *legitimises* that compulsion. Which is *delightful*.'

Various French absurdists, who previously created fine nonsense humour, now say that there is no such thing as nonsense. They say to *have* nonsense, you must first have sense – and there is no sense anymore.

'That's a very interesting point, which is really to do with age. It's absolutely right that you can't have nonsense without sense. The Absurdists were very much part of a post-war existential movement which intellectually argued there was no true sense; but they made wonderful nonsense out of perverting the sense people had of the world around them. The reason they could now say "We can't make nonsense anymore" is that they are of an age when they can no longer delineate. Their bones have set, and the world around them has changed. The universe, of course, *is* nonsense – it's complete random nonsensical chaos. But what distinguishes the active intellectual mind is the ability to make *some* sense of that nonsense. It starts when we are born, when we look out of the cave, so to speak. We see a hill rising up and we call it a hill and make sense of it as a hill. And thousands of years later we call it levels of Jurassic and pre-Cambrian rock. But the hill is still a piece of bloody nonsense. *And comedians can play around very effectively with that nonsense.*'

Yes, but why *do* men have nipples?

'I'm sorry, you'll have to excuse me. I have a TV commercial to voice-over.'

STEVEN WRIGHT

Stranger

When I was a baby I kept a diary.
The other day I was rereading it. It said:
Day 1: Tired from the move;
Day 2: Everybody thinks I'm an idiot.

Steven Wright, for eleven years, has stood on stage, on an average night, telling 275 jokes in an hour. An example, 'Sometimes you can't hear me . . . (Because I'm in parentheses).' Whereas the majority of stand-up comedians tell their witticisms with a fluctuating level of vocal expression, Wright tells his – one after the other after the other – in a voice which is unflinchingly adenoidal, monotonal, dry and dead-pan. At the same time, despite occasional walks around the stage and to a glass of water resting on a stool, physical movement and expression play only a miniscule part in his 'performance'. He moves his mouth but retains a stoic and almost terminally emotionless face as he recites his short lines. He very occasionally forms a shape with his hand or narrows his eyes as if to be looking at an imaginary object. He incorporates the comic apparatus of subtlety and stealth but uses them in a one-dimensional fashion. Where there is surprise and recognition in his monologue (and there is much) it is entirely contained within the conceptual twists of his material. He restrains himself from elaborating his recitals with *any* shifting voices, gestures or facial and bodily movements; he simply unfolds an absurdist or surrealist notion vocally, receives laughter or applause, and then moves quietly on to another. Once or twice on stage he may hold his hand briefly on his forehead, with the subtly intended impression that the world is just too baffling. Meanwhile, aside from very occasional moments when he has to restrain the reflex, he never himself laughs or smiles in front of an audience. Although occasionally, at the end of an act, he may flicker one or two very swift glimmers of a smile to the front rows of his audience, this is almost instantly restrained. The impression this gives is that he is momentarily enthused, or feels obliged, to respond facially to an audience's enthusiasm, but that he still wants to remain, or be seen as remaining, very much an outsider.

Wright's 'jokes' comprise, or are built on, bizarre puns, analogies, conceits and mental aberrations. Seemingly simple one- or two-line

STEVEN WRIGHT: *'It's a small world, but I wouldn't want to paint it.'*
Photograph courtesy of Glenn Schwartz

tales, or epigrams, they provoke laughter through disturbing, or at least playing with, his audience's conception and unification of objects, knowledge and other folk around them. They defy science, medicine and general sense ('I was playing poker with Tarot cards . . . I got a full house and four people died'), and use received language and idiom to create new meaning ('Curiosity killed the cat . . . but for a while I was a suspect'). All create a newly-observed world which sometimes seems bewildering to Wright (or the 'I' of his stories), most often unexciting and almost expected. We are never sure exactly where his emotions lie, what he feels about the displacements in his world. It feels like a confusing world but also an intriguing one ('I've just had amnesia and déjà-vu at the same time'). In the world of Wright's imagination, there are midget dwarves, there is a man wearing false teeth *and* braces, and sideburns behind his ear, and there is a man with wooden legs yet real feet. In this world one can be gainfully employed as a proof-reader for a sky-writing firm. In this world – through which he walks, presumably with this general air of expressionless diffidence – button holes can be lost, a man may own a telephone bearing no number five and a calendar with no sevens, and 6,000 mice dressed as rice may rob a Chinese restaurant. In this world, which is at least half like our own world, Wright likes to 'reminisce with people I don't know'. He skates on the other side of ice, his dog is called 'Stay', he doesn't pay for electricity because he's never seen it and he has been the victim of a speed-reading accident which involved colliding with a book-mark.

'My whole act,' says Wright, talking offstage, 'is just a funny pack of lies.'

What mental activity is involved in the recital of a pack of 275 or more lies?

'Memory and a degree of timing,' says Wright succinctly.

Although your joke-lines occasionally overlap in topic, they exist largely alone within very short periods of time.

'About ten seconds each. Which makes it all the more difficult. But I am fascinated by the fact I can remember that amount of material . . . because I *can't* remember things well in real life, *at all*. But you practise your memory skills every time you go on stage. You do the jokes so many times that they are all individually imprinted in your brain over and over again.'

How does one of your performances unfold, or how is it *structured?*

'I know exactly what material I'll be covering before I go on, but I've no idea of the order I'll be doing it in. What I *do* have to help me though is my division of jokes into three segments. It's a way of remembering all the material and also a way of placing jokes towards the beginning, middle or end of an act, because – for whatever reasons – I've realised night by night they generally work better there. So my head is divided into three sets of jokes. But within the thirds I pick each joke off the top of my head, as I go. Depending on how a specific audience is reacting I decide which joke to do next. Each night the audience is always in a different mood constantly and you can *just tell* what joke should follow each separate reaction. Really, then, the audience run the whole show and they don't even know it. All *I* have to work out, to decide, is what they *need* at a given time. To this end I also divide jokes overall into *quality*. There is *A, B* and *C* material.'

Within each and all three thirds of the act?

'Yes. You adjust to the audience's reaction the whole time, using varying segments of *A, B* and *C*. I try to give them as much *C* or *B* material whenever possible, then – if I get in trouble – I still have *A* jokes to pull me through. After an *A* joke, or possibly two, I go back to *B* and *C* for a while, and so on.'

And those gradings are based on what? On past audience reactions?

'Exactly. Obviously they all work, or I wouldn't use them. But *C* is the average to bottom line.'

What is an example of a C joke?

'Let's think . . .' (Six seconds elapse.) *'It doesn't matter what temperature it is. It's always room temperature* . . . That's a *C*.' (He laughs, with a short but warm 'Ha!' never heard from him on stage.)

Has that joke ever gone over as an *A*?

'Once in a while, yes. I'll have a freak night and "room temperature" will become an *A* . . . Sometimes it might even be a *D*.'

What would be an *A*?

(10 seconds pass.) *'They say sponges grow in the ocean. I can't believe that. I wonder how much deeper the ocean would be if they didn't.'*

This is an *A*?

'Yes.'

Do you usually agree with the ratings you, or rather the audience, have applied?

'Often I think something that gets a *nine* reaction from an audience really deserves only a *five*.'

How soon after you get on stage can you tell the general mood of an audience?

'I can tell in half a minute. I can tell from how they react to the first two or three jokes what the overall mood is going to be for an hour. I usually stand in the wings and listen for two minutes. I *never look* at an audience beforehand – I just listen. I can feel how lively or dead the crowd is, what the acoustics are like – whether the room soaks up or vibrates the line and the laugh. Then, if the audience doesn't have a lot of energy *and* the room soaks up sound, I know before I go on. That way I protect myself against thinking it's just me who's doing wrong.'

How do you feel, though if there's a flat or low-key mood right from the start?

'Well, audiences have different levels of energy, and if they really won't react there's little I can do with it. If that happens it really makes the hour feel like an hour. The analogy I use is dragging around a boulder from a rope around your neck. The opposite feeling, playing to a very receptive audience, has the analogy of surfing. A good show just surfs along, and it feels exhilarating . . . in a straight-faced sort of way.'

What are your tricks if you sense or know it's a low-key audience; other than just stick to the *A* jokes?

'You can't do that. Because they would all be gone in five or ten minutes. You've got to be out there an hour. So, I don't know – I just do the best I can and keep trying to get to them, with whatever order of and combinations of jokes come into my head. *A . . . C . . . C . . . B . . . C . . . A . . . C . . . C . . .* When I was 26 years old I'd go out there and do *anything* to get them over. Dancing, falling over . . . Now, if they're really not into it, *they're not into it*. There's nothing you can do. It's just embarrassing.' (He produces his first real laugh now.)

Do you feel yourself speeding up?

'Towards the end, usually. I tell them much faster – or else their attention span is lost and it might all fall asunder.'

You speak in a monotone. How much more difficult does that actually make it to *pace* your material?

'I do far more pacing than people realise. Joke, pause, joke, longer pause, joke, shorter pause . . . I can feel each audience, feel the mood of each act or segment, I can tell how fast to go. I can tell when they've heard so many jokes they need a rest. I can feel how long I should deal with the water, how long I should sip. I can feel *exactly* when it's right to put the glass down on the stool again.'

So the drinking of water is largely for effect?

'It developed that way. They're watching you so much, so intently, that if you hold the glass for just the right length of time, everything is magnified. You can take the pause in jokes right to the edge – almost of boredom, and in doing so you create a tension which is palpable. If it's a very excitable audience you can't take the pause *too* long, actually, or someone will yell out. But if it's a receptive or *polite* audience, you can take that and s-t-retch it out. I found all this out, ages ago, simply by forgetting. In the early days I would tell two minutes of material then forget the rest. So I would be standing there, with the audience gazing, and somehow I held their attention. I was delighted. I realised right then I could use silence to my own benefit.'

You never do encores.

'*Never*. Absolutely. I don't know whether they're going to want me to come back, so if I've saved some material and they *don't* want me to come back, then I'd be forever considering how much better the show would have been if I *hadn't* saved it. I can't risk that.'

Have you ever walked off stage mid-act for lack of approval?

'Only once. It was in a disco club near Boston where, one night a week, with absolutely no announcement, they shut the music off and paraded comics one at a time. People were shouting abuse, so I left. Equally horrible was performing to students eating in a noisy cafeteria. I got through 28 minutes of material in just over seven.'

Is your dead-pan face something you have cultivated?

'The reason I have a straight face on stage is because that's how I am . . . at least with strangers. I don't show much expression and emotion with strangers; and that's what the audience are. With friends I laugh a lot, I'm much more open – whether I'm riffing jokes or not. But with a bunch of strangers I'm just an introvert. And it's also to do, it grows out of, *concentration*. On stage I've always taken it all very seriously. There are so many jokes to remember, so many weird things to say into the microphone, that I've always gone on with a straight face. It's a serious task. But the effect of that style and my own natural monotone voice are entirely an accident.'

Occasionally, on stage, it is evident that you are laughing but swiftly – desperately – trying to stop yourself.

'When that happens, which is very rarely, it's most always me laughing at someone's laughter. I'm not laughing at what *I'm* saying. I'm laughing at the idea that I thought of something, and that some person on the second row is laughing in a particular way at it. When you see someone really laugh it makes *you* want to laugh.'

Does it have to be really strong laughter to make you laugh?

'It's more the person and the bizarre circumstance. Sometimes I'll see an old person – a 60-year-old woman, for instance – of which I get quite a few. And seeing her laugh at some fucking thing that I've thought up at 2am in the morning in New York, it just kills me. So it can appear that I'm occasionally laughing at my own material, but usually I don't even know what I'm saying. I'm completely concentrating, and not at all in a laughing mood, but then some old folk's laughter will distract me.'

Do you think people in the audience might take your straight-face as a comment on life in itself – that being bemusement, bafflement, concern or even *lack* of concern, in the face of the world your jokes inhabit.

'I'm not trying to do that on purpose, honestly. I don't *think* I'm looking sad out there. I'm perhaps partly trying to act like all those things did happen to me, like I just stepped out of a story. I want to come on for an hour and say "This happened to me, then this, and then this . . .", but I'm not complaining about it. I'm not saying "Oh poor me". I'm just acting like I just came home from work and I'm telling the family what happened today, only there's a thousand people in the kitchen rather than five or six.'

Steven Wright was born on 6 December 1955, in Burlington, a piece of suburbia 30 miles outside Boston, Massachusetts, to Roman Catholic parents he now semi-jokingly says 'are crazy, just *a crazy couple*'. His father is a truck-driver, his mother a nurse. Wright has two brothers and a sister. The title of his concert recording '*I Have a*

Pony' was, or rather is, true (he suggests '*I Still Have a Pony*' as a future album title). His active childhood memories revolve much around 'walking, riding horses, then motorcycles, in the woods, and playing hockey and middle-league baseball'. He also drew and painted a great deal, consequently 'exercising the part of my brain that would think in detail'. To wit, he explains that 'If you were going to draw two tables, you would notice the space between the two tables, and could actually draw that space – that's where the fun begins.' He remembers the time he first became aware, in high school, of surrealist painting ('waterfalls turning into roads'), how he wanted to paint like that but his teacher wouldn't allow him. 'It's a small world,' he now jokes: 'But I wouldn't want to paint it.' This did not, however, stop him realising that 'you could put two or three things together and the juxtaposition would create something *totally* diferent.' Meanwhile, the family did indeed 'congregate' in the kitchen after school or work, and there was often laughter in the air, although Wright remembers 'always feeling rather sillier' than the other children. At the same time, conversely, he also felt '*very* introverted' and worried excessively, 'so that *everything* in my life became a big deal – thinking *''Oh no, here comes the bus. Where am I going to sit on the bus?''* '

How do you look back on your mother's and father's moods and sense of humour?

'My mother seemed completely extrovert and really funny; she's a real character. She's crazy, like Lucille Ball. She can take over and dominate any room she's in, and everyone likes her. She talks to anybody, she travels, she writes, she visits . . . She's the complete opposite of my father.'

Were you distant from him?

'He's very unemotional. You really don't know what he's feeling. I *never* knew what he was feeling! My whole life I never knew. He doesn't show anything. But he did have a good sense of humour. He didn't talk to me much, but half he *did* say was funny, silly.'

He joked with you?

'He joked a lot . . . but I'm not convinced joking is a real communication.'

It isn't?

'It doesn't show your true emotion. *Well*, it does and it doesn't. Underneath it might do, but it's indirect communication. Really, my father never expressed himself emotionally. He doesn't know *how* to. It often feels like he's behind a big wall. He feels like a stranger. I just don't know how to get through to the guy. Haah!'

Do you think your on-stage persona owes a lot to his stoicism?

'I think that's it, *exactly*. I can't express myself with people I don't know, and I feel that wall between me and the audience. It began as severe nerves, which is still there really, but I soon realised audiences don't mind – even that they quite get off on that stoicism.'

Why do you think you became a stand-up comic?

'Being a comedian definitely has something to do with your early family life. Going on stage in any form has to do with trying to fill a void of attention which wasn't there. I mean – why else stand in front of a thousand people? It fills a previous void – in a huge way. Concerts, television . . . look at me, look at me, look at me. *That's* why I went on. And it's a really weird thing – one guy stands there and all those people look at him. It's kind of sick. If you know some jokes, why go on stage and tell them? Maybe some day I'll just be writing the jokes, thinking they're funny, and leaving it at that.' (He produces a hearty laugh.) 'No one will hear them. I'll just file them and pile them all up.'

Did you enter your teens with a very bizarre sense of humour?

'I don't really remember when it started – I just know it was unstoppable when I began. I do remember sitting in the library one day, at junior high-school, trying to put things together that shouldn't, like *a flock of false-teeth*. That was at eleven-years-old. I actually still use a joke I came up with as a kid . . . the one about learning Spanish from a record I put on at night, but the record's scratched, so now I can stutter in Spanish.'

Does it not go further back than age eleven?

'Probably, because part of that curiosity in looking at the world is like a little kid's. It's about seeing with the eyes of a child but talking in an adult's language. But for most adults that curiosity wears off . . . I was sitting in a restaurant yesterday watching a two-year-old kid playing on the floor. I was watching the baby watching other people, and I was dying to know what it was thinking. Everything that moved, with every nuance, its eyes played attention. With age that subsides. But I really identified with that baby.' (He releases an embarrassed laugh.) 'If a child heard that a telephone line was busy, he'd wonder what the line was doing. I know the feeling. Sometimes I even half-jokingly tell the press that my material is written by a group of three-year-old children whom I keep in my attic.'

When did you first decide the comic's life was for you?

'I was about fifteen. Because my older brother controlled the television set I had to watch Johnny Carson's *Tonight* show every single night. Everybody else was in bed and we'd be watching Carson. Gradually I got hooked on watching the comedians who appeared – Richard Pryor, Robert Klein, George Carlin . . . It became *my* thing. And I was listening to comedy albums, like Woody Allen's stand-up material, on a slot on late-night radio. Later I went to see *Monty Python and the Holy Grail*, and then their programmes arrived on television, and they were a complete revelation to me – a breaking of the old mould. And somewhere amidst all that, around fifteen, I thought "This is my fantasy . . . to go on TV, make comedy albums and go around the country making people laugh." I'm not sure why . . . I think I could tell there was an aloneness to it; a guy comes on and he talks about dealing with the world himself. I think at that age I felt alone, and I made a connection. I really decided that's what I wanted to do. I made it my goal. But I never told anyone, because I thought if I did the idea would somehow be *jinxed*. So, from age fifteen to 23, when I finally went on stage, I kept it as my secret goal.'

Did you often joke with school friends?

'On a one-to-one basis, or maybe one-to-two, but if anyone else came over I'd go completely quiet. So I was exercising being funny, but I'm not the Class Clown.'

What did you get up to between sixteen and 23?

'I went to Middlesex Junior College for two years and studied Liberal Arts. Then I went to Emerson College and studied Mass Communication – which helped me think. Getting a degree became a huge goal to me. Then, when I'd graduated, I parked cars for a while, and painted apartments. Then a comedy club opened in Boston and I said to myself, "I must go down and confront this dream I've had for eight years." I didn't want to get to 40-years-old, be selling insurance in Wyoming and thinking what it would have been like if I'd taken the plunge. So I made myself, *forced myself*. I did an open-mike audition (at Ding Ho's Comedy Club and Chinese Restaurant, in Cambridge, Massachusetts); I did two minutes or more and spoke one-liners very fast, just kept going straight over the audience's laughter. I was very nervous, but they took me on board.'

How did the first time feel?

'Just an incredible rush. They laughed at about half I said and I went home very satisfied.'

Four or so years later you were asked to perform on Carson's *Tonight Show*.

'Which was just the same feeling only more so. It came completely out of the blue, and – almost unheard of – Carson both called me over to interview me and then invited me back the following week. It was the highest point of my life. It's what I'd always dreamed of and it all took off in one week. (He has since appeared on Carson's show eleven times). All of a sudden I was playing clubs all over the country with people paying to see me. Then a year or two later it went on to a whole other level – larger tours, a TV special, an album, I was in planes flying all over, which I still don't like. I've always had a real fear of flying . . . And apart from the fact that all that commotion uses up your jokes *incredibly* quickly.'

How do you go about writing?

'I walk around, I hang around with a few people, I travel. I just go and do things. I have to feed reality into my head visually, and you can't do that in a room. I'm very visually orientated. Comedy is just twisting reality, so I have to go see as much as I can. It's harder, really, to come up with the set-up than the joke.'

Is it a mathematical operation, this twisting?

'I don't *try*; I don't go out looking to write a joke. It just happens. I don't look at something and think "Where is the joke in this?

Where can I find it?'' The entire thought appears in a nutshell; then I choose to write it down. It's instant, not forced.'

You've said you're 'visually orientated'; is that not *completely* at odds with your on-stage persona?

'Well . . . I'm behind a wall, but I'm painting the audience's brains out with what I say.'

You're forcing them to use their imaginations?

'I don't like the word forcing. I hope I'm not a forceful person. But the audience must make their contribution; they *must* respond.'

Do you make yourself laugh?

'Yeah. When I first think of it – most of it. I laugh right out loud. Then I tell it to a friend, maybe. Then scribble it down in a notebook. Then say it to another friend. And by the time I get round to saying it on stage I'm simply very concerned whether *they're* going to laugh or not; because only one in three jokes will stay. I'm taking it all very seriously. All that matters is that they laugh. It's almost as if the actual sentence has no meaning to me any more.'

Your key emotion on stage is worry?

'Yes. It's like gambling, especially with new material. I'm not even thinking that I'm talking about *a guy with wooden legs and real feet*. I'm simply concerned with the response.'

(Wright remembers a time when he was lying asleep on a couch, in New Jersey and woke up hearing his own voice. Looking through the window he realised that the people in the house close next door were watching a show of his on their television. His reaction was to lie back on the couch and listen intently to exactly which jokes the neighbours laughed at.)

Is it not quite bizarre, given your straight-faced and monotone persona, that you appear to be so loved by audiences, especially the *whooping* American variety?

'Yes, although I've never really thought of it that way before. There's something that they obviously identify with. They think people feel there's too much going on in the world, that there's too much happening; and I come on and say short things one after another. They can relate to the subjects, if not the twists . . . they can identify with the idea that the world is simply insane. I have a line where I say ''You know when you're sitting on a chair and you almost fall over, but just at the last second you catch yourself? . . . I feel like that *all the time*.'' The world tries to pass itself off as a sane place, but I confirm what it really is. I don't know if I even exaggerate it much, because real things are quite as crazy as what I make up. It's kind of weird, because audiences shouldn't really have to come and see me at all . . . They should just *watch the world*.'

Are you suggesting it's strange that a comedian's job is to encourage or allow an audience to laugh, as opposed to the audience finding the world funny on its own merits?

'Yes, it's *very strange*. Sometimes I look out on the audience and

I feel baffled that they come to hear me say these things I made up. Why don't they just laugh and talk and make things up themselves? Why do they have to come *here?*' (He chortles now.) 'Not that I blame them. I make my wage from this. I think up weird shit and get paid. It's *unbelievable*. I'm very grateful because to make a living from your imagination is tremendous. But I'd still be thinking up all this stuff even if I gave up the job.'

Steven Wright, a man in his mid-30s, of average height, with a high, balding, professorial forehead, a prominent nose and very dark eyes, lives – when he is not on tour – in a New York flat almost bereft of furniture or ornamentation except wall-hooks and a few paintings which are frequently swapped around on them. He buys very little; 'Everything is given or borrowed . . . making a purchase is such a commitment.' He has a girlfriend, to whom he sometimes strums a brief song on stage, the only point in his act in which he suggests a small degree of emotional attachment. Aside from the jokes, it appears that she is his true salvation. He works a lot, with determination, but does it gently, gracefully – forever presenting a mental, rather than physical, guise. His comedy – from clubs, auditoria and television – now increasingly turns to film, a medium in which he can paint with a more elaborate brush. Nevertheless, his persona remains at the hub of his work, whether in the filmed segments opening and closing his live video (he leaves a house in a barren desert, misses a bus, walks to a performance; he leaves the performance, he catches a bus, he meets a girl from his imagination), or – more at length – in the self-written short film for which he won an Oscar award. The latter, titled *The Appointments of Dennis Jennings*, involves Wright visiting and then plotting to kill a cold (father-like?) psychiatrist who barely remembers his (Wright's/Jenning's) name and has minimal interest in what he has to say. 'I spent the afternoon trying to day-dream,' Jennings announces at one point from the proverbial couch, ' . . . but my mind kept wandering.'

How have you changed since your childhood, your youth . . .?

'In one sense I'm much more extrovert, but in another sense I'm very much the same. I've changed completely and I haven't changed.'

Being based in New York, as opposed to the countryside of Massachusetts, how does that effect your comedy? Does it make it harder or easier to make sense out of nonsense?

'It doesn't affect *how* I write, although the tension of the city makes me write more, perhaps. I've lived here for quite a few years now and I think now I *do* want to get out. Because there's just too many people, too much going on. There's too much going on in my cranium anyway, without having to deal with much else.'

Do you live a fairly normal life?

(At this Wright laughs for close to a minute, partly in what appears to be a lightly sarcastic tone, partly in joyous release. I am slightly taken aback.)

Why did you laugh just then?

(Wright takes his time considering the question.)

'. . . Because my mind has two ways of looking at things. *Part* of me knows I'm an artist – at least someone who uses his imagination to write and create. The way I live as "an artist" has no structure at all, really, except for a timetable of shows and even that is based on my own decision. I get up when I want, spend most of the day doing exactly what I want, go to bed when I want . . . Yet the *other* part of me, having grown up in the suburbs and all that, wants structure. That part of me concludes that I should be going nine-to-five, that I should be married, have three children already and be mowing the lawn. I laughed so long because the part of my head that heard your question was the part that still thinks I should get a regular job. It was saying, "Are you kidding me? He lives an insane life?!" So I laughed so hard because I haven't come to terms with it.'

Is it guilt?

'Oh yes, are you kidding? It's Catholic guilt running rampant! It's driving me *insane*. I have conversations with myself all the time – about what I do, about the money I make from it . . . about whether I should be loading a truck.'

The Pope says you should mow the lawn?

'Exactly! Making money from my imagination and telling jokes just doesn't seem decent, really.'

GERRY SADOWITZ

Born-Again Comedian

Do you think that's controversial?
I couldn't give a shit.
A joke's a joke, isn't it?

Contradiction seems very much one of the comedian's stocks-in-trade. The twists, the turns, the irony, the schizophrenic leaps, the sheer unapologetic contradictions in their work are devices with which they can achieve the seemingly central aim of their lives – audience laughter, the nervous, shocked or joyous laughter of realisation and release. At the same time, contradiction is evident between their on-and off-stage lives, and within the off-stage life itself. On stage Gerry Sadowitz, comic and magician extraordinaire, has quite frequently exclaimed, with measures of irritation and ingratiation, that 'You're not supposed to take me seriously – I'm a comic.' At these moments he will expound his theory that '*A joke's a joke*'. What he is saying is that a joke's *just* a joke, that he doesn't really mean what he has been saying with great aggression; that comedy isn't serious, that the comedian can be offensive and yet not really 'mean' it; that to laugh is *just* to laugh. Then, as if to contradict himself completely, Sadowitz will state off-stage, 'I think that "stand-up" is a very good medium for expressing *exactly* what you think. It's still very overlooked as an "art" in this country. For me, though, it's not an act. I go on stage so I can be *myself*; while off-stage I put on an act – being nice to people, talking pleasantly to folk so I can get bookings. Then I go on stage and say exactly what I really think.'

'There should be different types of philosophy in comedy, just as there are in life,' he proposes. 'Personally, I genuinely believe that life is absolute fucking shite; that to live is to suffer. I don't believe anybody is happy. So I think that idea, that realisation, is a perfectly acceptable basis on which to form comedy. Why assume that everybody is having a nice time out there – of course they're not! So I'll say whatever I fucking want, and if people want to agree with it, or laugh at it, they can. It's true, whatever. That's how I feel.'
You hate everything?

'Everything. I hate white people, black people, women, yellow people, old age pensioners, young people . . .' (Gerry adopts a vaguely caricatured voice now.) 'I hate anyone who opposes

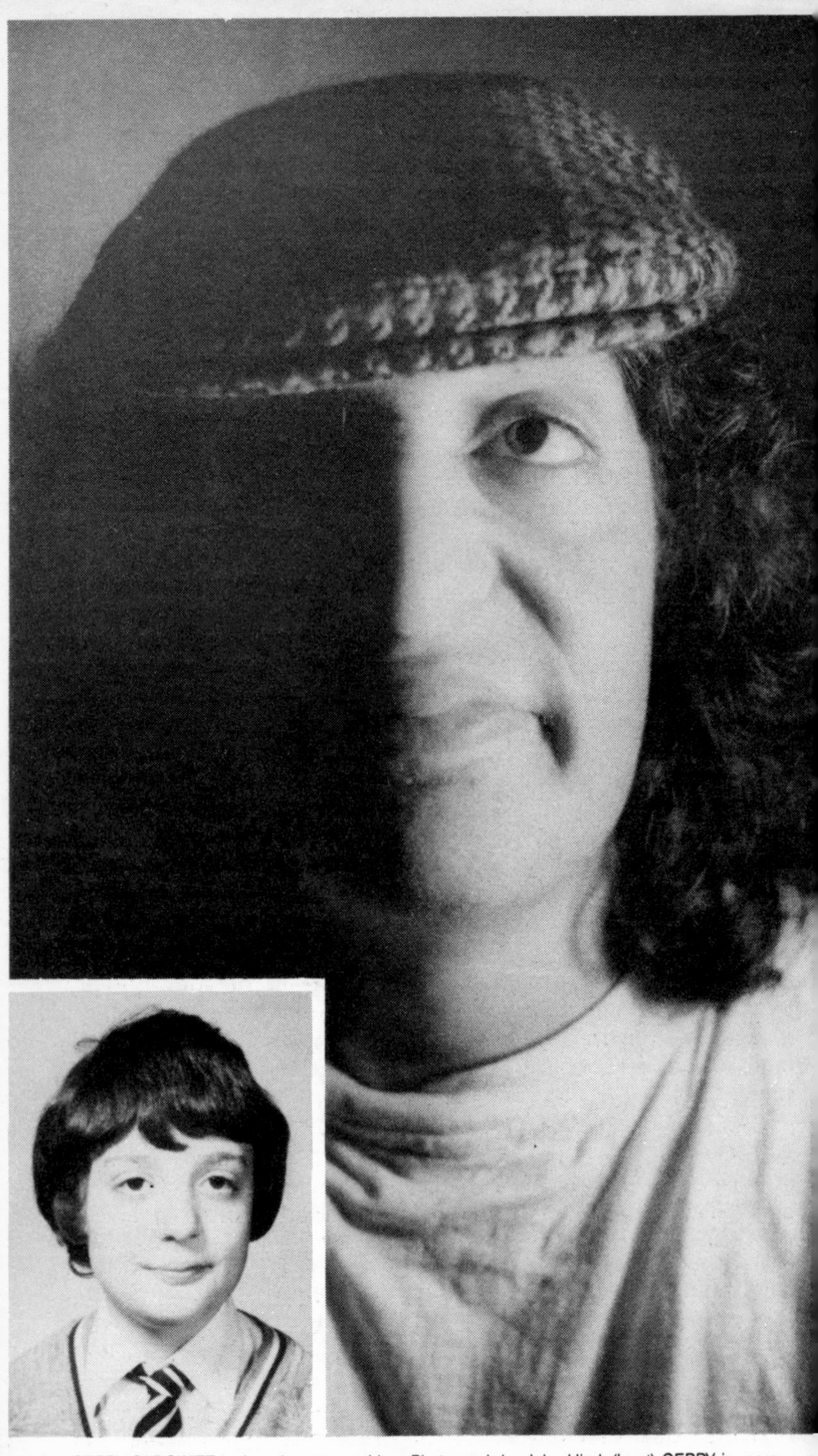

GERRY SADOWITZ hating almost everything. Photograph by John Hind. (Inset) GERRY in more optimistic days?

my will of becoming the greatest stand-up comic of all time. I am actually the Fuhrer of Stand-Up Humour, the Chosen One. And I'm on a crusade.'

He's not joking too. But then he is.

'I hate students,' he offers, when there are students in his audience, 'I fucking hate them. They're all completely brain-dead, right, but they've got this brilliant excuse that they're still studying . . .' (Pause.) 'I don't hate them really, by the way,' he goes on. Then, *very* swiftly: *'Yes I do.'*

Gerry Sadowitz, in a sense, is an illusionist, a trickster turning the tables on his audience and himself. Parallel with a sense of humour he developed, in youth, elaborate skills at table magic; magic in fact was the performance from which his comedy evolved. The result is that by blending and quick-changing between the two forms he creates a drama and dynamic which makes each form doubly aggressive, sly, clever, contradictory and relentless. His 1987 stage-show *Total Abuse* should rather be called *Total Abuse and Sleight-Of-Hand*, because the two skills (somewhat like in Steve Martin's shows in the 1970s) become part and parcel. The last third (20 minutes) of Sadowitz's *Total Abuse* show, encapsulated in a video release, shows the slow but eventful unfolding of one grand Sadowitz trick, set to 'jokes'. He begins by 'borrowing a five pound note' from a member of the audience, a necessity which involves slouching off the stage (parodying a drunken Glaswegian beggar), insulting a man in the first row ('Are you an actor? No? Well get your feet off the fucking stage!'), then trying out his charms on an attractive female ('You're very nice looking . . . Any chance of a fuck?'). He walks off, rejected, turning briefly to ask, 'I suppose a blow-job's out of the question?' Someone ('a bald person') rather nervously offers a fiver for use in the trick, having previously been promised that double the amount will soon 'return'. Gerry abuses the bald person, tells him not to take the abuse seriously, returns to the stage, at which point – double crossing – he now admits fiercely 'I was *lying*'. Audience members relish the abuse of one amongst them, especially – most nervously – when Gerry then *does attempt* the switch over from fiver to tenner, resulting in a blank piece of paper, which he rips to pieces. Within the next ten seconds, unbeknownst to the crowd, as he moves a table for another trick – before leaping into abuse of a political and economic flavour, attacking one category of human being or another – he has already (in a *moment*, behind a bag) placed the irritated audience member's money within the core of an apple. Ten minutes later – as the grand finale – this apple will surface underneath a cup, one of three apples miraculously replacing small balls which came 'from my nose, just this morning'. In the intervening ten minutes he has been doing six things – making numerous jokes, abusing a man in the audience, spying a 'great bit of underwear' viewable up the man's companion's skirt, returning balls to cups with sleight-of-hand, explaining *how* he does it, and – all the while – secretly setting up the surprise apples ending. The effect, after tomfoolery, abuse and self-abuse, is ultimately to have the complete professional upper-hand.

During his 1989 show *Lose Your Comic Virginity* Sadowitz took much the same course, turning the tables on his audience a dozen times. In the last three minutes on stage, having previously just *savagely* abused the reputation of the female sex in a welter of exclamations and observations (largely improvised), he set off into the audience, selected and dragged out a woman from their midst, showed her a disappearing-trick box to get into, chased her as she ran nervously off stage and then out through a side door (of the auditorium), carried her back over his shoulder, *then* attempted to get her into the large wooden box from which he himself had appeared at the beginning of the show. The audience laughed and disapproved almost simultaneously. She, however, somehow over-powered Sadowitz, he fell into the box and she walked to the microphone shy but victorious. *Within seconds,* from the opposite side of the auditorium Sadowitz appeared, totally re-dressed in Highland garb and sporting a motorised three-foot strap-on penis which ejected liquid across 30 rows of the audience. He revealed the box to be empty, and for fifteen seconds, as he sprayed, he stood triumphant as a man, an abuser, an illusionist and a clown. The audience laughed with communal amusement and bemusement – from the combined force of their gasps within the previous 75 minutes' escapades, the ultimate penis outrage and their lack of understanding over where Sadowitz had come from. How did he get out of the box? Why was he not still in the box? Was there, briefly, a double of Sadowitz in the box, the box from which the real Sadowitz took to the stage? Surely there couldn't be *two* men who look, amuse, behave and *degrade* like Gerry Sadowitz?

How do you feel prior to a performance on stage?

'Before I go on I imagine I'm making love to a gorgeous female. And the reality that this is after all merely a fantasy gives me the determination to get through the show and be totally evil . . . Haaa. Let's see – I'm sitting in a box which is pitch black, with a bowler-hat on my head plus a dove attached to a curvy-grip which is digging into both sides of my temples. I have underpants and playing-cards in my pockets. I'm sitting there for 25 minutes, unbeknownst to the audience whom I can hear filing into the theatre. I'm feeling that they're very happy, that they have wonderful lives – and I know, by the way, that contradicts what I feel about everyone in the world being unhappy. I hear them laughing and happy and jolly and I'm sitting there as miserable as fuck, as miserable as absolute fuck. For 25 minutes before each show I'm folded up in there thinking "What vestige of dignity is left in my life? I should have been a clerical officer, living in Glasgow with my friends and having a nice time, instead of reading terrible things about myself in newspapers." I'm thinking, "What *have* I been made into?" '

You don't relish the work and attention?

'I don't have any good feelings about tours or anything. I don't look forward to them. Honestly. I'm working my guts out and getting ripped off. So what? At the end of the day people laugh at you and you go home and you're *still* miserable. It doesn't mean anything to me.'

You nevertheless choose to get into the box.

'If I had decent respect from the public and critics and acceptable *financial* remuneration maybe I'd feel less of an arse and enjoy it more. I think I'm a latent capitalist, do you know that? I want lots and lots and lots of money or it's just not worth it. All I see is the grief. I don't get a chance to enjoy it, all I can think about is the problems I've had from it. I feel like a moron half the time. I don't know exactly *who* is appreciating what I do. I know every night people will misunderstand me. That's what's going on in my head.'

Would you enjoy performing much more if everyone appreciated everything you did?

'. . . No. The fact is I realise nothing is going to make me happy. That's the truth. I can't think what'll make me happy. I'm a sad and unsatisfied person . . . *finito*.'

Each Sadowitz 'performance' is explosively funny, from – perhaps – an opening index-finger raised aggressively in 'tribute to the Queen Mother', to the last dramatic, gleeful/angry tarnishing of his audience. The act comprises barrages of one-line put-downs, character assassinations, ludicrous and violent tricks produced from hold-alls and carrier bags, vivid minimalist comments on the awfulness of life, obscene rhymes, cruel impersonations, libellous opinions, balloons, flowers, rubber doves, cards from the crotch, cocky and angry expressions and jokes at the expense of all and sundry. Assassination and disasters are fair game, in his book, for jokes, so are old age pensioners, right wingers, left wingers, Irish, Pakistanis, Arab hijackings, miners ('I won't support anyone going down a mine . . . it's a stupid fucking job'), TV charity, ugly women, feminists, royalty and himself. Obscenities flow thick and fast; indeed they are an integral part of the whole texture, pacing and effect of his material. They kick-start the laughter and give the jokes their impression of heart-felt belief. Sadowitz will demolish Christ in 45 seconds. He begins by mimicking the moment when Mary the Mother announced to her husband that God came down and impregnated her in a blaze of light. Surely, Sadowitz proposes, Joseph (a carpenter) 'would have had the sense to look in the cupboard'. He then ridicules the idea of Jesus going round changing people's names ('This guy wants to change my name . . . You'll call me John yer fucking hippy!'), vaguely elaborates on how religion could be cheered up a bit and then attacks with vitriol the whole premise of religion, seemingly all-serious now.

The stage around him becomes a battle-zone, littered with tricks, objects, props, ripped cards, occasional spit and breakages, water, a blow-up doll (which he assaults 'in case there are any feminists in this evening'), towels, a fake dog-turd, a floating ball, a Sooty glove-puppet (which has earlier been administered to the comic's crotch with the cry of 'Izzy-Wizzy, Let's get busy') and much more besides – the litter and shrapnel of his angry-child tantrums. He sometimes opens up his jeans (mid-act) to expose his pitiful but proud manhood. At this point most folk paying to be in his presence are so bewildered that they do not quite *believe* what they are seeing. Sadowitz is as bold as brass, prancing and storming with violent and sexual frustration.

'I just won't censor myself on stage,' he posits. 'As far as I'm concerned when I get on stage I can *do* whatever I like and *say* whatever I like. And I will, thank you. Once I'm up there I won't stop myself, and I *can't* stop myself, doing *anything* – however much trouble it'll get me into.'

Gerry has a scabby scar at the top of his nose – the result of 'an accident' on stage a good year ago, plus much subsequent 'picking'. On stage he wears red jeans, a T-shirt, a battered bowler hat and a black jacket with strategic rips and the odd badge attached.

Off stage he replaces the bowler hat with a Northerner's flat cap, is generous, gentle and genial, but then throws you a serious line like 'I *never never* ever want to have children!' (There is, however, a coda: 'I maybe wouldn't mind adopting one.')

'I was born in America in 1961, and lived there for a while – which I remember virtually nothing of. My parents separated and I was raised in Scotland, from three or four years old – in Pollock Shields, Glasgow, on the edge of the Gorbals. Pollock Shields has a large Asian community and a lot of poor Jews. The rich Jews live in Newton Mearns, and we never mixed with them, except at dances where I went to find a nice rich girl. But they were so ugly. Ugly big-nosed Jewish bastards – just like myself.'

A tough upbringing?

'A very tough upbringing. We were so poor that we used to go to the Samaritans for tea. Haa! It's so classic it's corny. Just shite. My mother brought me and my younger sister [now a philosophy student] up in a flat, at the end of a block, and my uncle once said it was colder in that flat than outside.'

Where's your father now?

'He's in the States somewhere. I hate him. That's why I hate myself, because I see him *in me*. My parents divorced when I was five. He's gone. I don't think about him *at all*.' (Pause.) 'Actually, I've been thinking of giving him a ring.'

Did you enjoy school?

'I think I was pretty scared at school; I was terrified of the teachers. I went to a Jewish primary school where there was a teacher called Mrs King, an evil old whore. I was terrified at night of going in the next day. I really longed to leave school and grow up – I *really* thought life would get better. But it didn't, it hasn't, *so there you go*.'

Did you have a religious upbringing?

'Sort of, but I'll tell you something about that – the whole concept of being a Western Jew is one of pretence. My mother is like any other Jew in the hemisphere – she pretends to be Jewish. Candles on Friday, new dress for Passover. I think *all* religion's shite by the way – it's the single biggest scandal on this planet. But I'll tell you something – Jewish old age pensioners are brilliant. All they talk about is death and illness; it makes them happy. My Auntie Mary is 80 or more, in a wheel-chair, and her conversation is superb. If you ask her "How are you doing Mary?" she replies, "*Oh, did you hear that Ethel Nernacknowitz died yesterday, she had three kids – they all went meshuggah* [crazy]. *Her father had salmonella poisoning. Oh, Heidi Braintumouritz – she died three days ago, and her son's just died in a motor-bike accident. Sophie Picklevavavvadowitz? Oh, she's very very ill – she's had half her lung taken away.*" Then you ask her, "And how are *you* Mary?" and she says "*Fine, fine – you know me. I always like to keep cheery.*" This isn't made-up material; she actually says it. It's *very* funny.'

Did you enjoy your bar mitzvah?

'I believed that'd be when I'd get my foreskin back – but no chance. The idea is that, after bar mitzvah, at thirteen, you're now considered a man. Yet I didn't lose my virginity until I was 22. The problem being I was *absolutely* ready for it at thirteen. I was *more than* ready for it. There's no point in standing around in some holy place when you don't understand a word of what you and everyone else is saying and singing, and getting no presents whatsoever, getting absolutely nothing out of it. I should have at least got my oats!'

When did playing-cards enter your life?

'Ahh yes, card-magic as a form of masturbation. I took up card-magic at eleven – most magicians start around eight, apparently – and it's since been a constant factor in my life. I saw someone on television doing a trick called the "Six Card Repeat", then went to the library and got out a book called the *Amateur Magician's Handbook*. At thirteen a genius called Gordon Bruce started teaching me and I began to treat it with great respect. At that age I had colitis (ulcers in the colon), which still haunts me today. I was in hospital for most of my childhood in fact – from nine to sixteen I spent half my time in hospital, seeing doctors about my arse-works. Ememas a go-go. But it gave me a lot of spare time to do card-handling. Whereas in school I'd always get into trouble for it . . . for practising under my desk. *Wwwwish-flitt-wwwwish.*'

It was uncontrollable?

'Yes. At about sixteen I used to go into pubs – I don't even drink – with a bowler-hat on my head, cards in hand and my pockets stacked with tricks, and go up to tables to try them out on people I didn't even know. I did it for practice, but partly because I was insane. Bringing out toy-ducks and hoops and cards, making a real show of myself. Funnily enough, I can't do that anymore – I've become reserved over being a prat in public. Now I think it's all saved up for the stage.'

Did humour play a large part in your youth?

'I adored Monty Python. That, and card-tricks, got me through schools and hospitals. It gave me a respite from being a miserable bastard. I went over to America at one point, but my Dad chucked me back on the next plane. I had a breakdown – I didn't know what was going on. My mum was now in London, trying to set up home, so I went there – I was seventeen. I got a job at Selfridges (the shop) and the council put my family into separate bed and breakfast accommodation. At one point the three of us were put in one tiny room, for three months, three beds cramped up together. It was a very unhappy time of my life – I had *nothing* to look forward to. But I bought a crappy record-player and then I chanced upon a "Derek and Clive" album. And not only did I find that funnier than Python but they became my companions, at a time when I had no friends. I knew nobody, had no social life, but "Derek and Clive" were in my head – as friends *almost*. They were a safety blanket.'

Describe the joy of 'Derek and Clive'.

'I just think they're the poetry of comedy. It's like beautiful music really, like Lennon and McCartney in tandem – Peter Cook plays rhythm and Dudley Moore harmonises, adds melodies. They were beautiful – absolute poetry. They knew how to use swear-words. "Shit", "wanker", "fuck off" – they're all great words, with wonderful consonants. "Cunt" and "fuck" combined is poetry . . . pure attack. The point is, how come I can listen to "Derek and Clive", which is racist and sexist, laugh at it and *know* they don't *really* mean it, and yet people can't accept what *I* do? When I was in Glasgow, playing cards with a friend, if one of us won the other would say "You big-nosed Jewish bastard" and it was perfectly acceptable. Just a bit of banter between friends. You've *got* to be able to laugh.'

Yet you've said your aggression and misery are real. When did you first decide or realise that 'Life Is Shite'?

'Around seventeen or eighteen I definitely realised. This is why I call myself a Born Again Comedian. Before then I was a nice kid really – I never had any nasty thoughts, or things to say, about anyone. As a kid I was as good as fucking gold. I was *always* nice . . . Then something turned . . .' (He flips his hand over) '. . . and I went like that inside. I turned inside out 180 degrees. In the years leading up to that I'd had a great faith in life, a great wide-eyed innocence and naïvety, which was slowly questioned one step at a time, every single hope or dream I had, until finally it was like the straw that broke the camel's back. I'd believed my health would always get better, that my friends would always be there, that I'd have a decent job in Glasgow, that I'd pay my mother some money each week . . . and so on . . . that life would be quite good. Then I realised life is *utter* shite and you really can't win. Name anything, and I'll prove it. Life's so predictable.'

I can't predict what you did next.

'I moved back to Glasgow when things didn't work out, got a little bed-sit on my own, did some busking, went to college (Shaun's Academy) to do O-Level Maths and Higher English . . . I felt cold and very unhappy again.'

What did your busking involve?

'Standing like a fool on the street, saying "Ladies and Gentlemen – the greatest trick ever performed!" and doing some pretty good card-manipulations and other stuff which people watched, enjoyed and clapped at, but then didn't give me *any* money for. That's just not on – it's *outrageous*! My response was to start abusing them, either saying "Hold on a minute, ladies and gentlemen, I'm just going round the corner for a prop" and then pissing off and leaving them waiting in the pouring rain, or shouting "Did you enjoy that? Well give us yer fucking money then!" I really hate the idea of people thinking buskers are *happy* people . . . of course they're not! I hate those who pretend they are. They're not doing it for community spirit – they just want your money, thank you. So somewhere between standing in the pouring rain, not getting any money and policemen moving me on all the time, I became *really violent* with the props and the people. I really hated it anyway, because I was prostituting an art that I greatly respected – so I was doubly resentful. Thus I think of myself, in a sense, as a product. I'm a monster created out of a nice shy child.'

How did things evolve thereon?

'I was living alone and writing card-tricks down for posterity, hoping people would read them after I was dead. Haaa. I was at my lowest ebb right then, but it was at this point I heard the third stage, the third style, of comedy to have an effect on me. It was Alexei Sayle's Cockney stream-of-consciousness piece (*Knockitonthe'ead-dowhat-wanker-turnitupasit'appens-Millwall*), and from that everything suddenly came together in my head. Every force of my being said "Right, I'm going to die in a blaze of glory, I'm going to do something like this and say *whatever I like* . . . take every feeling, every tiny darkest thought and express it on stage." I started performing a little at college – magic plus vicious monologue, and I also practised at a wee pub owned by the uncle of a friend. I was becoming far more aware of politics, and I incorporated all that. I realised just how predictable politics is . . .'

You surfaced at London's 'Comedy Store' in November 1985 – how did you fit in there?

'I felt I was a genuine comedian with a genuine world-view and most of the others there were happy people just trying to make some money. I was on a mission – a comic mission. I headlined there twice a month for two years and was a cross between Godzilla and Hitler. The very first night, I went on as the thirteenth act, at 4am, and was brilliant, and none of the other comedians there could understand where I'd come from – "Why is he so good?" I didn't have to work out material – it just came to me. I did a lot of anti-Scottish material, anti all the things in my life, the things I disliked . . . Malcolm Rifkind, George Younger, Glaswegian OAPs, the [Scottish] *Sunday Post* . . . I had a line about how *News at Ten* always gives the last word to Princess Diana; "Bong . . . Unemployment escalates to a record 10 million . . . Bong . . . 350 die in plane-crash . . . Bong . . . And Princess Di puts her hair in a bun." At this point I would add "And puts her fanny in a toaster – if there were any justice in the world." '

How did you go down, in the club, with the 'alternative comedians' who espoused non-sexism and non-racism in comedy?

'There were a lot in the audiences too. I got continuously jabbered by women. The club was firmly engulfed in a tight concept of what comedy can and cannot include. It was when I realised what fake nonsense that was that I really started challenging it – I associated that restraint with all the other bad things that had happened in my life. I decided very consciously that I would go against it, for the sake of comedy and also because I could see the other comedians were hypocrites, yapping on to the crowd about sexism, then walking off and going home with a drunken woman they'd just met. I just wanted to say how *I* felt, what *I* had experienced. It was purely empirical – real beliefs tailored to be funny, and a few nonsensical ones just to see whether they *really* had a sense of humour. Far from giving in to restraints, I thought I would open it all up completely.'

Just for its own sake?

'Sort of. And then someone – a happy person – ripped off my style and act and watered it down; so I went even more extreme. I became a double monster. Many clubs had already stopped booking me – "The Comedy Store" sort of let me go after two years – I was getting a lot of stick, a real reputation . . . And then I did well at Edinburgh, sold out for two weeks and released my album (*Gobshite*). This, I finally realised, was libellous – that it could get me into a *massive* amount of trouble. It had to be withdrawn, so consequently I have thousands of the bastards in the cellar.' (Gerry explodes now.) 'Don't that make you sick? That jokes and opinions should be censored? It's absolutely ridiculous. Why the fucking hell can't I say whatever I want?! I'm a comic . . . and no one's getting off the hook.' (A pause for a ponder and a comic effect.) '. . . And certainly not women. I have a line that goes "I'm non-sexist and all that. It's just *women* that I hate." '

Who's your favourite philosopher?

'Schopenhauer! The pessimist. I read him well after I'd constructed my own views on things, but it's very similar and meant a lot to me. It's one of the greatest moments in life when you come across someone who feels the same way as you. I quote – *"The most effective consolation in every misfortune and every affliction is to observe others who are more unfortunate than we, and everyone can do this. But what does this say of the condition of the whole?"* . . . You've got to larf, though – haven't you?'

Is there anything that you don't think is 'shite'?

(Gerry does not answer for 20 seconds) '. . . My mother . . . She's much more of an anarchist than me, by the way. A lot more aggressive. *She* should be a comedian, not me. If she could channel it she could make a fortune. I spent the afternoon with her today and she's just outrageous. She really hurts people. We went into a shop, where I needed to buy a pair of trousers, and she was extremely rude to an assistant who was being perfectly pleasant to her. My mother walks down the street tearing posters off the wall, she's smashed the television, she walks on the Underground and shouts "Zimbabwe!" . . . She never lets me be, never stops pestering and cloying. She's got plastic covers on all the furniture, and sheeting across the carpet. She wants everything clean. I'm terrified of her – absolutely terrified. She's *brilliant*.'

Why is she thus?

'Because life is shite. It's from being shat on so much that after a while you don't trust anyone at all.'

You love your yiddisha mama but you proclaim you don't take kindly to other women?

'I just don't think *I'm* of interest to *them*. Consequently I've become rather misogynistic. I think, let's face it, if someone is painting their nails they can't be using their brains at the same time . . . I can remember being assured in my teens, by the way, that magic was *the* way to pick up women. But really it just makes them run a mile. "Here's a card trick, darling . . . Whooooosh. Where's she gone?" '

Don't women like 'a man with a sense of humour'?

'Ohhh, I can't *stand* that line.'

Do you like yourself?

'No! I hate being me. I hate myself. If you don't believe that – phone my mother. Phone her right now and ask her. I've no self-esteem at all. I'm pathetically sad.'

And guilty?

'I have guilt-feelings. But, surprisingly, not about things very connected to me, nothing I can quite put my finger on.'

What are your friends' virtues?

'A sense of humour, perhaps. Or rather the fact that they're friends. Because *that's* virtuous – to be *my* friend.'

What do you enjoy doing?

'. . . Gambling (horses and the wheel), playing chess, shuffling the old playing-cards.' (Gerry has had several specialist books of highly progressive card-magic published which are praised internationally, and which poured out of him in 'an almost paranormal way' in 1983.)

What's the link between comedy and magic?

'I don't know if there is one. In a way they're like chalk and cheese, although I know quite a few other comedians have also used magic. To me they feel different, and I enjoy the aspect of melding them together. I love the idea of telling the most disgusting, gratuitously offensive joke and then turning around and picking up a silk handkerchief.'

Other than during your magic tricks you leave *very* few silent moments on stage. Is this the result of nerves?

'The reason I speak so fast is because I want to give the audience total value for money – three times the material. I also want to make everything explosive, like an Alice Cooper show – he was a great influence of mine. I want drama, mess, strength, power, energy. Because the comedy is so negative I want the show to be really ''up'' visually. I want everything to just . . .' (Sadowitz stands up now, shakes his arms, expands his chest, contorts his face – mimicking a man seconds away from self-combustion – but does not complete the sentence.)

Is your aim to entertain?

'To me the definition of an alternative comedian is, or should be, to entertain with *what* you do – *without compromising*. Doing that involves many things – making what you want to say funny, organising lights, dragging bags to theatres, setting up props (which takes considerably longer than the act itself), doing everything well, improvising well, putting up with all the crap that flies back at you, and – at the end of the day – expressing exactly what you want.'

How much are you aware of the audiences before you?

'I concentrate on the middle section – especially if they're laughing, so I can take my timing off them. Actually, I find if I don't look at a section of an audience for quite a while they don't laugh so much . . . They like to see my cheeky face.' (He's being sarcastic.)

Do you get pleasure from an audience's laughter?

'. . . Yes. When I know they're laughing because they understand the joke completely. The best laugh to feel is one in which you know they realise the full irony. That it's a joke. Like, ''I don't actually fuck seven-year-old girls . . . *Not any more*.'' I'm really proud of that line.'

Ummm. Do you care if people walk out?

'I try and stop them. You can't let it go without a comment, because then you would be planting the idea in the rest of the audience's heads that he was *right* to walk out. I've even had someone come on stage, take the microphone and start admonishing me and the audience for laughing at me. I had to try and explain all that I was doing. But I *think* I won him over in the end.'

So you say you want to entertain, that you want to speak outrages *and* make people laugh, that you are telling your true feelings, but it's a joke really (or is it?), that you get pleasure from a good response, that you want and like money and want and like to give value for money . . .

'Yes. All that, and there *are* moments of vague pleasure there. I admit that. But I still retain the theory that life primarily consists of *bad* and *worse*. There's not *bad* and *better*, or *slightly better*. It's really just *bad* and *worse*. This is The Gerry Sadowitz Paradox . . . For example, "The Americans are bad, but the British look up to them so *they're twice as bad*."' (Gerry, of course, was American-born.)

Don't your feelings go from *good* to *better* from the beginning of a show to the end?

'I don't feel happy before a show, and I certainly don't feel excited or happy afterwards. During a show I try to give the absolute best of my abilities, I try very hard, but if anything I feel *more* miserable after a show.'

You're a real *pro*, though aren't you?

'Well . . . there's that old cliché that performers should go into each and *every* show imagining that it's the first time they've done it . . . so that it will sound fresh. When *I'm* on stage I pretend it's the very *last* time I'll ever be doing it. After that I may be arrested, I may give up and become a croupier, I may drop dead. I give *every* ounce as if it's the final performance. Because if you truly believe you're up for death you're going to *really* make sure you say everything, and do everything, *exactly* the way you mean it.'

But what would they inscribe on your comic tombstone?

'Oh . . .' (long pause) '. . . I'd like it to be, "I WISH I KEPT MY MOUTH SHUT."'

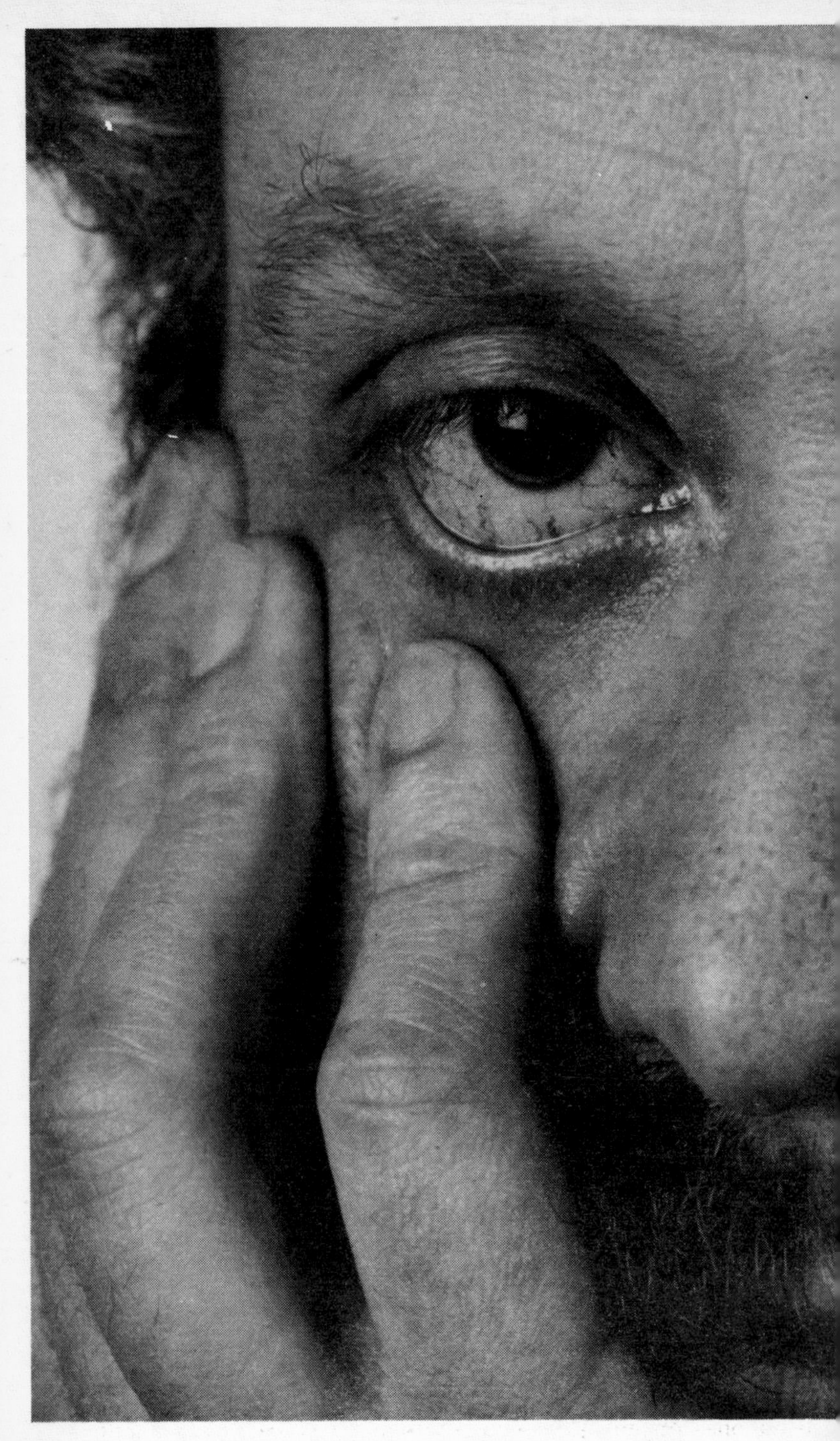

Film-maker and playwright MIKE LEIGH, 1988: '*It's good for a laugh.*'
Photograph by Gino Sprio

MIKE LEIGH

The Naked Ape

I just think it's funny how people treat each other.

Mike Leigh is remembering a discussion panel he once sat on. 'It was a piece of bullshit called *Whatever Happened to Political Theatre?*. And someone said "Can I ask each of the three speakers what their plays are about?" And David Edgar replied very dryly, "I like to write plays in which it's important you *don't* know whether the character is married." And David Hare said "I write plays in which it's *not* important you know whether the character is married." Which left me wonderfully open to follow through with, "I write . . . or rather make . . . plays in which it's *essential* to know whether the character is married." At that point the discussion got interesting.'

If the most effective drama exposes common truths, if the human face holds the key to bliss, torment and death, if the finest comedy derives from actors being involved in the bulk of the creative process, through some kind of cathartic play-acting, if 'reality' is, in truth, as surreal as surrealism, if humour works best when it keys into, and explores and challenges, the workings of our pedestrian drives . . . if all this is true, then it may be fair to conclude that Mike Leigh – who *never* appears in person in his own work – has his finger on the pulse of laughter and life. From his first play, in 1965 – through theatre, one film in 1970 and over 40 television works 'conceived and directed' – to his return in 1988 after 'a bit of a crack-up' with an anti-farce play and his second film proper, the nervously titled *High Hopes*, Mike Leigh has carried with a vengeance the torch of so-called 'improvised drama'. He has also influenced and inspired several generations of performers and humorists, and regularly encapsulated the *changing* essence of our times . . . and the ever-present foibles of humanity. Most importantly, perhaps, Leigh has offered up more finely tuned comic moments than it is reasonable to expect of one miserable man.

When Lawrence Moss, of Wibbley Webb Estate Agents – a small, hard-working, mustachioed husband character in *Abigail's Party* (Leigh's best-known play) – appeals rather tersely down the telephone, 'I'm not asking you to bath in cold water, I just want the key to 15 Clittingham Avenue', and comedy veers from the domestic to the erratic to the surreal to the sexual, *and* back again, *in one half-second*, before the story has barely got underway . . . When this happens, it almost seems too ludicrous to attempt to dissect the work of Mike Leigh. But, as in life, one is driven to swallow a cup of tea, then throw oneself into it.

Tea, the tritest but most refreshing of British panaceas, whether prepared, drunk or just mentioned, plays a role in almost all Leigh's darkly comic plays, and furthermore is the most frequent tool in his early improvisation with actors. Leigh's TV play *Grown-Ups* (1980), which began with the discovery of a cracked cup, managed to make reference to tea 29 times. Through 'Any tea in the pot?' and 'It's a teapot – *without any tea in it*', to 'I'm telling ya – *make me a bleedin' cup of tea!*' and the (weeping) 'I don't take sugar, Mrs Butcher . . .', tea symbolises the essentially humdrum surface of Leigh's drama. *Grown-Ups* ends, after physical and emotional commotion on a bemused Religious Knowledge teacher's staircase, with our grown-up 'working-class heroes' sitting next door, nine months on, listening to the heart-beat of a new generation shortly to arrive . . . whilst drinking another 'nice cuppa tea'. *Grown-Ups*, furthermore, contains 23 references to alcohol, eighteen to babies, four to milk bottles, and shows 45 cigarettes-to-mouth movements.

Leigh's comic, or tragi-comic, dramas are always very much *dramas*, but they grow within and out of seemingly dull, *domestic* environments. They revolve to a great degree around kitchens, living rooms and bedrooms, and they adopt a street-level 'wart and all' approach to acting, structure, dialogue and camera-work. Yet within such confines the human experiences and politics take on meanings of national, global, even mystical, proportions. Cultures, classes, sexes, neighbours, work partners and – most frequently – relatives co-exist and clash over everything from 'Who's making the tea?' to, perhaps, ' . . . UFOs, paranormal phenomena, telepathy, ectoplasm, life-after-death . . . GOD!' Doors are slammed, post is delivered, coats are put on and taken off, bacon is cooked, brooms hit ceilings and folk stumble out of bed, bullshit and stick their noses 'up bleeding people's arseholes'.

The beginnings and endings alone of Leigh's comedies show something of the work-a-day nature of their worlds, but also of how this fascination for detail evolves into higher meaning. *Home Sweet Home* (1981) begins with a tired postman scratching his testicles, and ends with a social-worker's hackneyed Trotskyite riposte to the question: 'What's the kettle for?' *Abigail's Party* (1977) begins in the living room of 13 Richmond Road, to the orgasmic moans of Donna Summer and a Gin and Tonic, and ends – still in the living room of 13 Richmond Road – with the earthly demise of an estate agent to the pomp and ceremony of Beethoven's *Fifth Symphony*, together with the painful leg-cramp of his unsuccessful reviver. *Four Days in July* (1985) commences with a camera-shot of children (and a dog) playing down a pathway in Northern Ireland whilst army jeeps crisscross the frame, and ends in a maternity ward with small-chat and mutual suspicion between a Republican mother and a Loyalist mother. *Nuts in May* (1976), meanwhile, opens to the folky middle-class singing of Keith and Candice-Marie Pratt as they arrive for a camping 'get-away' in Dorset . . . and draws to a close after Mr Pratt (a vegetarian who chews everything 72 times) chases Finger, a spirited Brummie lad, around a field with a stick screaming 'Get away from me . . . Get back I say, I'm warning you! I'll knock your head off – I'll knock your head offff! Come on then, if you want a fight! Come on thennnn! Come on, come onnnn – Let's fight!!!!' The actual end-credit sequence of *Nuts in May* involves the rich comic creation, Mr Pratt, squeezing between barbed wire, with a shovel and a roll of toilet-paper in hand, to defecate in a field of chomping pigs whilst his wife strums a ditty about human waste.

Nuts in May (which the BBC discouraged Leigh from titling *Eaten by a Pig*) is an interesting exception that proves the Leighian rule, in a way, because it takes part almost entirely outdoors – 'in harmony' with nature, and with its characters removed from their domestic environments. But this serves to actually heighten Leigh's on-going anthropological exploration of human characteristics – territorial, urban, sexual and otherwise. Its camp-site tents, the get-away homes of its battling characters, come to symbolise Stone-Age caves, and when teacher Keith Pratt unleashes his hysterical (funny ha-ha *and* funny-peculiar) attack on protagonist Finger his face bears striking resemblance to the apes battling in Stanley Kubrick's epic film *2001*. Thus Leigh mixes the minutiae of life with the monumental, the prat-falling with the profound . . . so they become a comic whole. Early on in *The Kiss of Death* (1976) the central character, Trevor (an undertaker's assistant), discusses girlfriends, clocking-in and chocolate sponge cake whilst preparing a corpse for viewing by its relatives. The TV film ends, within an Oldham high-rise, with reconciliation between Trevor and his best friend as they laugh nervously, then rather joyously, in a roar, at the sheer ludicrousness of life.

Mike Leigh comes to the door of his terraced London house with a barking dog and the offer of tea. He then points out the visual similarity – almost synchronicity – between two separate pictures of his offspring as babies, crying as one, which hang on the hall wall, and then climbs the stairs to his office, 'The Flea Room', where he apologises for the light whiff of canine excreta, and settles down to talk, rub his beard and sip Irish whiskey. His eyes, at once alert, weary, angry, scholarly and playful, have great power.

Can we talk humour?

'Oh yes. It's good for a laugh.'

Stephen Leacock said that laughter – 'Ha ha!' – began as the sound cave men expelled when they whacked each other over the head.

'As it's Leacock, who was a very funny writer and not at all intellectual, I think we should accept that as being *it*, really. I'm glad that the truth has finally been rumbled.'

Oh alright. But is humour the ingredient that makes your dark dramas digestible?

'Well . . . it works that way certainly. But I don't consciously decide "I'd better make this funny." A humorist is what I am, yes, and you know what that means. I love the tragi-comic, and I am a lampooner in a way. And yes, I'm a student of humour and how it works, of timing and structure, feeds, gags, punchlines, pay-offs and double-jokes. But that humour is never in script form – it grows *organically* out of discussion and improvisation and my structuring.'

Is it reasonable to equate your methods with Laurel and Hardy, Chaplin . . .

'Keaton, too, did what I'm doing *many* years ago; show up, say "OK, let's get a collapsing car and see what we can do with it", and if it doesn't work, do it again. It's exactly the same thing.'

Apart from yourself and a few others aside, why has that comic process fallen by the wayside?

'Well, that's a huge question. Read William Goldman's *Adventures in the Screen Trade*. Partly it's about systems, institutions, money, about people knowing what they're going to get. I was lucky until recently in that the BBC, once they would give me a slot on television, allowed total freedom. But since *Four Days in July* they haven't given me a look in. I've directed ten or twelve TV films since *Bleak Moments* in 1971. And to do a feature film then have a gap of seventeen years until *High Hopes* is *bad* news. And the reason precisely is that it is, or I'm, not safe . . . Buster Keaton was ruined when talkies came along and the industry became script-bound and literature-orientated. In England too, drama, and a lot of cinema, have roots in a theatrical, literary context. So there's a huge amount of prejudice. I mean, during final rehearsals I'll debate full-stops, commas and syllables until the cows come home – as long as it has all developed in 3-D, organically, through the actors. And you can be sure that's how the original Shakespeare theatre worked.'

When actors arrive to begin a project with you what knowledge do they have of what they'll be up to?

'Everybody agrees to take part without knowing *anything*. Not the size of their role, the type of role . . . *nothing*. Because I believe the only *actual* way to create a comic character with an actor, when the chips are down, is with him or her *doing it*.'

Leigh was born in 1943 in Manchester. The writer/director's 'career' began, like his dramas do, in acting. 'By some fluke, at seventeen I got into RADA on a scholarship,' he recalls, 'which was a pretty horrible experience as it was rather sterile then.' Leigh is remembering 1960, a time when the work and influences of John Osborne, Stanislavski, Beckett and Joan Littlewood's Theatre Workshop were disparaged within academia. When Leigh, in his second year, directed a student production of Harold Pinter's *The Caretaker* ('about an arse-scratching tramp and two other blokes in a grotty room'), his senior teacher dismissed Pinter as 'rubbish'. Leigh remembers only two occasions at London's Royal Academy of Dramatic Arts in which he witnessed any form of improvisation, and on departing the academy he found 'equally sterile' his year spent as a bit-part actor, although this included a keenly-observed and – perhaps unintentionally – very funny appearance as a dumb boy in the 1963 BBC series *Maigret*. Shifting direction, Leigh thus enrolled on a foundation course at Camberwell School of Art and it was there, in life-drawing classes, that he finally felt he was 'looking, first-hand, at real-life and arranging it creatively . . . I began to realise that acting could potentially be *that* creative. The inspiration he thereafter received set him on a path to conceiving and directing theatre productions in which actors develop and intensively research their characters and evolve a story through group improvisation. The results have been some of the sharpest and most 'honest' comedies in the last 20 years.

Let's start at the very beginning. What spawns a Leigh project?
'I start with a *complete blank.*'
How do you audition actors?
'I meet a lot of actors for half an hour each, then ask some back, for another hour each. I do certain things with them I'm not inclined to have in print – only because it can throw people up in advance. But from those techniques, 99.9% of the time I know whether each actor is right. I then begin to decide, for example that actor X, Y and Z have certain possibilities together. At that point the project, within the strictures of funding, is rolling.

'I take notes at the early stage. I talk to each actor about numerous people they've known in real life, then we eliminate some character-sketches from the list and finally I choose one to form the basis of the character . . . Sometimes actors say, "Shall I go and find the real person," and the answer is definitely *No*, because I'm interested only in the actor's *conception* of that person. One actor I was working with came up with this very public school guy he once knew – a City bloke, very straight, a Tory from his gullet to his gut. I told him not to look for him, and he did. He discovered he had dropped out, been through the Royal College of Art and was now a glass-blower in East Anglia. It totally threw him off the scent. So just as the original cornfield Van Gogh painted is irrelevant, so is the *actual* person.'

Leigh's characters therefore evolve creatively from a name, through the drawing of an *extensive* family-tree (often back to the nineteenth century); the actor's research into relevant matters; elaborate discussion with Leigh and his questioning of actors on all manner of 'random' philosophical, social, sexual, medical and cultural points relating to their character ('What is your first memory of a room you slept in? . . . Has your character ever eaten a Mr Kipling cake?');

solo improvisations (creating a 'Running Condition') and physical and mental interaction with others. Leigh meanwhile feeds his actors suggestions, takes *copious* notes and forms a narrative awash with his darkly comic world-view. Under his egis actors produce powerful characters whose credibility and humour are hard won. Actors explore how a new personality boils tea, whether it would wear spectacles and what its accent, phrasing, walk, hairstyle, posture, taste, terminology, consciousness, clothes and home-environment would be like. The results are poignant and idiosyncratic. Where Leigh's process varies from Stanislavski and The Method is that actors are not really building on their own experiences but on 'another's'. And the whole improvisational process, Leigh is keen to add, 'is all to do with liberating possibilities . . . But the *actual* finished artifact is something else again.' His style of improvisation, he is somewhat tired of explaining, has nothing to do with 1960s-style happenings, but on working around to a time when atmosphere, interactions, dialogue and narrative can be perfectly structured. Leigh demands that his actors will – at a nod – move in and out of character, so that Leigh can discuss, comment and gain technical control. 'The kind of actors I can't stand', he explains, 'are those who can't control what they're doing, can't play for laughs, and can't come outside it all so they can work on a personal level with me.'

What he is saying is '*I* am the dramatist.' He is the giver of freedom but also the one who obsessively hones and moulds it. He is the Comic Catalyst. More significantly he is the Comic Controller.

'The fact is I'm *very* dictatorial' he confesses, 'but it only works because – in the meantime – I'm in the business of giving actors a great amount of space to play, which they find immensely refreshing. And as for my relationship to the industry and why I don't work *their* way . . . I'm *just not interested* in working in a hack studio system, or any of its modern degenerates.'

Leigh's process of interactive improvisation (and narrative evolvement) is encapsulated in his description of working on *Nuts in May*. 'We rehearsed in a real field in Dorset. Alison (Steadman) and Roger (Sloman) got into character (as the Pratts) and drove from London with all their crap, and camped. Then at a certain point Anthony O'Donnell (playing Ray, their first camp-site 'enemy') was dropped off at Wareham station, and – in character – found his way to the site with a map. They all met, and at that point the two factions knew nothing in advance about each other's characters . . . So, all the time this is happening *I'm* sneaking around or sitting in the corner of the field with my bollocks freezing off, *clocking it all*.'

When a project's filming-period is arranged, Leigh arrives on location with what he calls 'The Premise' – a brief listing and structuring of choice scenarios taken from, reworked or inspired by extensive earlier improvisation. There are no 'wads of A4' (scripts), but thousands of words in the actors' and director's minds which have been whittled down for this the final sculpture – the clashing and resolution of characters before the cameras.

*

John Cleese said that, although he thought you were 'the finest creator of comic characters', he often felt your stories could be resolved *only* by someone dying of a heart-attack. (Or procreating?)

'Well, I certainly don't agree. In fact it's the beginnings that are the tricky parts. The endings almost always feel very easy, very natural.'

Your work isn't exactly naturalism though, is it?

'No, it's *heightened* realism. It's not a slice of life so much as the creation of the illusion of a slice of life, which I shoot fairly classically . . .'

Actor Gary Oldman said once that, after much worry, he suddenly *clicked into* his character as Coxy (his extremely chilling and funny skinhead in *Meantime*, 1983), when actor Tim Roth accidentally shattered a light bulb in his face during improvisation. Instead of saying 'Oh, hold on a minute, loves,' he beat Tim up – in character, *as Coxy*.

'With all due respect to him, that isn't really an illustration of anything normally relevant – because it was an extremity. But, as for the story, I just remember blood spurting from Oldman's head and saying "OK, come out of the character now." By then he'd been shaved and was dressed in gear, and he looked *very* real . . . We rushed out, jumped into my car and raced to a hospital. And as we ran in Gary said "For fuck's sake, Mike, tell them I'm an actor!!" But they didn't believe me. He almost lost his eye-sight, and – frankly – if that had happened I really don't know whether I could have gone on with all this. So that was a very traumatic occasion, *but very untypical*.'

How are close character relationships evolved – say, between two actors playing lovers, a husband and wife?

'I start improvisation at the beginning of their relationship, then follow through. The two actors learn everything they would know about each other. But there are also things they keep secret from each other that only the individual *and* I know.'

When actors are playing blood relatives though, such as siblings – which must be decided at a fairly early stage in your direction – are there ways of getting to the nub of those relationships?

'Well, I've got various exercises, some of them derived in another form from Lee Strasberg, which are slightly mystical. They're "hands-on". There are some primal improvisations, so they can experience what it was like to be with the "parent" at only six-months-old.'

Do you think a lot of actors are weary of your whole process?

'Some I've met, when they're drunk in a pub, say things like "Oh, it's all a load of method crap, Mike – just *do it*! What is the point of all that fucking information, if it's not in the film?" But of course it's in the film!' (Leigh sounds angry now.) 'It's not mentioned, *but it's there*! The *only* way we arrived at those moments of Cyril and Shirley (a couple for ten years) in *High Hopes* was through *weeks* spent discussing all the rockers they'd known, all the trips to Brighton on a motor-bike, all the Greasy Spoons, all "those heavy guys we met'', all the dope smoked . . . it's all implicit. We even had improvisations surrounding the illness and death of Cyril's father [Leigh's father had recently died] in hospital, and of course no such character appeared in the film. The details are *so* secure when the actors arrive on location we can concentrate completely on the creative stuff, the comedy, the refining. It's all got to be perfectly in place!'

Do the actors have to be so in character that they don't laugh at the material, at what they do?

'Oh, I don't mind giggling and cracking-up – certainly not in rehearsals and development. There's usually lots of corpsing. Which I think is absolutely great. It means we enjoy ourselves.'

You seem to relish the moment of choosing characters' names; Desmond Shakespeare, Samantha Cart-Walker, Colin Pollock, Caroline Stormont-Grundy . . . taking joy in the phonetics and the pictures the names paint.

'I keep a little book of them. I've got it in a drawer right here. I take this book into rehearsal for ideas and also so I don't use a name twice. There are hundreds of them, used and un-used . . . Vernon P. Staines, Jackie Sprag, Irvin Gammon. I spend a lot of time making up names.'

How much are your films about 'you', Mike Leigh?

'Obviously there is an idiosyncratic perverse auteur level to *everything* I do . . . And directors, in a sense, have to fall in love with actors – I think there's sympathy there for almost every character I evolve – and that's a whole matter one has to cope with. I mean ''falling in love'' with actors in different ways, including *actually* falling in love. And *everything* connects, I'm sure, into how I'm feeling at the time, on the day – how your sex is, and everything.'

Hard Labour, your first BBC play in 1973, was set in Salford, Manchester and utilised the two areas you grew up in. (Simply put, its central character, a working-class cleaning woman, is set against both her own arrogant husband and the middle-class lady she cleans for.)

'Certainly that's the closest I've come to direct autobiography. It was inspired by a woman I once knew, but it was the television producer Tony Garnett who coaxed me to refocus politically what I was doing, and indeed that whole class theme of my work has developed since.'

Do you always think consciously, 'This character is someone I like, but this one isn't'?

'It's very clear cut I would have thought.'

Before you said you had sympathy for almost all your characters. Are you now taking sides?

'Well, when I'm having a go at people it's really at ''us'', not ''them.'' '

Isn't that contradicting what you just said about it being clear-cut?

'Mmmm. The point is, I'm getting at things, like upwardly-mobile bourgeois affectations, which in fact can be found in *all* of us – at least a bit. It's about ordinary lives. But I create a dialectic by setting varying types or styles of characters against each other.'

Leigh is a master of 'twist and tics', of exploring 'ordinary lives', how in reality – as in the title of one of his plays – *Babies Grow Old*. Babies grow old to become, of course, grown-ups, the semi-ironic title of another Leigh play. This invariably involves families interacting, rowing, encouraging, complaining, fighting and drinking. It almost feels at times as if Leigh wants to explore the very darkest edges of how kith and kin behave towards each other, to take their relationships to the limit of exposure. By doing this, and playing with it and controlling it as an artist, he perhaps has a finger on the source and the roots of humour – 'the family', only on top of which is then placed society. In effect Leigh is the Comic Controller of the Family. In his 1988 stage-play *Smelling a Rat* a father, a son, the son's girlfriend and the father's employee and wife learn opinions of themselves from others who are ignorant of their existence hidden within nearby wardrobes. The resolution of this anti-farce comes abruptly, at the end of a brief second act, when the father suddenly accepts his son for what he is. But the son – a perpetually inarticulate boyish clown – is too bemused or numbed to respond to a new freedom. In Leigh's film *High Hopes* his themes cover society's politics as a whole, but they are personified within the families he playfully names the Benders, the Burkes and the Booth-Braines. The slightly grey optimism which surfaces at the end of *High Hopes* comes in two forms, both related to the family. One is the two central characters' decision *finally* to procreate – forcing themselves to adopt the optimistic approach for producing a new generation. The other is their new-found fondness for a grandmother, one of an older generation equally baffled by the world, her bafflement having previously been encapsulated in a exquisitely funny *and* horribly depressing scene in which members of the Bender family argue remorselessly around her. Their hysterical group-torment is only heard, however – it is never seen. Throughout the darkly comic cacophony, Leigh filmed only the unspeaking old woman's baffled face. He homes in on it, captures it and films it at length, uninterrupted, in tight deeply-wrinkled close-up. Leigh, with this shot, challenges all viewers quite simply either to slump into melancholy, or laugh heartily. His films frequently return to the theme: Families – to have or have not?

The points in your films where you close in on anguished, bemused or embarrassed faces almost resemble the eruptions in sex-films.

'That's what they are – exactly!' (He is amused.)

Can you explain where that keen observation for faces and human detail derives from in you? Is it a reflex to understand faces and moods for your own safety? In essence: Did you find your parents funny?

'Oh, they were hilarious. But I don't know where to start really

. . . I was born during the war (1943) and my dad was away – except for one visit – until I was three and half. He was a socialist but unpredictable and fairly suppressive towards me, which leads into my thing against teachers in varying forms . . . Mr Butcher the teacher in *Nuts in May*, Peter the teacher in *Bleak Moments*, Keith from Social Services in *Nuts in May* – they're all characters who unconsciously are my dad and school-teachers. As it happens, I spent five years at school in detention. They had me fully booked up.'

What were your childhood surroundings like?

'Dad worked as a doctor, but I both went to school and lived in a middle-class home in the same building as his surgery *within* a working-class part of Salford. I didn't know where I stood. And that could explain the class clash in my work . . . I suppose I was a big *observer* . . . At home I remember, even as a very young kid, watching over-weight or over-dressed or over-loud or over-smelling grown-ups *performing*. In the 1950s, which must have significance too, we moved surroundings to a more suburban middle-class area and I sampled *all that*.'

And reacted to 'all that'?

'Well, I finally rebelled, dropped out, whatever you want to call it. I escaped to London. And I'm still sitting here wearing a pair of jeans and all that. I'm still a beatnik, protesting against the 1950s, the Brylcreem, the suits and anything else you may choose to mention. Haaa.'

There are quite a lot of actual references to humour in your works – lines like 'Who does he think he is, Ernie Wise?' and 'You're a bloody comedian, mate.'

'It's true – the subject crops up rather a lot. Did you notice the teacher referring to her school-project about humour in *Bleak Moments*? She asks the man without a sense of humour, "I wonder if you've got any ideas?" '

As a character in the more heroic – even moral – characters in your plays, you often include more intentional, *conscious* humour. The deceived husband in *Home Sweet Home* and Clive in *Short and Curlies* tell jokes with gusto, the Republicans in *Four Days in July* are wonderfully droll, and actor Phil Daniels' older-brother character in *Meantime* was almost an urban surrealist. He asks 'Have you ever read *The Lion, the Witch and the Wardrobe*?', then disappears, ' . . . See ya!'

'And in differing ways those characters *are* my mouth-pieces, yes. I'm fond of people with that humorous spirit; whereas most of the characters have little immediate sense of their own humour.'

Were you a humorous child?

'I would say I was always very much a comedian as a youngster – an eccentric, clown and cartoonist. I was preoccupied by *loony* humour, and my mouth got me into a lot of trouble. In a peculiar way, though – by dint of what I do – I've actually become less overtly *loony* as the years have passed.'

How much does directing and filming feel like being a child?

'A lot . . . when it's working properly.'

Do you, like the Pratts in *Nuts in May*, often feel the desire both to control and to get away from people and real life?

'It's there certainly, and it's one of the things I've battled with . . . But in the last few years, after a rough patch, my father dying and other things, I've come to terms with all that. It's something you could feel in *High Hopes* – more optimistic. I'm more optimistic personally . . . especially in comparison with *Bleak Moments*, which started me in film and certainly was rather melancholic.'

So despite the character Cyril Bender's social comments in *High Hopes*, such as 'I'm scared of getting bitter', and ' . . . The thing is – change what? By the year 2000 there'll be 38 TV stations telling you what to think . . .', despite this you actually feel more optimistic now?

'Well I'm still as depressed, politically and socially and environmentally, about the things we're all depressed about. But somewhere inside I'm more optimistic. I think it's partly, or even mostly, to do with having children – which the central characters decide to do at the close of *High Hopes*. [The male, Cyril, also becomes closer to his mother.] You're pessimistically concerned about their life in the 2020s, but they make you less nihilistic – less doomed. Because children take things ''beyond you'' in more senses than one. And they rearrange the pecking order.'

There is a character's line in Leigh's short film, *Short and Curlies* (1987), which alone says a great deal about the comic director's nature. It is spoken by Clive, a half-romantic, half-realist urban youth who is far from averse to sprinkling his conversation with eager jokes and small playful riddles. The joker's words (Leigh's really) are illogical but to the point:

'I wouldn't be joking', he explains *'. . . if I wasn't being serious.'*

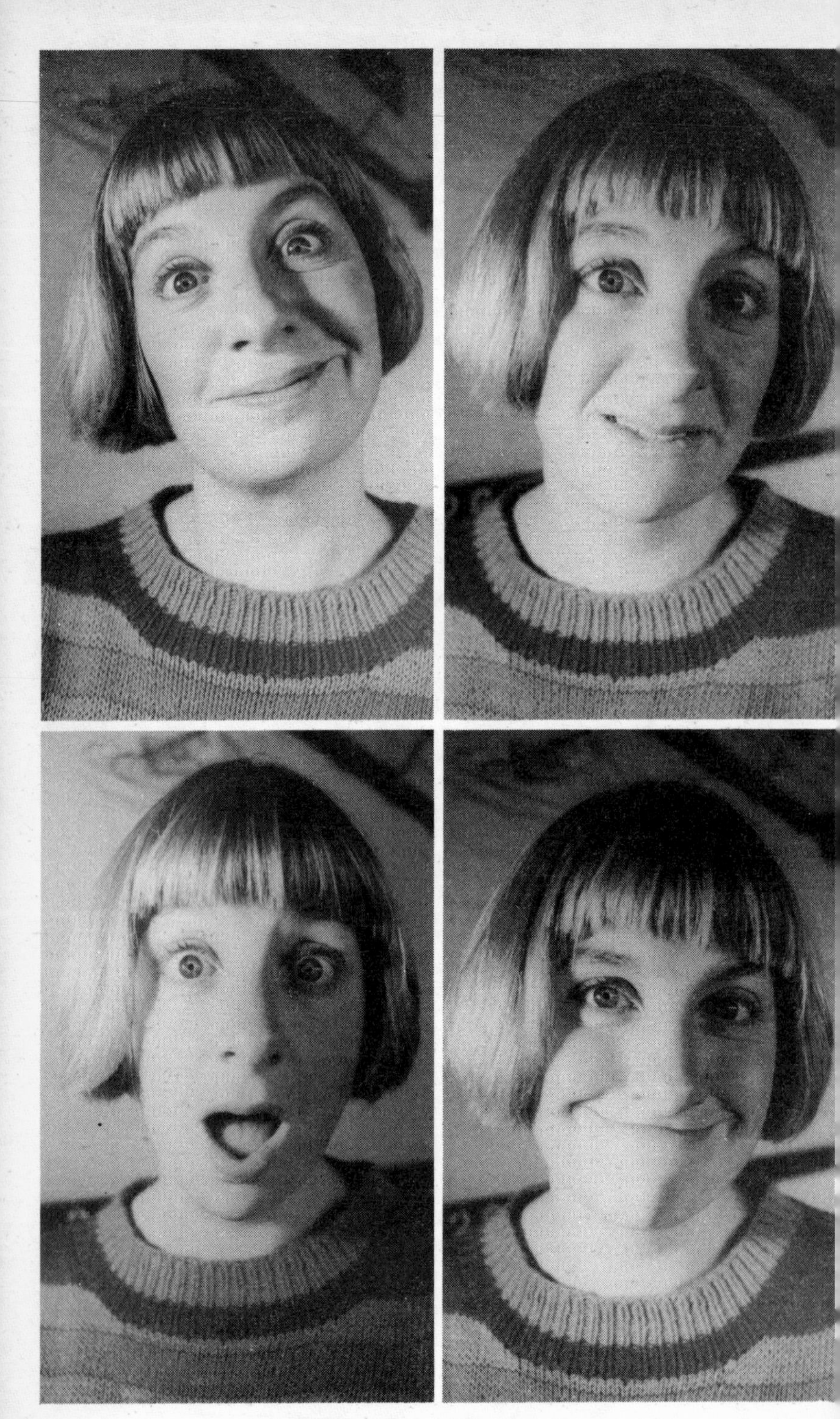

VICTORIA WOOD warming up for rehearsals, 1989
Photographs by John Hind

VICTORIA WOOD

Sister

It's like being continually poked.
Can you imagine that?

Victoria Wood's comedy inhabits a world in which the smallest and most trivial details are important, an artificial world (rather close to the real one) in which having one's hair dyed the colour of 'Varicose Violet' rather than 'Burnished Beechwood' is more than a woman can stand. It is populated partly by outspoken (or moody) urban girls or housewives and dull or self-obsessed local television presenters. It is a world in which people will expatiate on the state of their health at the drop of a head-scarf (gippy kidneys, a dicky bladder, a touch of groin strain or a grumbling ovary which once 'flared up during *The Gondoliers*'). They will further explain how they've scoured a shop from top to bottom looking for a side-winding thermal body-belt ('Could I find one? Could I faffoo!'). Their names are Samantha, Ariadne, Joan, Sharon, Kimberley, Madeleine ('Mad-e-lin'). In this strange world one's husband's funeral is greeted resolutely with the declaration: '72 baps, Connie – you slice I'll spread!'; and one can be gainfully employed in supermarket pricing ('It's quite a responsibility') calling out *'Red Cabbage! No idea!'* to a cashier's inquiries. It is a world in which a great day out will involve trying shoes on, eating salad, watching *Mary Poppins II: The Revenge*, then witnessing your drunken best friend Kimberley play chop-sticks on a pub piano '. . . wi' one nipple'. A world of bingo, macs, food-blenders, a body-support with a built in wolf-whistle, Dralon-effects and shopping-trolleys. In this world, when someone asks 'How is Life?', they are not referring to human existence so much as 'Life', *the new fragrant panti-liner for those inbetween times*; when someone asks 'What do you think of Marx?' the reply is most likely to be, 'I think their pants have dropped off but you can't fault their broccoli.'

Does Victoria *like* her characters? (One is never quite sure even when, more recently, she has played 'herself' on television.) These people are social animals, consumers, often creatures who are envious, pompous, gossiping, squabbling, blunt or unquestioning. Nevertheless, all Wood's characters – whether described by her or performed – can in one sense be seen as proud 'individuals' with glorious quirks and rare obsessions. Their power and humour come through the way Wood plays with their potential mundanity, sending them into flights of fancy, yet still ties them with elastic to the workaday. 'Good evening,' says one such lady, 'My name is Kitty. I've had my boob off and I can't stomach whelks, so *that's me for you* . . . They've asked me to talk about aspects of life in general, like nuclear war and peg-bags.' This jolts and teases our perceptions of, and deceptions about, the lives we lead. Are we being controlled? Are we all completely barmy (a good Wood word)? Is everyday human activity and conversation profoundly interesting or is it just immense gibberish and game-playing? And finally, when it comes to the *ultimate* crunch, just *how* important is a perfect panti-hose within the vast universal scheme of things?

Victoria Wood is one of few women in Britain to have both developed a strong comic vision of her own and succeeded in selling and *controlling* that comedy with large-scale success. We meet outside a theatre, where she stands sheepishly reading the *Guardian* dressed in thick denim with an assortment of cheerful decorations attached. She has large powerful eyes which much of the time lie half-secreted beneath a fringe of clean, wispy hair. Without cutting an inch from this fringe (which, actually, she does before the photograph herein) she is perpetually forced to spend a great deal of each day running her forefinger across her eyelashes to bounce the hair upwards, so she may occasionally see higher than five foot six inches.

We sit in an Italian restaurant and she eats a large bowl of her favourite pasta in under five minutes, while expounding on the general pleasures of food and motherhood. Then we sit on some grass in a park.

Why do you live in a little village outside Morecambe?

'It's rather *beautiful* – that's the main reason. I like the people and the comfort and the space. I like the fresh air, the walking and the weeding of the garden. Me and my husband (Geoff – a fake Spanish magician professionally known as ''The Great Soprendo'') ended up in Morecambe to do with his work ages ago, and so we set up near there and it just seems fine. We're on the Lancashire-Cumbria border. We live a very quiet life.' (Suddenly she changes tack.) 'There again, it's not a fairy tale world. There's awful sewage on the beach and a nuclear dump just up the road.' (Again.) 'But I do like the people. I'm not saying they're better people than others, but I feel much more comfortable with Northerners. I just love the way they talk. The way they use language . . .' (And again.) 'But I do like to get away from them, and it, fairly often.'

On stage you've said 'I come from the dullest place on God's Earth'; and indeed that 'This country is just essentially *dreary*'.

'Well, this country *is* very dreary I suppose. The place I live is very nice – although I live near to a *very* dreary town. The point is, I don't tell the truth on stage, you know. It's fiction . . . Although I suppose I write about a world existing fairly *near* to the truth.'

From the minor details in your comedy – the turns of phrase, the lingo of shopping expeditions, all the minor points of characterisation – I assume you spend a lot of time observing or spying on people?

'Well, if you're doing things you're not really observing them. I don't think I'm such an observer *nowadays*. I don't *observe* myself observing too often. I never take notes, and I never walk out to get material.'

I don't believe you're not a snooper.

'Well . . . I'm very interested in things, and I do *occasionally* hover.' (She laughs – sharp and swift.) 'I had a cross-line on the telephone recently, and I stayed on for literally hours listening to some guys speaking. So I certainly love hearing people talk.'

Is it true you actually peep inside other people's shopping-bags?

'Well . . . *not really*. But I just love the way people use jargon and product-names in conversation. First off, the words are funny in themselves, as sounds. When people refer to "Oxidol" in normal conversation, in a very straight way, I get amused. I mean, it's not as if I'm imagining it all – am I? That *is* the way people speak. They've seen so many adverts, they spend *so* much time buying things, thinking they should buy things and planning to buy things.'

So, when one of your characters sees an actress trying to wash her hands in Shakespeare's *Macbeth*, she naturally feels impelled to call out 'Try Swarfega!'

'Yes. I *rarefy* it. The fun there comes from the sheer sound of Swarfega, and because of the ridiculous – but fairly down-to-earth – incongruity between what's on stage and Swarfega. But what *is* important to me is that, beyond all the product name-calling, there is a *real* inner life within the characters I create that audiences can almost believe or identify with.'

My question is – do you get inspiration from ordinary folk you meet and pass by?

'I suppose I must do; but it's very difficult to understand. People and conversations have gone into the brain in some form and come out as part of something else. I could go through one of my scripts and say "Oh yes, that's *slightly* based on a woman I met last March"; but it's so convoluted by the time it comes out that it's almost indistinguishable.' (She pauses and reflects.) '. . . I think *if anything*, most of my inspiration comes from much further back, during my childhood in Bury and school-days. From stuff that's all tucked right at the back of the head.'

Victoria Wood had ordinary beginnings?

'I come from a pretty ordinary place. I was born in 1953 in Prestwich, which is just outside Manchester, and then was brought up just outside Bury, on the hills between Bury and Rochdale – Northern country. Bits of moors, bits of barns, bits of factories – Bury is a little cotton town. I live 80 miles away now; I haven't been back there for years. It wasn't pretty country, *at all* . . . but it was space, it had space.'

Your father sold insurance.

'He still does. He won't stop!' (Mr Wood is in his 70s.)

What's he like?

'He can be *very* funny.'

Funny ha-ha, or funny peculiar?

'I think if times had been different, if he'd been of a different generation, he would have been a musician or a comedian instead of an insurance salesman – something in that field. He writes – he's had some plays on the radio, he used to write songs and tunes and he plays the piano *very* well.'

What form does his humour take?

'It's quite hard to describe. The things he writes are quite ironic, quite wry, *rather English*. He has a very big way with words – he writes very funny letters to me. It's not dissimilar to how I write, in some ways. My mother, meanwhile, is a teacher – she is now. When she finished raising, when I went to school at eleven, she went back to college. She'd left school at fourteen, so she returned to do exams, then university. She was at university the same time as me practically. She even did a little drama herself.'

Do you note characteristics you acquire from both of them?

'My mother's very hard working and I get that from her, and my father's creative, and it's quite a good combination to have. I can see a lot of characteristics I get from them both, *plus* whatever's thrown in on top of that to make me an individual.'

Is your mother amusing?

'Well, she doesn't *know* she's funny.' (Wood laughs with gusto.) 'She's *very* funny when she shouts at my father. She's rather, umm . . . indomitable! I often think of her when I write older roles.'

How important was humour in your family?

'I think it was more my own thing. Obviously I gradually realised how witty my father was, but humour wasn't a particularly frequent thing. We didn't all roll around on the floor together. I have one brother and two sisters – all older than me. We were spaced out in ages, at least it felt very much that way. My brother is 49, sisters 45 and 39, I think. My brother left home when I was five – so he was gone and I felt distant from my sisters anyway through them being "older children". So comedy didn't feel to me a family thing, but something *I* was into. I didn't think "Oh yes, comedy is my baby", but whenever the family was going to the cinema I'd say "If it's not a comedy, I just don't want to go!" I liked discovering comedy programmes, reading humour books . . . it was quite private to me.'

Did you try to amuse or spin jokes off your parents?

'Well, I don't know really. I wasn't an attention-grabber; I kept to myself. Although when I was very very little I pulled faces a lot – it was what I could do, what I was good at. They used to say "Go in the kitchen and make up a face", I used to go out, come back with a new expression and be very amusing to people. I was probably the funniest of their four children. But I'm not sure it was my way of making a mark on the family.'

You said you were a loner.

'Yes, *very* much. I felt that my sisters were much cleverer and much better at everything than me. It *never* occurred to me that it was just because they were older; I thought they were naturally endowed with more brains and more looks . . . just better at everything. So I tended to disassociate myself from the things they did. I stayed at home, and often sneaked round their rooms – privately taking an interest in their doings. The sister above me is three years older – and she's a brilliant dancer, she used to go to all the clubs in Manchester and dance and meet boys. There wasn't that in me – I couldn't have done it, but I *was* very envious. I think I wanted *her* approval. She went to art school and used to make all her own clothes. And I felt *very* pathetic in comparison.'

But did your sisters ever tell you that – did they make you feel beneath them?

(A hearty laugh.) 'Oh yes – *but of course*! They were *horrible. All* sisters are horrible. Well, mine were. Very bossy, and they treated me like a nuisance. They were very proficient at giving "young Victoria" a good quashing, telling off and bossing about. And it made me, *has* made me, very competitive – so I'm glad really. Because it's made me want to get even with them!' (She emits a jokingly sinister laugh.)

Did you desire to prove yourself similarly to your parents?

'I don't think so, too much. I'm glad to be doing something they like, but I always did what *I* wanted to do . . . I didn't do it for them. I love them and I'm very proud of them, but I can't ever remember really trying to please them. Although I'm certainly glad they like it now.'

What did you get up to as the semi-loner of the family?

'I read – I was a mad reader. Well, I either read, played the piano or watched the television. Which is almost exactly what I do now. I just did much more then! It was quite a big house, and I had my own room – aside from my bedroom. It had a television and a piano. And I used to go in there and no one would see me *for days on end*. And I used to write music.'

Where did the piano come from?

'Well, we had a piano in the house anyway. But when I was fifteen my father bought me my own, which is great . . . And I bought him one for his birthday last year, so I've paid him back.'

You once said, 'By fifteen I wanted to be an actress, a performer.' You also once said, 'I *always* wanted to be famous.'

'I *did* always want to be famous, yes. I can remember thinking it at about four years old. And someone said, "Oh, but *everybody* wants to be famous" . . . but I *really* did have the feeling for it.'

What did the word 'famous' mean?

'I suppose being somebody of importance. I didn't feel important and I wanted to. When I started watching television a lot, I wanted to do that. To "do television" as a job.'

Were you a humorist at school?

'At junior school my thing was *being clever*, being high in the class.

'But when I got to Bury Girls' Grammar School everyone else was quite clever, so I gave up on that – except perhaps in English lessons. I'd say I was quite a joker from eleven onwards. That was my way of giving myself an identity. Because I didn't have much going for me apart from that – I wasn't pretty, I wasn't good at games, I wasn't *loads* of other things which give people a good pathway through school.'

Were you still a loner?

'I was to start with. But I *wanted* friends. I had *some* friends. But until later I was never in the groups I wanted to be in. I used to look at the girls who rode horses, or were good at games, or those who went out with boys, and I'd think, *"Oh, I wish I was one of you."* ' . . . (Laughs.) 'Now I think, Thank God I wasn't! But I did get in with some amusing girls.'

What do teenage girls joke about?

'That's very easy to answer – sex. It was the main theme of conversation . . . there was a boys' school just over the road. We were very good at spreading malicious rumours, about the most respectable girl in the Scripture class, for instance. Actually, we used to joke about *absolutely anything*. The best thing about being at school is the jokes, surely . . . the jokes *all* the time. I used to hurt myself from laughter. Always falling on the floor and banging my head from laughing. Either laughing at other people's behaviour or appearance, or making jokes about other girls, about teachers . . . but mainly about sex. Only five pupils in the sixth form had "done it", and we kept an elaborate chart of how far everyone had gone.'

This was comedy?

'Oh yes – it was a scream. They're my favourite jokes, in-jokes. They're the ones that make closest contact, communally.'

You tell a line about a school-acquaintance coming back from the shops at lunchtime and saying, in a very guttural tone, 'I couldn't get ya Ras'berry Yoghurt, so I got yer meat p'tato pie!'

'That was true. A true story. Not really in that voice but I remember it *very* well. I was sitting on the fire-escape stairs with someone called Sweeney, sunbathing. That's an in-joke really. I don't know quite *why* it's funny but it certainly made *us* laugh, thank you.'

One Wood character-piece may suffice as an illustration of the pedestrian and yet ultimately free-flying nature of her comedy. 'Welcome to the wonderful world of Sacharel. This is Mad'laine sp'kin' ' introduces a solo stage routine in which Wood puts on the antiseptic perfumed persona of a cosmetics saleswoman with a microphone, and then gradually teases out the very human qualities of error, arrogance, sarcasm, self-obsession and exacerbation. What she speaks is at first merely badly-worded sales-speak with minimal meaning ('We have a special offer on special offer . . .'), concerning pieces of nothingness ('Free gift comprising of suede-effect poshette packed to the draw-string with handy-size oddments') and reducing all beauty and life to jolly jargon ('mouth-blot, eye-wipe and shimmering cleavage enhancer'). The imaginary customers she is speaking to in the cosmetics department are, it seems, perfectly *dis*interested in having 'a full beauty make-over' which is 'totally free of charge, which so ever'. The saleswoman is neither in control of what she is saying nor particularly interested. She is doing a well-rehearsed job in a rather dull place. *Ultimately*, though, she is clearly not one to evade her own personality, making cruel digs at her ugly assistant ('Take yer muzzle off') and making comments about her predicament ('So this is Mad'laine, asking for the last time, for just one frigging volunteer!'), or the truth behind the mask she is purveying ('over-priced bits of grease'). Like most or all of Wood's comic faces, Mad'laine is a small lost soul still pumping with character and resilience.

Was there any comic actress who made a strong impression on you as a youngster?

'I saw Joyce Grenfell (Queen of Gaucherie) on stage in Buxton when I was about six. It was the first time I'd ever seen anyone stand on their own on stage. I didn't realise there were jobs like that before – that one could stand on stage and speak, with no props except a nice frock, and people could die laughing. I was very taken with the idea. The idea of working alone, doing something for yourself but also for all those in attendance. I can remember much of the dialogue even now. Grenfell was terribly observant and her voice was superb. Using humour to communicate rather than attack – which I think women generally can do better than men. She made a great impression on me. Indeed I actually met her that night. My sisters had gone backstage to meet her *without me* because my mother decided I was "too young". But Joyce came out to find me, to say hello.'

Did you do drama classes at school?

'Earlier on, the odd class – rolling about on the floor, pretending to be the wind or whatever. But they didn't have any at Bury Grammar; I couldn't do it at all there. But my sister went to a school in Rochdale. Rochdale was much more liberal, and they had a theatre workshop in the school-holidays there, plus a small drama festival. So I sort of followed her along one day, when I was fifteen. I was lucky, because there was nothing vaguely theatrical in Bury.'

What was it like?

'It was absolutely brilliant, sincerely. Very professional. They did three productions during the summer and you could do anything you wanted – design, lights, sound, costumes . . . There were workshops going on all through the day, mime and clowns and masks and movement. It was wonderful. I was in there before anyone else each morning – 9am, waiting to get going. There was a marvellous atmosphere, it wasn't like we were children at all. You were treated as an adult.'

Teenage days are normally the time when people become more inhibited in performing.

'But it was the first time *I'd* ever really done it. The first thing I did there was a play called *The Rising Generations*. It was a sort of post-nuclear tale about people in a spaceship; and I played a comedy charwoman. I don't think I had anything to say, but I had padded bosoms and I wore football boots and a funny hat and curlers. A small part. I just loved it. I just loved it all. I did a bit of writing. Prompting – I was brilliant at prompting.' (Laughs.) 'We did a version of *Dracula* where I was a wolf *and* the prompter. I had a really big nose on which made if really hard to see the script. I was just *so* happy when I was at that place. I had the main part in *The Caucasian Chalk Circle* at the end, just before I left to go to university. Pity you have to move on, really but I finished in a *blaze* of glory.'

You left home, moved to Birmingham, a drama degree course becoming the centre of your world, and had to make your own way . . .

'Yes, and I took another dive then. At university everybody could act, and they could *all* do it better than me . . . or so I imagined. I've had this repeated pattern throughout my life of always thinking people are better than me, which perhaps has faded more recently. But I definitely felt it very strongly then. I felt I just couldn't compete academically.'

Was it very serious?

'A lot of Shakespeare. The whole gamut right from the Middle Ages up to Noel Coward. I just felt out of my depth. If I'd had a lot of bottle I could have gone in and done anything . . . I could have taken charge. I was writing plays but I never went so far as even to suggest they were put on. Often, though, instead of writing an essay I would submit a play on the same subject. Lecturers would say ''Well I'm sorry, but I asked for an essay,'' and throw the play away. Instead of writing an essay on Joe Orton I wrote a play which had something of his style. But they just *weren't* impressed.'

Did you perform *anything* at university which was humorous *and* written by you?

'The first good thing I did, the first time I ever felt I was making my mark, came when I was up for a part in *Loot*, but another girl got it. As compensation they said I could play the piano ''. . . in the interval and at the end as everyone's filing out''. So I thought ''O.K.'', and wrote this very evil song about how it should have been *me* on stage playing the part. And I got a huge round of applause for it every night.'

A *bitter* song?

'*Yes* . . . But a joke!'

Did you then set out to perform solo?

'Oh good God no. I was never that dynamic.'

The story goes that you were plucked from obscurity as a pianist in a small bar.

'I wasn't performing. I was a barmaid, the only "job" I've ever had. It was in a pub where BBC producers used to drink in Birmingham, and one of them invited me to a party. Because I was a barwoman! I was a stray woman to fill a place at a party. And for some reason I ended up playing a piano there. I was always eager to sing my own songs, given encouragement. And someone said "Oh, oh marvellous girl. Come down the BBC and audition tomorrow!" Then, the next day, the guy rang me up at the time stated and said *"Umm . . . Where are you?"* So I woke up, got down there, and did an audition before lots of producers. And one of them gave me a job. A Local Arts slot at 10pm Friday night for which I sang three songs and got paid £33.'

To rapturous applause?

'To complete apathy. But I thought it was wonderful.'

For the next two years or more Wood became a purveyor, almost a hack, of rhyming songs on topical themes. She took to it as a craft, forcing rhymes from her head – many of them barely relevant, some coy, some bizarre. 'They weren't songs I particularly wanted to write,' she says, 'I just wanted to be on television.' (She'd won the heat of a corny TV talent show in the early 1970s.) She still incorporates similar songs in her act today, but they have more inner-life, more sense, more sex and more perversity – 'completely', for instance, being rhymed with 'weekly', as in '. . . beat me on the bottom with a *Woman's Weekly*'. She sees it as an exercise, born in teenage days, which forces the 'musician' to make sense of nonsense. 'You've got to have a good rhyme, be realistic, yet surprise them.' She does much the same now in sketch, TV play and monologue form, albeit without piano or obvious rhyme. There is, however, always a strange sense of warped reason. In her monologue Mad Woman (1984) she took this flow-of-consciousness to an extreme, composing a ludicrous drunken monologue in which an alcoholic tramp spouts words of confused wisdom inspired by the sight of anyone or anything that passes her. 'Oi! Where's your meat-balls, Mister?' she howls, 'We don't need you maggoty old men, you wanna crawl back under your manholes. Just leave us girls the sherry and the duvet. I bet *she's* got a duvet, old jiggle-tits there. They're coming off, bosoms – it's the council. *Bosoms are off this spring, I hear!* Lucky for you, pleated-skirt! Oi! Shirley! Shirley Bassey! You're a bit of a blackie, aren't you?' This is human observation and human insistence on perpetual comment taken overboard into madness. Yet it was written by Wood, a nice 'still rather shy' country woman who says, 'Oh, I quite *enjoy* the simple things in life.'

It's said that you 'disappeared' from the media for two years in the mid 1970s.

'The song-writing work dried up, I was 23 and I thought I'd never work again. I thought I was too old. I sat in a bed-sit in Birmingham . . . making the odd hundred pounds, maybe. But basically doing absolutely nothing, for two whole years, except eating . . . and pondering. I started getting hauled in by the DHSS, who said "You've claimed dole for so many years, you'll have to stop."'

You were fairly poor?

'But that side of it never bothered me *at all*. I found the dole quite easy to live off. But I got *very* depressed in the end. I thought I'd started with a blaze of glory, and now it was all down-hill. I was quite a loner. Maybe I should have moved to London . . . yet now I'm glad I didn't. I wanted to work, to do a day's work . . . but I was absolutely gripped by lethargy. I couldn't make myself do *anything*.'

What saved you from that?

'First of all, meeting Geoff, my husband – who had a much better idea of show-business and what works. The initial result was that I built up a six-minute act by 1977 – it doesn't sound a lot but it was a great step. It was my husband who first said, and made me think about – "Well, what the fuck are you going to do? How are you going to walk on stage? What are you going to wear and say?" Those questions had honestly never occurred to me.'

Do you have a 'show-biz marriage'? You once said 'We meet when we can.'

'It's not quite as bad as that sounds. But there's much travelling involved. I didn't feel destined for that sort of relationship. I don't like that side of it – I'd prefer if we could work out a way to be together more. But it's just impossible. Most comedians are men, of course, and the norm is for their wives to spend their lives travelling *with them*.'

Has husband Geoff been a consistent supporter?

'He's 100 per cent enthusiastic. When I lose heart he's always there. He loves my show. He's totally obsessed by magic *and* by what I do. He encouraged me with all the plays I wrote and performed in the late 1970s. I did the revue *Funny Turns* with him (in 1982) and he's always been in the background supporting all the stage and TV stuff I've done since. He's already talking about my next tour, nine months hence. Asking what I'm going to do, say and wear. Geoff means everything to me; he writes none of it, thinks of none of the ideas, but if he didn't like it I wouldn't care to carry on. His enthusiasm is such a charge. Without it I would get very cold about what I'm doing. I'd very quickly decide "It's no good, I'm going to stop doing it." I wouldn't be able to gather myself up to write. It would go dead on me.'

In 1978 you wrote the play *Talent* which you performed with Julie Walters. What was that – your first major work – saying about talent?

'It was really just "The Story of the Fat One and the Thin One" – about a pretty girl who takes a more boring one out with her. Manchester gals. The thin one's going in for a talent contest. But it wasn't about talent so much as being trapped in a situation you can't get out of, except perhaps by using whatever you've got . . .

It certainly worked for me, because I never stopped working after *Talent*.'

Do you feel powerful sympathies towards certain characters in sketches and plays you write?

'I have characters I like and others I don't like *so much*. The ones I like often get it right – certainly that's the direction I'm going more now. You create sympathy for one character and direct laughter at the other. And I've done that in the plays I've just written – I want people to like me and the people who play my friends, and not everybody else.' (At this she laughs in earnest.)

Would it be fair to say you're shy?

'I am rather. But after a certain age you can't go round telling people you're shy.'

What makes you moody – as a person or artiste?

'If anything goes wrong around me, if people don't do their job, if anything stops the smooth running of the show or makes it less than professional, when people don't learn their lines, if they give a worse performance than I'm expecting . . . anyone that doesn't come up to my expectations.'

Do *you* normally come up to your expectations?

'I miss myself out of my expectations.'

I noticed you just did that.

'I have very high expectations of the script, certainly.'

You've said many times it's very difficult writing comedy.

'I've decided to stop saying that, because people think you're just moaning.'

What does a working, *writing* day involve?

'The most recent case was having as my starting point the decision and contract to write six separate TV plays and knowing I would be playing myself, as opposed to being particularly in character – it's something I want to do more of now. So, anyway, I set about thinking up eight or ten ideas – in a health farm, an airport delay, etc., etc. Each day I'd pick one, I go into the room at 9am and do my exercises, then collapse down at my desk at 10am.'

You sweat before writing?

'I think I probably do it to put off the start of work. Then I write letters, then I go and see the baby . . . then – at some strange variable moment – I finally think, "Health Farm, Day One, the Start, They Arrive". I write in long-hand; I can't type very well. What appears on paper is usually very bad, not funny, *terrible* even, at first – but at least I've started . . . I get miserable when I think the writing isn't going well. Every time I've ever written anything, the first months or so have been *just awful*. Even though I know it'll finally sort itself out, I get miserable. But it has to be gone through. Because – as for the performing side – I really love that.'

What's the essence of that ultimate satisfaction?

'It's the feeling of communicating with all those people. It's the *only* time I ever feel people are understanding what I'm saying. It gives me a kick. Because I spend so much time with people who, when I'm saying things to them, go "*I'm sorry?*" – not knowing that I'm joking. But on stage they've paid to see me, and they *know* I'm joking. I enjoy it extremely . . . it's quite wonderful.'

Is being a comic as perfect as you make it sound?

'It is. It is. *When you get good at it*. But there's nothing worse than *not* being good at it.'

What are the more specific good moments?

'When you've got a piece of material and you know it really really well. You've played it for ten or twenty shows already, you know how to do it, you're confident with it and in yourself, and then you get a particularly nice theatre and a particularly warm audience . . . and it's like flying. You can do *exactly* what you want with them. And you know it's going to be alright. You can tease out all the gaps for just a little bit longer, before going in for the kill. *It's absolutely wonderful* . . . But then, some nights, you get all these lousy old gits and you can't imagine them getting going unless you begged them. They won't loosen up, won't concentrate, won't laugh and you really have to work at it. But I don't mind that either, really . . . Haaa.'

Are you standing there considering how well your performance is going?

'Yes. You're doing that, rating it, I think, all the time. While one side of your head is performing the other half is thinking "Oh, that didn't go so well, I'm going to miss out the next bit" or "I'd better speed up, some quick laughs are needed!" You check what the audience is doing, what they're up to, deciding how you can get a better grip on the proceedings.'

It's a battle of wits?

'Yes. Indeed, during my last tour, I sung a very serious song about dead babies at the end of part one, and it always felt like a challenge to shut them up . . . to halt the gigglers. I quite enjoyed seeing how soon I could shut them all up.'

So it's a battle for misery, as well as humour? Why, then, is there this desire to move suddenly from humour to 'a tearful earful', as Ken Dodd calls it?

'Well . . . it shows another side, I suppose. It's mainly for theatrical effect. And it gets you off in a black-out. Throw them a shocking last line, and then out goes the spotlight! By the time they realise what's happened, zap, you've disappeared. Gone in a blaze of glory; nowhere to be seen. They're still there, feeling disturbed, and you're in the dressing room with the kettle on.'

What kind of audiences do you attract?

'Well, I never really see them much. I get fan-letters from lonely old men who collect autographs, and *lots* of fifteen-year-old boys and girls. People knit me sweaters, middle-aged women write to tell me things they've heard at bus-stops. People want to be my friend and invite me for tea! And then there are those who say that they too want to "stand on stage and be funny". I write back and tell them they must be mad.'

Are comedians generally fairly healthy people?

'It's quite a stressful life. A travelling salesman's life really. The failures and successes are very immediate, yet they don't feel tangible off stage, where you become rather anonymous. There *are* a lot of nutty comedians, certainly.'

Towards the end of the television special you recorded, titled *An Audience With . . .*, your eyes were popping out to the extent that a level-headed viewer might have considered you were being administered with narcotics.

'No, no, no. Haa. It was adrenalin; excesses of it. If I seemed extra happy it was probably just from being pleased about making it to the end. I'd recorded 90 minutes of material non-stop in front of an audience with lights on them as well as me. When you're on your feet for 90 minutes and you're flapping your arms around and making faces and telling stories and playing the monkey and there's all these expectations on you, people staring at you and on top of that you're six months pregnant . . . that's bloody tough.'

But you couldn't do without it?

'. . . Well . . . I'd certainly like to hang on to it.'

Life goes on remorselessly. You're a mother now.

'Yes, we have a girl, Gracie, who is one year old.'

Does she have a sense of humour?

'Yes, but *of course*. She smiles, she laughs. Babies are wonderful. Gracie enjoys funny noises and singing. If I stick my tongue out at her she knows it's supposed to be a joke. She even invented a joke herself just recently which involved lying down and pretending to go to sleep. She play acted it as an absolute joke . . . And I rather like that idea – a bit of pretend tiredness.'

(Top) PETER COOK in the lamplight. Photograph by Liam Woon
(Bottom) COOK as Premier: *'I used to be cynical when I was young, but by God it's worse now.'*
Photograph courtesy of ITC Entertainment Ltd (*Whoops Apocalypse*)

PETER COOK

Moody

Tea's up, Dud.
COME ON!

I show Peter Cook, a man with an improviser's spirit who once savagely parodied Bruce Forsyth, a press-clipping which contains a picture of the comedian plus the caption 'Bruce Forsyth, 56 – a new wife and a new wig.' I ask if Cook will provide a caption in a similar vein to place under a photograph of himself.

'Bruce Forsyth . . .', Cook responds, 'a new wife. A new wig. That's rather nice really, and rather accurate. He's got a very *nice* wife indeed. Her name's Winnie, she used to be Miss Puerto Rico, she's very very attractive and very pleasant. Fairly good at tennis, probably better than Bruce, but she is not so foolish as to let him know that. I think Brucie made an *excellent* choice with Winnie, with whom he seems very contented . . . Ummmm, I seem to be ambling on about Brucie and Winnie, rather than discussing my own caption, for obvious reasons. I'm slightly *envious* of Brucie. It *is* a wonderful looking wig, isn't it? Are you sure that's the newest one? It makes me almost want to go bald.'

But what about your caption?

'"Peter Cook . . . 49 . . ."' (pause) 'and just leave it at that. I think that news is remarkable enough, thank you.'

Peter Cook, no longer 49 or 50 but around 51, holds several illustrious positions in the history of comedy, most notably for: being 'the' father figure of modern 'satire' in the early 1960s; forming a link between the Goons' 1950s bizarrity and the Pythons' 1970s surrealism; being the tall half of what was Britain's most natural comic coupling of the 1960s and 1970s ('Dud and Pete'); and investigating new comedy shock tactics ('Derek and Clive') in the 1970s. The most important point to be made about Cook is that he is neither, on the one hand, a satirist, nor, on the other, a nonsense-comic; he blends them both perpetually, so that one tempers and nourishes the other. His major talent is being – in John Cleese's words – 'the world's most quick-on-the-feet developer of comic ideas', although perhaps Cleese is forgetting Robin Williams. Much exercised, Cook's mouth – which barely opens to speak and which he licks the lips of slyly but *constantly* – often takes on the guise of an offensive weapon. He is a natural, if slurred, conversationalist for whom comedy is only enjoyable when he can do it improvisationally. He converses with a slightly nervous and sweaty self-consciousness but, on form, his words can be as razor-sharp and/or profoundly ludicrous as any man's. He is a wag, a cutting merry-andrew . . . a chain-smoking *card*. He seems to be constantly either cross or highly amused by the world and he claims that he has no ambition any more and even *dislikes* ambition. An unrepentant cynic or at least a severe sceptic (a quality essential for owning *Private Eye* magazine), he is an angry man who comes from the establishment and yet scorns it, a middle-aged rebel who has carved a niche for himself as comedy's Lord Chancellor.

Cook was born on 17 November 1937 in Torquay, Devon, to where his mother had travelled, for the event, from Nigeria. His early years were 'uneventful' save for a German bomb blowing a female neighbour (plus the bath she was in) clean into the middle of the street. His early years at preparatory school were spent ingratiating himself with bullies, developing 'wit and sarcasm' and attempting to 'go sick' on Fridays so he could listen to the *Goon Show* on the infirmary radio. Much of the time he saw little of his father, a colonial officer working abroad. 'He used to receive news six months after it was published,' Cook recalls. 'It went to Africa by boat, then up the river . . . He'd then open up *The Times* and exclaim "*Gooood God! Worcester are 78 for six!*"' Cook's father is now deceased, but Cook has increasingly realised in later years that 'a lot of my sense of humour comes from my parents, dad particularly – and that's quite humbling in a way.'

> 'My father did something quite extraordinary actually. He left Cambridge University and went off, very young, to Nigeria to be a district colonial officer. He had no knowledge of any of the three main languages spoken in Nigeria yet was suddenly in charge of 100 square miles of territory. This was his life – at least as I understand it from reading his diaries. He travelled around from village to village with trunks or whatever, and was entirely reliant on a local interpreter, and the trick of it was to hope you'd chosen an honest interpreter because otherwise it was all nonsense. They were tremendously alarming circumstances to live in – to have to reach moral or judicial decisions over a society of which, at least when you arrive, you know absolutely nothing. He did that, on and off, for 20 years. But I don't believe there was *pomposity* in him, and – as far as I can judge – no desire to impose a personal viewpoint. I think he just believed Britain had a good judicial and parliamentary system and thought that it was good and wise to act on that in foreign parts. I don't think he had any objections when the Empire vanished. After all those years he realised it was right to let Nigerians get on with it on their own. The thing is, most people there realised that – come independence – one

Nigerian section would attempt to wipe out another. And Whitehall in London took absolutely no notice of this whatsoever, so there was the appalling Biafran War . . . It was all very confusing and sad.'

Did you spend much time in Nigeria?

'Well, I went there during some school holidays to visit father. The rest of the time I spent in boarding-schools and things.'

Were you an only child?

'No, I have two sisters – one seven years older and one seven years younger. We came in seven-year waves. Which may have something to do with my father's leave-periods.'

Did your mother travel around with your father?

'She divided her time. Which is something I think she found very difficult. She didn't like sending us off to school but, on the other hand, she didn't want to take us to Nigeria which – certainly during my early days – was a big health-hazard for children. So during my childhood my mother divided her time between here and with father.'

Was the Foreign Service something you imagined you'd join?

'I was always aiming at it, definitely. That's why I eventually took languages at university. But anyway, we were fast running out of colonies. My father retired quite young, in fact. He'd moved from Nigeria to Gibraltar, where as financial secretary he introduced the lottery, as it happens. I always believed *I'd* be a diplomat or whatever. I quite liked the idea of trundling round the world like him.'

Were you bred for it, in a way?

'. . . My grandfather indeed had worked in the Foreign Service too, in Malaysia, or Malaya as it then was. He was stationed in Kwalalumpa. He died very young and nobody in the family seemed to know what he died of. My father's mother had never told him about it. I always assumed grandfather had been a black-sheep or a womaniser or something. But the truth is he shot himself. I eventually traced the details through *Debrett* and newspaper clippings of the time. And according to the obituary he'd been very nervous about being promoted and had decided to shoot himself. I've worked out this whole picture of a group of English gentlemen out there with their club, their homes, their garden, their little world. If you visit any old colonial city you'll always find the same things the British have left behind. A parliament house, a large pitch for cricket . . . across from which is the club-house, and there's a golf-course – always. They had their little England but of course they were far away from their real home. So I never knew grandfather and my father barely knew him either. And I never really knew *him*.'

Did you enjoy your school days?

'I didn't enjoy my first couple of years at public school. I enjoyed the remainder . . . perhaps because I wormed my way to the top and became a bossy prefect. But I just felt the usual things you feel at boarding-school . . . disliking being away from home. I didn't like to get on the train with weeping mum on the platform. That part of it all was horrid.'

Were you rebellious at school – an even younger version of the 'angry young man' you were later billed as?

'When I was thirteen,' he remembers, pausing now for a laugh which sounds self-deprecating, ironic *and* outrageous, '. . . I wrote this absolutely ghastly essay which won a prize. As far as I can remember it called for the chemical castration of the working-classes. I think it was chemical castration, nothing cruel! The idea was to prevent their breeding. So *those* were my thoughts at thirteen.'

This won a prize?

'Exactly.'

Was it written tongue-in-cheek?

'Oh no. Absolutely not – it was *not at all* tongue-in-cheek. I was just pompous, witless and hopeless. All the while surrounded by similar public-school (Radley) types talking about "awful people who can't speak English", inferior people who "can't do this", "can't do that". Tyrannical attitudes! I had fags [young slaves] at Radley.'

Do you feel guilty about the past?

'Well, nowadays, whenever I find myself having awful thoughts against Hooray Henrys and all those frightful people, and all the other folk I complain about – I really shouldn't you know. I should pull myself up with a start and think what an . . . *idiot* I was. Idiot is the best word I can think of.'

Was there a sense of fun at Radley School, though?

'Oh yes. Especially when I started performing. One of my biggest successes was a challenge to the Marionettes Society's "Gilbert and Sullivan". Me and another boy decided we'd write and put on a musical of our own – we even produced an album of it. So I was, indeed, *Mr Show-business* by fifteen. It was called *Black and White Blues* and the plot concerned an Englishman who decided the way around the hearts of the Africans was to go out there with a jazz-band.' (Cook chortles.) 'It was rather jolly, and pretty bloody good for fourteen or fifteen! I still have people who come up to me and say it's better than anything I've done since . . . But I also wrote sketches and material around then, some of them rather smutty. My earliest attempt to make money out of humour was sending a parody *Goon Show* script to someone at the BBC. He pointed out that it *was* a complete parody, but was still very encouraging. I appreciated that.'

What were you thinking about as a teenager?

'I was thinking that I was quite funny.'

What did you do in the year you took out between school and university?

'Well, I was turned down for national service by the army because of an allergy to feathers. They had it on my medical record that I'd had asthma as a kid – but I'd grown out of it at puberty. The officer said to me, "If you were in a barrack-room full of feather pillows would you sneeze?'' As if a barrack room would ever have feather pillows – a likely story. But I sort of said ''Yes sir'', and was declared unfit. But I almost pushed my luck, adding ''Oh, but if there's an emergency I will be called up, won't I?'' Very luckily I was rejected, and instead I travelled around Europe – Paris, Hamburg, Berlin. I stayed with friends of the family and worked as a waiter and beach photographer. I was still aiming for the Foreign Office – the whole idea was to get some language experience. But in the main I hung about trying to get to know women. That seemed to be the usual procedure. I was less aware of the beauty of the European landscape than the new-found qualities of womanhood. I attempted to trap an Italian lady, I seem to remember. She was called Floriana – the daughter of the man who controlled the Milanese shoe-trade . . . or so Floriana told me. It was a rather stilted one-way romance.'

She was a good Catholic girl?

'I imagine so. But indeed one of my chatting-up techniques during that period was quoting Blaise Pascal (the ironic moral Jesuit philosopher) to her. Pascal didn't have too many hints for seducing eighteen-year-olds, or women, but he did tell me a little about getting them drunk.'

Cook, the tyrannical young wit, anti-philosopher and alcohol-imbiber, entered Pembroke College, Cambridge in 1957 to study Modern Languages – French and German. What surfaced over the next year or two was a complete restyling of revue comedy at a time revue was locked remorselessly into cheery musical numbers and light teasing sketches (often in drag) focusing largely on personalities. Politics now entered the fray. The 1959 Cambridge Footlights show, *The Last Laugh*, which included Cook amongst its performers, was the first to take an aggressive social and political line (director John Bird, says Cook, was at that time 'an extreme left-ist'). Cook had witnessed political cabaret in Paris and Berlin during his earlier travels and was vaguely questioning the establishment ingredients within his upbringing, but around any polemical elements in his humour he then – and has always since – wrapped a colourful cloak of absurdity. Indeed, 'Say something silly' has always been his greatest motto, either in the guise of satirising authority or pomposity or else simply for the purpose of not wanting to sound that way himself. Absurdity goes above and beyond politics. Cook says comic things, it often seems, '. . . simply because they're there.' His E.L. Wisty character, which so enthused fellow students at Cambridge, was the sort of conversationalist who could flit from the topic of the Royal Family to bees in under a sentence. Likewise from nudism to Deirdre, Beryl and Margot the Tadpoles, and from Hitler's skill at ball-room dancing, to the idea of ringing up the Minister of Technology to exclaim 'I can't *stand* these machines everywhere!'. E.L. Wisty, in one of his more tyrannical moments, even proposed to his audience that he intended to achieve 'Total

Domination of the World by 1958'. This date, fortunately, had already passed.

E.L. Wisty . . .

'That *awful* man . . . yes.'

The park-bench philosopher and moaner; he of the mac, hat and dull monotone – how did you develop his character?

'It just occurred. I don't know where it came from or why. It's been in my head for years and years. Whenever I sit down and stare ahead I just go into that voice . . . it's the easiest thing in the world. A bit of an alter-ego. I started it at school, and eventually half of Radley were walking round speaking in this dreadful voice. So this was all well before half of Cambridge ended up doing it.' (Cook pauses then receives a pristine memory rush.) ' . . . I think if there was any basis for Wisty whatsoever it may be a man who waited on the high tables during mealtimes at Radley. Radley was a very pretentious school; the headmaster and head boys, including me, sat at the high table. Mr Boylett I think was the waiter's name and he served the table. And as far as I can remember he used to come out with occasional strange remarks when he was hovering, remarks like "I saw this pebble in the driveway . . . and I thought I saw it move. So it's probably very valuable, that pebble." I sort of built up this character who, in a slow precise voice, thought he saw things move. And if they move – *ipso facto* – they must be valuable. It was an utterly barmy creation and I've been doing him ever since.'

When did comedy overtake your Foreign-Office intentions?

'The "career" was always there, but after a year or so at Pembroke I got hooked on "It" [performance]. I was already selling material to radio shows during my first year. And what I had thought would be very hard to get into – this elitist club, the Footlights – was actually very easy. I did a monologue before chairman Adrian Slade, and I was in. And in 1960 I became chairman. All that went on, but – came the end of university – I was still going to take exams for the Foreign Office. Yet first it was agreed to do Edinburgh.'

The revue *Beyond the Fringe*, which was mounted at Edinburgh Festival in August 1960, moved to London's West End, jubilantly ignited the new(ish) decade and was performed almost constantly through to April 1964, when it ended a 'triumphant' New York Broadway run. Teaming four ex-undergraduates – Jonathan Miller (Cambridge, middle-class, 6 foot 2 inches), Peter Cook (Cambridge, middle-class, 6 foot 2 inches), Alan Bennett (Oxford, working-class, 6 foot 1½ inches) and Dudley Moore (Oxford, working-class, 5 foot 2 inches) – *Beyond the Fringe* was an outing with small production values but containing big brash nonsense, tasteful piano inserts and topical politics, all written entirely by the performers. Cook's presence was most notable in a Wisty park-bench monologue concerning working as a miner and reading *The Universe and All That*

Surrounds It: an Introduction; and also in a spoof TV political broadcast in which Cook impersonated (very snootily) the then Prime Minister, Harold Macmillan . . . rattling on about Skybolt missiles, foreign travels and what he plainly wasn't doing for pensioners on fixed incomes in Fife. The revue elsewhere attacked capital punishment, civil defence, religion, self-absorbed intellectuals and much more besides. The grand effect of this venture by these four gentlemen in grey pullovers was to make the word 'satire' fashionable.

Every satirist did Macmillan for years after you.

'Yes. It was a breakthrough because no one had impersonated a living Prime Minister for years and years. But Harold was just a natural for me to do. In many ways I was actually very fond of the old sod. I did him again on TV a couple of years ago, decrepit, going up and down on a moving chair and talking about his future plans for appearing in Vegas. Even after 25 years he was great fun to do again. I just like him. I clicked straight into it.'

It says something about the early 1960s that the Prime Minister felt obliged to come along and see you impersonate him on stage, in 1961.

'I knew he was present and, according to my colleagues, I went a bit further, a bit more over the top than usual, that evening. And apparently, throughout the *entire* piece he hid his face in his theatre programme, as if he was trying to find out what was going on. He never looked up at me once.'

Do you feel in a way you were satirising your own class and background?

'Well, that's all I had to go on. Yet I still feel a lot of it came from within, rather than being based on anyone. I can remember Jonathan Miller, when I first met him, telling me how well I observed and could reproduce "the schizophrenic speech-patterns of a judge"; but really it was just coming straight off the top of my head.'

How did you feel during the times of *Beyond the Fringe*?

'I just very much relished being funny.'

You were after laughs obviously, but what else were you desiring?

'Well, I was a bit of a mogul in those days. I put money into *Private Eye*, eventually buying out partners and becoming Lord Gnome – in theory – with grand shareholdings therein. While *Beyond the Fringe* took London, I set up the "Establishment Club" (1961), made that the place of the moment and called it "London's First Satirical Night-Club". I was certainly quite ambitious . . . dashing around, building an extra floor on top of the premises of the old El Morocco Night-Club. I was generally zapping around being a whiz-kid.'

Broadway beckoned?

'One day, over there, our Broadway producer rushed round in a state of excitement saying "President Kennedy has asked us to perform at the White House" – in some state drawing-room. What a nasty thought!' (Cook scowls and spits.) 'My reply was, "We're not some fucking cabaret! He can come to the theatre.

So Kennedy came to us, and this wonderful security operation took place; they went through everything, yet they completely failed to notice a prop replica of a .45 resting on my dressing-room table.'

During the early 1960s did you definitely feel humour could have a political effect?

'I don't know if it had any *specific* political effect, but humour's a useful encouragement for change on occasions . . . And by God these people need taking apart! They're awful, aren't they? I wish I had more energy to do it myself. Whenever I see anyone young and funny I feel it's almost their *duty* to have a go.'

Is this irritation with the establishment something you've felt consistently since youth?

'For whatever reasons I definitely find the current Government more offensive than *ever* before. Before Thatcher my previous most disliked Prime Minister was Callaghan. I just can't bear these people's aspirations – to boss people around and have a farm in Wales. Maybe I should give them more credit as humans, but the sheer notion that you should impose your opinion rigorously on a nation just seems complete lunacy to me. When these people get the idea that their notions are right and should be forced through no matter what, when they feel themselves so tremendously important . . . I just can't bear it! They're worse than film-stars, believing *so strongly* that they should be well-respected.'

During satire's heyday Harold Wilson was looked on as a potential saviour.

'But really all Wilson wanted was to mingle with lots of famous people, to have important parties at Number 10. And – as Lord Wilson – he's evidently got what he wanted. It's that awful desire for respectability and respect. The perfect example of this behaviour can be seen in Lord Mountbatten's Diaries. All *he* wanted of life was to travel round the world being treated with tremendous importance, wearing the right uniform, being given a better room and treated with more prominence as royalty than someone like Kissinger . . . it's just pathetic.'

On his return from Broadway to London in 1964, Cook began regularly injecting his language skills into *Private Eye* magazine, which by then was somewhat flagging and – along with 'satire' – becoming institutionalised. Richard Ingrams, then editor, once recalled Cook's presence at the magazine's offices thus: 'He would stalk about the room saying ''Good evening!'' in an intense way, and then embark on lectures about enormous snakes – ''many of them millions of miles long''. Or he would impersonate a zoo keeper attempting to recapture a very rare type of bee which had become lodged in a lady's knickers.' A surrealist on heat, Cook would walk the floor dictating (never typing), relishing every moment spent spouting vaguely topical nonsense-news-spoofs, and tales about pungently named persons (Basil Nardly Stoads, Sir Arthur Streeb-

Greebling *et al.*) which, he says, were 'not a million miles from the truth'. With similar intent he performed solo on television as E.L. Wisty, the park-bench ponderer on the meaning of life ('a thought that continually crosses my mind but never stops there long enough to resolve itself'), and viewers took the intensely pedestrian – but subversive – character (and his imaginary friend Spotty Muldoon) to their bosom. Cook's greatest success, though, came by developing his relationship with Dudley Moore, fellow performer in *Beyond the Fringe* with whom, each night, he'd re-improvise a Civil Defence lecture (Cook on stage, Dudley as a plant in the audience who harangued him). At that time, says Cook, 'Miller was worrying himself that he should really be a doctor and Bennett was wondering where being a history don would take him . . . but Dudley and I just thought "What the fuck are they bothered about?" '

Cook and Moore were to play many different characters and sketch settings together; they ad-libbed with relish, for instance, through the simple (but highly schizophrenic) set-up of two men in the same drab office making inane, unproductive but determined telephone conversations with 'Docketing', 'Central Docketing', 'Lengths' and each others' desks. But the duo had most impact simply by positioning themselves at a table and clicking into 'Dud and Pete', two pedestrian gents with Northerners' caps, scarves, warm jackets, a sandwich box and a cup of tea or pint of beer. They formed a perfect comic cocktail together: Cook, the tall thin middle-class smart-arse sceptic eager to dress up as a man of the street with a moustache, and Moore, the tiny but perfectly-formed mother's boy ('I've seen your little ticket') from Dagenham, eager to sound sophisticated. Moore was a perfect melodist and harmony maker for Cook, both on the piano and in conversation. What they shared was a joy of the finely-tuned sounds and words of comic friendship, plus – it must be said – a strong obsession with nudity. 'Hello nudies', 'You're nude', 'nuuu-ude', 'nude as ever', 'Take off all your clothes-es' and many other similarly naked phrases were sprinkled throughout their work, almost as if the pleasure of comedy, and language itself, felt to them akin to the pleasure of going naked and getting physical. As this duo they often virtually became as one; each individual's voice took on a schizophrenic control within the other. And quickly – through the TV series *Not Only But Also* – they became, in combination, celebrity household names. Or rather, down-to-earth, 'horny', anti-celebrity household names.

What was the initial inspiration for 'Dud and Pete'?

'I wrote a sketch, which was just two blokes sitting in a pub complaining about how they were being molested by film-stars ('Get your huge bra out of here!'). When we came to choose costumes it just sort of happened. They arrived fully-formed. They were an absolute natural, I think. Easy to do, and a tremendous amount of pleasure. Looking at them again recently I thought Dudley was *so* wonderful. He had the twitching face and projected this . . . ' (Cook slips effortlessly into Moore's Dud) ' . . . this tremend-ous eagerness to sh-ow knowledge and of course humility, tinged maybe with a bit of gen-er-osity, Pete, and a little bit of savoir-faire, and all the other *condiments* of the elite. By God he was funny . . .'

How did you work together?

'We'd sit about and ad-lib into a tape-recorder. If we couldn't get anywhere we'd fuck off and have lunch. The script, or an outline, would derive from studying and editing the tapes. By the time we'd written it, it was almost fully rehearsed. On TV we didn't have an autocue or anything, we just had bits of cardboard with six headlines around which we'd steer ourselves, feeling free to re-ad-lib. We always had a show ready to do but then we'd discard a few things, through boredom – ask for new sets which were nothing to do with what we'd planned.'

Did you have abundant confidence together?

'Well, once we took over an anniversary programme of *Newsnight* for 45 minutes, start to finish – and what gave us the confidence to do that I just don't know. Because it turned out *absolutely terribly*.'

It was through their creation in the early 1970s of 'Derek and Clive' (inspired on a bored day-trip by Cook and Moore to a recording studio 'just for fun') that the duo perfected the art of (as a buddy duo) not even needing an audience, and brought an extra dimension, or at least strength, to their material. Derek and Clive, perhaps, were the tyrants tucked within themselves; certainly the characters' excessiveness seemed like a reaction against, and total liberation from, the restraints put on them previously as the nation's cuddly TV comedy stars (having said that, their film *Bedazzled* (1968) had been a vehicle for their 'evil' sides). *Derek and Clive Live*, and its two follow-up albums and one video, made comedy shockingly funny again, unsettling liberals on the issue about which they are most vulnerable – censorship. Derek and Clive were men-on-the-street turned iconoclasts – powerless reactionaries spouting obscenities as a reclaimed folk language. The duo mastered small-talk once and for all, leaping at the hack of a cough from 'the blue tit on Mrs Coletart's roof' to the agonies of eternal 'horn' (perpetual penis erection). They blended arrogance, honesty, bitterness, nonsense and lavatorial matters in equal measures. If we can assume that Cook was the main creative force behind this material (he opened and steered most of the sketches), then 'Derek and Clive' was really his cynical snort of disgust – an utter (seeming) rejection of the normal conventions of humour, those being stealth, subtlety, anticipation, climactic delivery and 'the big laugh' . . . Nevertheless, it all somehow worked, raising a guffaw over the most bittersweet matters. No topic was too trivial or too taboo to escape Derek and Clive's course contempt and perverse intents; they made fun of everything, from the Queen Mother to Jesus, from their mothers to Russia, from dead Popes to Derek Batey, from masturbation (lots of it) to cancer to death to nothingness and beyond. Applying a new thick skin to listeners' backs, it almost felt as if 'Derek and Clive' had stretched Cook and Moore to their limits, even exhausting comic boundaries perhaps. Copies of the video (*Derek and Clive Get the Horn*), meanwhile, were seized by the police, but – interestingly – no prosecutions ever occurred.

'I think that was close to the edge of prosecution' Cook considers. 'The Board of Film Censors advised us we could be prosecuted for obscenity and *certainly* blasphemy.'

It's comedy that is 'likely to deprave or corrupt'?

'Once, indeed, a muddle-up in the record company's distribution or packing department meant that a few hundred people (some children presumably) got *Derek and Clive* when they thought they were getting *Black Beauty*. To which I replied "It would be equally alarming expecting *us* and getting *Black Beauty* . . . But as far as I can tell, much of it's still obscene – and if it isn't I'll have to have another go. I think if I was setting out to make an offensive record I could be a *bloody* sight more offensive than that!'

Did Dudley ever play his mother the track on *Come Again* which goes '. . . My Mum came into my bedroom and sucked my tiny knob'?

'I *hope* he didn't. *My* mother read about them, knew she wouldn't like them and avoided them. Which is perfectly fair, I think . . .'

What did the *Get the Horn* video session involve?

'As always – just getting blasted and going to the studio. Only I'd arranged three cameras, and Dudley wasn't keen. In fact that was a very bad night for us, because I was rather cross that Dudley wasn't eager and he was being moody in return. That we still came up with what we did says, I think, a *tremendous* amount about our relationship.' (Cook notes that only recently has he realised '*just* how much I bossed Dudley about.')

Is it true that Dudley later stopped the video's release in America in case it damaged his career?

'Ummm . . . well. I don't know whether it *was* released . . .' (A pause.) 'I really don't know about that . . . It *was* re-released in Britain, with special specs, so you can get the full 2-D experience. I haven't watched it for a while actually. But, by God, that was fun to do!' (Cook swells with enthusiasm now.) 'Just to sit down and be *that* unpleasant was such fun.' (He adopts a critic's voice.) '"*Oh, what a shame. To see Peter Cook and Dudley Moore, the sophisticated wits, reduced to this!*" I think *Get the Horn* is very interesting alone as a film about a relationship . . . I just think we were dead lucky that the two of us could combine so effortlessly.'

How did the Cook/Moore team come apart in the mid-to late-1970s?

'We'd done a New York stage show and tour (*Good Evening*) and I was a bit disappointed that he didn't come back and continue the duo . . . because it was the most enjoyable time of my life from a professional point of view.'

A void?

'*A divorce!* It produced a gap in my life which is probably still there today. I wasn't envious of him because I didn't want that

(Hollywood) life, and I certainly didn't wish him ill as newspapers claimed. But when people asked, ''What are you going to do now?'', I really didn't know – I still don't really. I've written and performed with many other comics but I can't really imagine doing films and four TV series with *them*.'

In the 1980s Cook has moved in mysterious ways, carrying eleven newspapers under his arm and wearing trousers which look as if lines have been ironed into them. He has placed his solo monologues wherever they seem fitting, has become an 'expert' television interviewee (cigarette in hand), has applied his nonsense and news skills at frequent *Private Eye* dictation sessions, hosted numerous odd television shows (including a music show as an offensive God-like club proprietor), appeared in the one-series American sitcom *Two of Us* (as a servant *foil* to a female), acquired a pot-belly, quaffed his fair share of beverages, retained his profound dislikes ('Young people? Sod them! I mean, aren't they awful? . . . Why? Well, they're younger than me, aren't they?'), done one (and only one) solo TV special, written and made the unsuccessful pirate comedy *Yellowbeard* with the late Graham Chapman of Monty Python, and lent his character skills to the works of numerous younger humorists who were coming up the rear. In a short film made with members of 'The Comic Strip' team he played a blood-drenched homicidal man in an office with a picture of Adolf Hitler on the wall. In the film *Whoops Apocalypse* he portrayed Sir Christopher Mortimer, imaginary current Prime Minister of the United Kingdom – a mind-numbing prophet of perdition and vacuity, oblivious to all complaints even being howled directly outside his door, blabbering nonsense about 'evil leprechauns lurking in bread-bins', distributing nuclear fall-out umbrellas, throwing the unemployed off Beachy Head cliffs and then initiating mass crucifixions at Wembley Stadium. As the older statesman of satire, grey hair and all, Cook took to that role with authority and inebriated charm.

'I was inspired by Anthony Eden hyped up on speed and all kinds of drugs after his operation at the time of Suez. But Mortimer's slightly more optimistic than Eden, with Thatcher's resolve and Macmillan's airs and graces . . .'

Mad?

'Yes . . . *confident* in his own madness.'

What's your favourite newspaper clipping about yourself?

'They're all in a huge heap in my garage – sackfuls. The Italian press have had me in lots of affairs – Raquel Welch and Candice Bergen, I seem to remember.'

What about the tabloid story a few years ago in which a teenage girl said something like 'Peter always cracked gags while we made love'?

'Ahhh, yes. My only kiss and tell! *Haven't* I been lucky? All the rest have kept their mouths shut, or else my hit-men have been effective. She didn't even notice the affidavits she signed and the lawyers round the bed . . . That headline was *MY CRAZY NIGHTS*. I thought she was very flattering, actually.'

Is it true in the 1960s that you once turned down a romantic lead in a film with Brigitte Bardot?

'Bridg-itte, yes indeed.'

Why?

'Out of stupidity. I thought she was the most attractive woman in the world, but I didn't like the script. In those days it was almost mandatory to go to bed with her . . . and I turned her down. I mean, how fucking stupid can you get?'

What's next for Peter Cook? How about Broadway as a solo-performer?

'I've conquered Broadway twice – in the 1960s and 1970s – and I've got *no* wish to conquer it again, thank you very much!'

New television?

'I don't have that desire to be on TV for its own sake any more – *if ever I did*. I've chat-showed myself to death . . . And I don't want to do six 30-minute shows on my own in a row – I don't have enough ideas. I really don't think I have enough ideas to write *one* one-hour special! Maybe 45 minutes, but that doesn't fit any slot.'

Do you find it hard to put pen to paper?

'I just think that things which are thought of *on the spot* come out funniest. I'm useless at repeating funny stories. The skill of embellishing a story every time it's spoken is not really a skill I'm interested in acquiring.'

How much do you do at *Private Eye* now?

'I go there twice on a regular week, to write with two or three others. I love it – it's just sitting around and chatting, with a list of topics to cover. Whoever has the pen writes down what we come up with and composes it. I'd *like* to think the best lines get written down, but a lot of them probably don't.'

Do you write humour with conscious messages in mind?

'No! I just flare off intermittently without conscious thought.'

Freud said that once a joke is pondered right to the core it looses its humour, in a similar way to the exorcism of a neurotic symptom.

'Yes, and knowledge or memory of your own past jokes, and other comics' jokes, is also inhibiting – when you start thinking, ''This is so obvious, I must have heard or seen or read it somewhere else.'' Whereas, when you're young, you never think such thoughts.'

Did you ever argue over comedy with Dudley?

'Well, one of the most depressing things in the world is to try and *defend* a joke. If they don't like it, that's it. Once you start arguing, ''No, no – it *was* funny, *because* . . .'', it becomes *sooo* depressing.'

Do you take comedy apart when you watch it?

'Well, American sitcoms are so technical, and I watch TV so much anyway, that I find myself working out the lines myself. I get quite a bit of pleasure from sitting at home pre-empting other people's jokes.

'I've written another TV special, which I may or may not do – the linking scenes of which involve a psychiatrist trying to work out what is funny. "Every komic idea in ze world" he explains, "was first invented by a German couple called Fritz and Boris." Part of the script involves different numbers of people slipping on bananas. First one person – "We laugh . . . haha! The gag is here!", then it builds up eventually to "But is it funnier if 4,000 men are walking along and slip on two bananas?" '

Have you read many books on the theory of comedy?

'Quite a lot . . . One of the worst books is by Doctor Arthur Legman – he did an *enormous* volume about "The Rationale of the Dirty Joke", a history and analysis of the dirty joke which is *really* depressing to read. Legman analyses them all one by one . . . It covers sex, death, syphilis jokes . . . There's been so many disease jokes – it's awful. Jokes that would suit Bernard Manning on his death bed in a bad mood.'

The last time I met Cook for the purpose of grilling him for this book he was seated in an empty Hampstead restaurant near his home. Working his way rapidly through numerous margaritas and cigarettes, he was wearing a jacket covered in today's cigarette ash and a pair of jeans tailored out of a hundred pieces of different denim and patterned cloth. He looked a *little* rough. He proposed that his key contribution to this book would be to compose a title for it. After one or two minutes' reflection he finally announced that the best possible title for a tome concerning comedians would be *Fuck 'Em All.'*

This is the man who once defined himself, societally, as 'a GUPPY – a Gloomy Useless, err . . . Pessimistic Prat'. He is tired; 'I didn't get to bed until six this morning . . . I don't know why.' Most of the day he has been drinking and writing 'lots of *very* offensive material' at *Private Eye*, '. . . most of which will probably be cut'. He is in a mood. The mood of a true cynic?

'I used to be cynical when I was young. But, by God – it's worse now. I just really dislike going along with what's going on. I hate this current attitude of "Oh, grow up, join the real world, don't be so stuuupid . . .! This is how the world is, so don't be so childish." I can't *bear* those awful ideas.' Cook *is* in a mood, but still has his enthusiasms – one of them being Rolling Stone Keith Richards. 'The biggest star in the world is Keef, I think,' he offers, noting a kindred decadent anti-authoritarian spirit. 'He defies death – and has such *wonderful* make-up. I always like people who kick heroin and switch to Bourbon.' (After a more sullen pause.) 'Actually you've caught me on one of my Dislike of Comedy Nights tonight.'

Really?

'Oh, I don't like it *in the least*,' he scoffs. 'I can't think of *anything* I like about comedy, really . . .'

Later he lights another cigarette, takes another large hit on a margarita, struggles out of his seat and drawls a departing punch-line:

'. . . I'm going to have a lie down now – all this comedy's worn me out.'

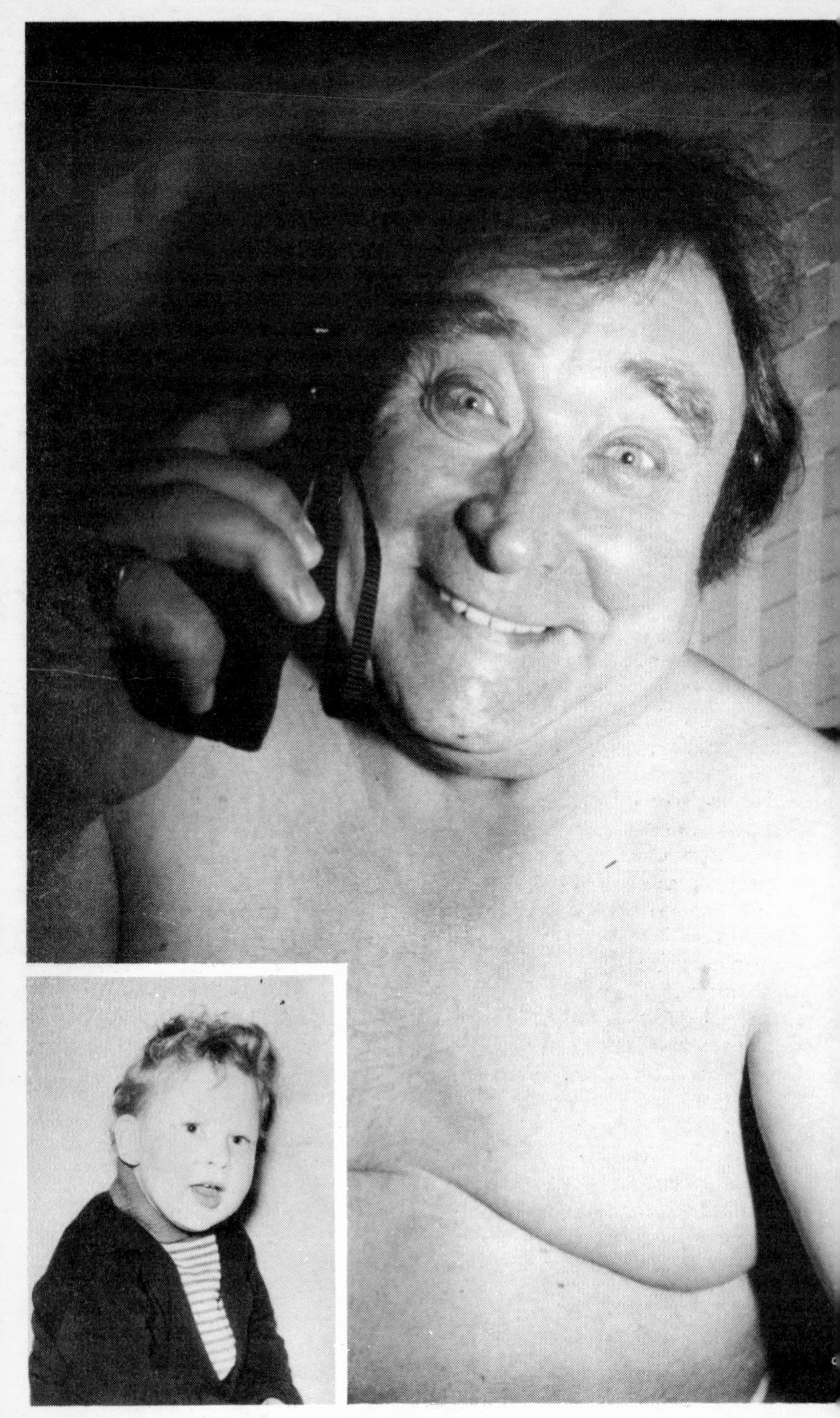

BERNARD MANNING ten minutes prior to a show-stopping performance. Photograph by John Hind
(Inset) BERNARD aged about three
Photograph courtesy of Mrs Manning

BERNARD MANNING

Mr Nice Guy

They can't stop us laughing, can they?
It's the only thing we've got left.

'I'm a Northern comedian really – a blue act; very risqué, with four-letter words dotted *all over the show*. If they want the Archbishop of Canterbury, they should go down the road instead. But I can work any way, which or where, me. If I perform at the London Hilton I still tell the same stories and get the laughs in the same places. Harold Wilson was in the audience at the Hilton. I said to him, "You used to tell lies and prove 'em. Some Prime Minister *you* were. You got rid of the idle rich and you've replaced them with the idle fucking poor." Y'know – I ripped a few lines across him. What could he do?' He chuckles boyishly. '*I've* got the microphone.'

Bernard Manning, a rather gentle and generous man off stage, is bringing my attention to the illustrious moments displayed on the walls of his North Manchester venue, 'Bernard Manning's World Famous Embassy Club', where most evenings for 30 odd years he has performed religiously to a packed paying audience, as well as speeding across the country to do his act before a further large thirsty crowd. He points half-nonchalantly towards a particular framed photograph. 'This is me shaking hands with the Duke of Kent. What a gormless bastard he was.' He adopts a slurred posh accent. '"Oh, Mr Manning – lovely to see you. Enjoyed your splendid show." I laughed at that for ages.' He moves along the wall. 'I performed in front of the Duke of Westminster once. Him and I were sat on the top table before two hundred fellas in dress-suits. And I said, "I've got a message from Tony Benn for you." The Duke said, "What is it?" I said, "Get fucked!" And apparently wherever he goes he tells people, "You know, Bernard Manning told me to get fucked!" He *tells* people!'

Bernard explores more photographs and memories: 'This is me with Kevin Keegan, Henry Cooper, Derek Dougan, me backstage at the London Palladium with all those tuppence ha'penny comics . . . There's me as a young man, singing . . . Here's me shaking hands with the Queen. She put her hands in mine and said "I thoroughly enjoyed your performance." Nice old dear. . . . This is me topping the bill at the MGM Grand, the biggest hotel in Las Vegas, on the Strip – a standing ovation. I went in with both feet, son . . . There's me with John Conteh . . . Mrs Thatcher . . . And this was a highlight – getting my own show on television, five or six years ago. A full hour with full orchestra. I delved into great comedians from the past, as well as my own career, and I sang "Memories" on that. But you can't tell *good strong* jokes on television, son – it's a place made for fairy stories. When I'm on screen I feel like a horse held back at a starting-gate . . . it's a terrible feeling. You have to tell all these soft tales about the car, the dog, the aeroplane and all that fuckin' nonsense. . . . I won £25,000 on that horse. It won the Ark.'

You're a gambler?

'Oh yes – I like a good flutter . . .'

We move on. 'This is some declaration from the Jewish National Fund' says the man known for making more than his fair share of 'racial' jokes. 'I raised thousands and thousands of pounds for them.' He passes through a door at the back of the club, reaches for a container of old perfume on a shelf and sprays his neck and wrists. He now suddenly begins singing, briefly but warmly: 'Some enchanted evening . . . Yoooou may see a straaanger.' He has a fine smooth voice which belies both his image and his intake of cigarettes. 'And this is me little dressing room, where we all sit and have a talk, the musicians and me.'

What thoughts do you have before taking to the stage each night?

'Well, I have a stroll round, look at a crowd. I'm just mentally thinking – are they young, old, mixed? I see where the characters in the audience are . . . the bald-heads, the thin 'uns, the ugly bastards. So I can say later, "Look at the state of *him*. If *he* gets a fuck in here tonight, there's a chance for all of us." I'm an American type gag-man really. One gag after another. I bring the audience into it – I have a go at someone. I have a go at *everyone*.'

Everyone?

'Including myself, . . . really. If a fella walks in here with a gorgeous looking bit of stuff, I go the other way. I'll say "Is she better than that old bag you brought in last Thursday night? Your taste is getting better son. God, he's fetched some fucking dogs in here!" Then I'll look at her and say, "But I bet you've flattened a bit of grass in your time, haven't you love? . . . I bet she's seen more ceiling than Michelangelo." The place is in uproar, because she's a gorgeous glamorous bit of stuff, and half the time I might be saying she's a dog. It's ridiculous really. But that's the funniest part, *I* think.'

On the stage of the 60-foot Embassy Club lounge that evening, before a packed house of 300 Mancunians sitting around small drinking tables, Manning creates – with apparent ease – a truly joyous atmosphere of communal *and* anti-communal laughter. His stage-act, in effect a vast store of jokes practised, restructured and newly paced twice a day, is an incredibly powerful and crude comic *tour-de-force* which leaves few icons and taboos intact. Manning, who is just under 20 stone in weight, smokes numerous cigarettes on stage, sweats a lot, and wears clothes in the order of a light pink shirt, brown flared trousers and black shoes, or (for slightly formal occasions) a white suit from the 1970s with a bow tie. He woos the audience with immaculate pacing, with perfect pauses, with a brusque swagger which is offset by sparkling eyes, occasional cherubic smiles and almost impromptu singing segments 'the fundamental things apply, as time gooes byyy . . .' Anyone in the audience can find themselves personally or generally abused, from those who stroll to the toilet during his tunes ('You bastard!'), the waiters who serve the clientele at their tables ('You better buck your ideas up, or I'll put you down for tax'), to late-comers to the venue (You're not soliciting are you, love?' or 'You'll be starring in my next wank, love'), and even the band behind him ('Some of the shit they play – it's unbelievable').

His reputation, in a sense, precedes him (he is – for example – extremely rude about other comedians in the press), but there is little similarity in tone between what the audience will have seen of him on television, and his stage act.

'Fella giving this bird one . . . She said "You've only got a small organ, haven't you?" He said, "Yes, but it's never played in a cathedral before."' Then he pauses for only two seconds before leaping, for thirteen short sharp sentences, on to the topic of 'slitty-eyed bastards.' 'You Japanese never fucking laugh, do you?' he asks, gazing aggressively into the audience at someone who is patently not Japanese, 'You never fucking laugh . . . We haven't forgotten Pearl Harbor, pal, don't you fucking worry about that! What a shit-house trick that was. Sat there, he can't wait to go home and make another Datsun . . .'

A microphone, a spotlight, a stomach and a foul mouth. Manning is especially proficient at humour with both coarse corners and 'unacceptable' values, in which – for instance – vicars suddenly swear, or a Pakistani dressed in white at night (for safety's sake) is knocked down by a snow-plough. But, just when he has seemingly brought out the bigot or the patriot in his audience, he goes in for a rear assault. Here is a good example. 'There's two gentlemen in the audience tonight who fought at Goose Green in the Falklands,' he announces, fat finger directed to one of the tables. People cheer, applaud and/or gaze. Then Manning closes the comic trap, '. . . They're Argentinians.' Further pause. 'And if you want to clap for shit like that it's your own business.'

'Every time you laugh, love, your tits go up and down . . . Don't pick your nose, love – we just swept up over there . . . Put it all end-to-end, what she's had, and you could make a hand-rail for the Isle of Wight.'

He slips and leap-frogs between jokes – many of them sexual, perverse and ludicrous – concerning Zulus, a blind pilot, Durex, Billy Graham, pensioners, a sperm bank, 'two Jews' (although not normally anti-Jewish jokes), a blow-up doll, chipshops, Napoleon, a bionic arm, sex . . . hundreds if not thousands of jokes interrupted only by a melodious singsong, the weary wiping of his brow with a handkerchief, and the announcement of a raffle '. . . for the old folk at the back'. A minute later he's referring to a frail old man in the front; 'Has this old fella *gone*? Was it cold in the ground this morning?' He tells several stories concerning himself in the sex-act, but then announces (seriously) at one point that he has not had sex for two and a half years. He tells people 'Don't start taking Valium and shit like that,' philosophises on dogged determination, and – when knowing of a man in the audience who is shortly to be married – intercuts congratulations with sudden exclamations of the exact opposite. 'I hope you'll be very happy . . . *No fucking chance!* . . .Stop wi' yer mother, yer barmy bastard!' He is often known to make reference to his own mother Mary on stage. He speaks admiringly of mothers ('Marvellous . . . Bung her eight quid out of 150 . . . "Here, get some food in mum. Get some sauce for fuck's sake!"'.) In a slightly more directly personal moment he even reveals to the clientele that he is back living with his mother again now ('A lovely cook') and that each evening she tells him not to be 'rude' on stage.

Manning flows between jokes, between the segments of comedy stored in his brain, with split-second precision. The order is not rehearsed, only the jokes – time and time again, with embellishment, plus – and not forgetting – assorted effortless ad-libs prompted by a glass breaking behind the bar, a heckle or just a minor movement before him. The mention of someone who is Welsh leads to assorted Welsh material. 'I took the wife to Wales . . . to Bang 'er (Bangor). Nice day . . . They want to stop singing in Wales and get some coal up. You can all sing when you've got fuck all else to do.' He recalls a – undoubtedly imaginary – night staying in a Welsh hotel. 'I said to the landlady, "There's no lock on the lavatory door." She said "We've never had a bucket of shit pinched yet."'

'What kind of people talk like *that*?' he then asks with evident, growing irony. 'That's the way the world's gone nowadays,' he announces later. *'The world's gone fuckin' mad.'*

'It's not often I sit down like this,' Bernard says to me, as we repose in the Embassy Club late one afternoon. 'I pay lots of people here, but I do all the fucking work. I never stop.' He adopts a temper only for jest's sake, and it seems to clear the air, as – during our delve into his roots – he converses in a completely genial manner.

'I was born on 13 August 1930, into a poor family here in Manchester,' recalls memory-laden 'Fat Bernard' (as he often titles himself). He reaches for a cigarette. 'My father was on the dole, like everybody else in those days. He used to get temporary work as a breadman, driving a horse and cart. We lived in a two-up, two-down. There were seven of us. Me mum, dad, brother Frank, me, me sisters Rene and Alma, and brother Jack. I was the second child. My mother used to be out working a lot. It was a very clannish family – cut one, we all bled. And we still do.'

Was it a religious family?

'Roman Catholic. I was a choir-boy, in the altar.'

What did your parents expect of you, as you grew up?

'Well, we're working-class . . . they just expected their children to get a job and carry on like that – get married, have children, like people usually do. I went to just an ordinary school, and I left at fourteen to work.'

What do you think makes someone set out to be a comedian?

'Oh, I could never answer that, son! There's certainly no one in my family in the theatre business, and I can't trace back to anyone who ever was. There's nobody else in the family who can really tell jokes, *and* there's nobody who can sing either. My brother – fucking 'ell, does *he* sing out of tune. You've never heard anything like it! So I'm just a one-off, and I don't know how that happened.'

Were you a humorist as a child?

'Oh yes. I used to tell jokes in the air-raid shelters during the war, when Germans came bombing Manchester . . . laughing, taking George Formby off, and other stars of the day like Max Miller. Entertaining the neighbours at Christmas parties, I was always doing my bit – making people laugh. I made the lads laugh at school; I made them laugh in the army.'

What are your thoughts on bringing up children?

'Well . . . spoil the rod and spare the child.' He does a double-take. 'I mean, spare the rod and spoil the child . . . You've got to give them a crack now and again, so they know they're doing wrong.'

Did *you* have that?

'Plenty! Plenty of good hidings I had. Right across the arse with a slipper.'

What did that do to you?

'It made my arse sing, I can tell you! I got lots of hidings from me dad. He always wanted us in by a certain time. But I still loved him . . . I was all the better for it.'

Were you a 'naughty' lad?

'Well, there was a big gang of us. We pinched apples from trees, annoyed a few people. We walked to Blackpool, slept in a bus shelter, living on crab apples. Fifty-two miles I walked! I tell you, I got me face cracked when I got home.'

Was your father very much the boss of the house?

'Well, men *like* to be the boss. They *think* they're the boss, but the woman's the boss really. My mother was the boss in our house . . . for ever more. She's the greatest. Into her late eighties now, still alive. She's bloody lovely.'

That strong bond with the mother seems to be a common trait amongst male comedians.

'I don't know what it is son. It's just that you see your mother struggling . . . going to the washroom with a huge pile of washing, and all that. My father went out for a drink, and mum stayed in of an evening and kept the house clean, kept us well fed, she hardly ever drank – only at party times. And that's what's missing today – the old-fashioned mums who let the father think he was boss when he wasn't at all. No doubt about that.'

What role did father play?

'Well, he was the breadwinner. He went out to work. He even did golf-caddying, in the 1930s, and turned people's gardens over. Everybody in the North had a bad time then.'

What are your memories of him?

'When I was a young lad I used to watch him shaving . . . And we used to listen to the radio together – Tommy Handley, Max Miller. And he used to laugh at them a lot. He had a good sense of humour, but he was mostly a bit serious. He never told stories himself. *I never heard him tell a "joke" in his life!* I worked on a stall with him at Smithfield fruit market sometime after I left Mount Carmel School, up the road, when I was fourteen. We started with a horse and cart. Then the market was full of comedians . . . stall-owners, the porters. There was always jokes about summat in those days, plenty of jokes flying around about Hitler, Mussolini and all that fuckin' carry-on. We heard that banter all day, and I joined in.'

Bernard's humour survived the working world. At one point, as a general dogs-body in Manchester's Senior Service cigarette factory, he was voted 'Personality of the Factory' in the staff magazine. He remembers such employment thus: 'I told jokes, made merry, carried things, ran bets down to the local bookies and played the goat.'

How and when did you first take to the stage?

'I was called up on National Service. The Manchester Regiment, in Berlin, 1948 and 1949. I was considered the humorist of the battalion, and I sang with the regiment band on some tours. Happy times. After I got back to Manchester I went for an audition, as singer, with the Oscar Rabin Dance Band. That time means a lot to me – playing London's Lyceum Ballroom, getting £50 a week. Lovely.'

Was the humour retained, for later use?

'I was still joking with friends and in pubs, all the rest of the time. When I'm together with people I'm *always* first in with a couple of gags. I get on with everybody, me. It's just *natural*. You can't learn comedy. You're either funny or you're not.'

But when did your humour start surfacing on stage?

'I became resident compère at Manchester's Northern Sporting Club in the mid-1950s. The cabaret scene had begun, and the theatres were closing down. We had clubs, and wrestling and boxing, springing up all over the shop. And to be a compère it's no use just being a singer – you've got to greet or abuse people as they come in, you've got to sing their requests, tell a few stories, a few ad-libs. And that's how it began. A couple of ad-libs lead to a dozen, you bounce lines, you grow . . .' He clicks his fingers. 'And it's bloody marvellous when everybody falls about.'

What was your early stage material like?

'I used to write the jokes on the back of my arm! Sing a couple of songs then glance down. They used to be silly clean jokes. I think in retrospect it would sound very corny. There's one joke from back then which I'll probably use tonight . . . A guide-dog slashed up this blind guy's leg. A fella dashed up and said "What a lovely thing you've just done – that dog just pissed up your leg, and you've given it a dog biscuit." "Yes" says the blind fella, "I'm just finding out where its mouth is – then it's going to get a kick in the bollocks" . . . You could get away with *bollocks* back then. I even heard it used two or three times on the television.'

Were you a confident performer in those days?

'I was shy at first, doing comedy. *Every comic is*. You don't just go out there and think you're doing wonders. You work at it, slowly and surely. And being a singer was my crutch. Do a song, whip in a couple of quips and gags, have a go at a few folk . . . and one thing led to another and I could do two hours. *No problem*. It's infectious.'

How did you come to run your own club?

'I opened it with me Dad – all the family really. I was compèring down the road and I said "What I can do for them, I can do for us." So we scraped together the lease on this place . . . and 30 years on it's still in business and I own it lock, stock and barrel. We ran three clubs in Manchester at one time . . . the Wilton, the Palladium and this, but the others got cleared out with the slum-clearance. Before then I did three performances a night, sometimes four. Worked my bollocks off I did.'

Did it all go well from the start?

'Oh, good houses yes. Lots of supping. The Embassy opened on 11 December 1959. It soon became the swinging 1960s . . . what we here called the roaring 1960s. I sang and told some jokes. Dad looked after the bars and the cellar. My mother was on the till, my brother on the door and me sisters behind the bars. Everybody in the family pulled their weight.'

What did your father make of it all?

'I think he thought "absolutely marvellous". Because he'd been working all his life in greengrocery, for really a pittance. He was watching cauliflowers go rotten before his eyes, lettuces wilting in the hot weather. Even if you put them in a fridge they don't last. But put beer in a cool refrigerated cellar and that doesn't go off. *You* shift it, *I* pull the crowds in, we're always packed out . . . every fucking night. It's lovely.'

Manning remembers with uncanny speed a long list of performers who appeared in the early days at the Embassy, and the *exact* fees they received for their services: 'The Beatles – £44; Matt Monro – 30 quid; Freddie and the Dreamers – £7; Jimmy Tarbuck – £5 . . . I could go on all night. But most people came to see *me* – other comedians wouldn't draw flies. So now I'm the main-man, not just the compère. Which is lovely. Because I don't have to pay other people – oh no, son!'

He chuckles. With the mere mention of any other comedian or performer, bar just a select few (Jackie Mason, Don Rickles, Tommy Cooper, W.C. Fields, Laurel and Hardy) Manning unleashes two or three droll and razorsharp quips concerning their lack of talent, good looks and material, even referring to their homosexuality when it is quite evidently not the case. 'Seeing *him* perform' he says of anyone, and no one in particular, 'is like watching a coffin warp . . . *He's about as funny as a rabies epidemic in a blind folks' home.'* His comments and facial expressions veer back and forth between outrage and wide-eyed boyishness. He pulls his underpants up higher, rocks with laughter, shuffles on the seat, scratches his nose and lights another cigarette. 'Hold on a minute. I'm just going for a slash.' He burps. 'Do you want a pie, or owt? . . . *Get this man a cob and a drink will you, someone.* It's on the house, me old pal!'

'I've been in the business 40 years,' he offers on his return. 'I've been to nearly every club in England – there's not many I haven't worked. But it was only in 1971, when they put me on television, on a programme called *The Comedians,* that I became a real success. I went from £10 or so a night, to £2,000, across the country. It's all been hard work, but I got there. It's a great success story really. Because my mother lives in a £200,000 house, I've set up all my brothers and sisters in business and we want for nothing. But the *terrible* thing is, my father never saw *any* of that. He died early in 1971. But I think he would have been *dead chuffed* about me if he'd known.'

He pauses and reflects for a moment. 'I really went into a terrible depression when he died. He died on the bowling-green. I went to the hospital, I couldn't *believe* he'd died. I'd never seen a dead person. I was crying and shouting and bawling, "Don't let him die." This doctor sat me on a form and said "Your dad has gone son; there's nothing we can do about it."I just couldn't take it. And I went into a deep depression. And if it hadn't been for getting the television show, I don't know how I'd be now. I think I'd be in exactly the same depression today. We were like brothers really, y'know.'

Does not bereavement crush a sense of humour?

'The very *worst* times in any comedian's life are bereavement. When my father died I went to pieces. And a few years ago, I was due on at the Embassy Club one evening at 8pm and the phone rang. My wife Veronica was in Naples and she'd just collapsed from a heart-attack. And in four minutes I'd got to go on that stage there for an hour. The people sat waiting didn't want to know about *my* problems. And I went on, cut myself right off from the sickness in my stomach and I did it. After that I got Veronica flown back to Manchester, she went into hospital and I went in there every morning, and every night, before a show, taking her a few sandwiches and cakes, holding her hand, then coming back and doing me job. Terrible, terrible . . . I wouldn't wish that on anyone. But it doesn't matter how you feel – you've just got to go on there and do it.'

You still perform well?

'Yes, because when the spotlight hits you, you're away. It's only when you come off stage . . . whack!' He claps his hands. '. . .

That's when you're destroyed. You go home, you sob. I've cried myself to sleep many a time . . . I still do sometimes. Terrible. When you see that coffin go down . . . *Hiiiiya!*' (He has called out momentarily to someone entering the lounge.) '. . . When you see the coffin disappear, it's terrible.' He shrugs his shoulders and frowns. 'But that's *life*, you see.'

Do you have a general philosophy on life?

'Not to worry. Because there's nothing worse than death. If you're healthy and all the family's healthy, enjoy it while you can. If mum and dad are alive, enjoy 'em . . . enjoy your children. Enjoy the best times; there's plenty of rough ones ahead. Because there's nothing worse that bereavement.'

So there's quite a lot of misery tucked behind the laughter?

'Sad, yes, I'm a sad man in the house. I sit in the house and I watch television, and I go back and delve in the past, when I was care-free and gay, when I courted my wife for seven years, when my wife and father were alive, and I think . . . But I pull myself out of it. Oh yes, but I'm a sad man in the house, I must admit that. I'm not laughing and telling jokes all the time, oh no. You just *play* the clown, you see.'

Are *you* religious?

'I was brought up a Catholic. But I'm not a good Catholic. I never go to church. Sunday is a day for being lazy. I pray though. I pray many a time. But I don't know who I pray *to*.'

Are you superstitious?

'I don't believe in good luck or bad luck. You just have to take things as they come.'

But . . . *Once a Catholic, always a Catholic?*

'I don't know really. I think religion should simply be about doing good in your everyday life, whenever you can. I mean, there were two old age pensioners who live near here who were put in the nick for non-payment of rates recently. Can you imagine putting old folk away for that? So I got them out. No one *else* got them out; *I* did. And I'm supposed to be "Fat Bernard – the Hard Guy, the Baddie". I'm not an aggressive person off stage. I'm very kind. I've earnt millions for charity. I feel for people, I really do. I'm a fuckin' sucker for a sob-story.'

On stage you regularly perform a number of fairly outrageous 'religious' jokes, most notably the story of the nun and the punkrocker, which incorporates elements of homosexual disguise, menstruation, anal sex and more besides.

'Oh yes, *that* one. I haven't told that one for a while. Tonight I might start with . . .' (A three-second pause.) 'What's a good gag? A priest fell over this cliff and he's hanging on with his fingers, and he looked up and said "Lord, can you help me please?", And a voice said, "Let go of the cliff, your body will be dashed on the rocks below and – this time tomorrow – you will be sat on the right-hand side of God." And the priest said, "Is there anyone else up there who can fuckin' help me?" . . . That got a laugh, you see! Now, most comics would tell you a joke and you wouldn't laugh. They *think* they're comedians, they keep getting work, and while they're getting work they're keeping good comics *out* of work. They might have a good agent, but they die on their arses on stage. They should get arrested for talking to themselves.'

What do you think of the theory, proposed by Stephen Leacock, that early mankind began to exclaim 'Ha ha!' during the act of hitting someone or something over the head?

'It's very probable. Somebody stepped on a banana-skin or summat, went arse over tup, fell bang-slap on their arse, and everybody else started laughing. It's a natural thing to do. People are very cruel deep down.' (He chortles now.)

Comedy is aggression?

'It is with me. A lot of meek and mild comics just don't cut it. You've got to have balls and guts to do it, and you've got to have lived. It's about knowing you can carry off a gag perfectly, and making it seem totally natural. In actual fact a lot of thought's gone into it, but the audience wouldn't think that. They think it comes right off the top of me 'ead. But it hasn't. Every night you're trusting to luck, I suppose; you can't really pre-plan anything, but it's all in there somewhere and you have to know it's going to come out. You have to feel your way second by second. But I'll tell you now, son . . . the first time I go on that stage and I get booed off or given a slow hand-clap, *I will finish* as a comedian for certain. I've practically got to have a standing ovation *every* night, because that's the adrenalin. It's that what keeps me going.'

What do you think of the argument that subject matters such as some of your own should be avoided in comedy?

'Irishmen, Scotsmen, Pakis, West Indians, Tom, Dick and Harry . . . Nothing's sacred.'

A joke's a joke?

'Exactly. Comedy's all about laughing. If we're telling jokes we're not fighting, are we? I don't believe in rules and theories. You can't say *this* should be funny, that *can't* be. And you're either funny or you're not.'

You once said, though, that 'I do blue humour, but not sick humour.'

'Well, I wouldn't tell jokes about disasters . . . I don't want to know about that. Because I feel for people. Death and bereavement are not funny subjects. So that is taboo to me, because anybody who's been bereaved like me doesn't want to know a lot of bloody sick nonsense about death.'

Several weeks later I again meet up with Bernard Manning at a venue in Hemel Hempstead, where he performs to 800 or more people, standing on a high stage, at least 15 foot from the seated crowd. He abuses them, fields numerous heckles, points to me and calls me 'a scruffy bastard', tells 230 jokes and stories, envelopes the hall with sustained laughter, receives a standing ovation, returns for an encore and then retreats to the wings with an appreciative smile and a playfully abusive 'V'sign. What I noticed during this performance is that Manning *does* actually tell jokes about death, including one which quite blatantly laughs in the face of bereavement. 'I've had fuckin' thousands of jobs' he says, at one point, without any evident link from the previous joke, 'I've got sacked once for laughing . . . Mind you, I was driving a fuckin' hearse at the time.'

Twenty minutes before that performance Manning arrived in a chauffeured Lincoln Continental, with registration plate number 'BJM 1', from Manchester (his other car, a Rolls Royce, bears the legend '1 LAF'). On arriving in his dressing-room, carrying a portable telephone, he stripped down to his underpants and urinated in the sink, while his chauffeur/assistant took charge of the £1,500 he was being paid in advance for his performance.

Bernard makes light of the wads of money, but I'm eager to ask how important it is.

'Money? there's nothing I want to buy for myself,' he offers, 'I earn £7,000, £8,000 or more every week. That's outside what I take at my club. So I'm a very wealthy man. And I'm a wealthy man because I'm a *funny* man and I pull a crowd. I perform to 300 at my club and maybe 300 or 800 others *every* night.'

Are you a workaholic?

'I never stop. I'm working myself to death.'

Do you take holidays?

'I go away sometimes, but only to work. Jersey, Benidorm. I'd *never* go away to lie on a beach, because *I can't stand that*. I never move out of the room when I'm abroad – except to go on stage.'

What does your day involve?

'My day. I get up between seven and eight o'clock. I won't have gone to bed most nights until 3.30am. I go straight down to the Embassy Club, and I let the cleaners in. I help to set the room out, check the beer, see if anything's broken, see if we need anything, if a microphone is broken down, if a piano wants tuning. There's a million and one jobs and they've *all* got to be right for the night. When folk come in, they don't want a spot light out of place, a door hanging off, a toilet-seat missing or bog-rolls going short in the ladies.

'Then, when I've sorted everything, I go to my son's place in Rochdale – his roller-skating rink – and I have a game of snooker with me son, Bernard Junior . . . a cup of coffee to wake me up a bit, a round of toast, I'll crack a few jokes 'round the bar, make everybody feel happy. This is every day of my life, this! Then home to mum and have a bit of dinner – a few lamb chops, new potatoes, green peas, a bit of apple pie and custard, a cup of coffee. Then I might get my head down for half an hour in the afternoon, or more likely back a few horses if there's racing on the television. *Back a few winners, back a few losers*. And then it's back to the Embassy for 5pm.'

What happens if you're ill?

'I never am ill – I'm *never* ill. I have flus and colds, I suppose, but I always keep on going right through them.

Are you a foodaholic?

'I eat huge meals, me. I have a constant battle with my weight.'

Do you drink?

'No alcohol, no. I sell plenty, but I don't sup any. It would ruin your comic timing . . . *And* it ruins the audience's timing if they're too drunk. So I water it down a lot. The only time we had a strong pint from these pumps was during the water strike.'

Is the comedian's life an unhealthy one?

'Well, you're in smoky clubs half the time, packed in, with hardly the room to move your arse – sweating cobs. I suppose if I wanted I could make them laugh for an hour or so and then be on me way. The thing is, I'm getting no younger. I was a lot younger in the old days. I could get in bed at 3.30 and wake up at eight, no problem. Now I get in at 3.30 and it's hard to get up at eight every morning. It's hard. *But I do it.*'

You don't *have* to do it though – do you?

'I don't have to, but *I do*. Every day. I don't need too much sleep. You'd be surprised how little sleep people need. And, anyway, if I laid about I don't know what weight I'd be. I'm nearly 20 stone as it is. If I laid in bed half the day, and didn't sweat like I do, I wouldn't be so slim and lovely.'

But why do you have to join the rush-hour traffic to open the club doors each morning . . . to take care of everything at nine in the morning? Couldn't the staff run it without you?

'Well, I've seen the way other clubs are run. People coming up to the bar to ask for a toilet-roll, or you'll get hold of a microphone and it's as dead as a fucking door-nail. What do you do without a microphone? I have three spare microphones, me. And three spare amplifiers, like in Vegas. You learn as you go along. I've even got two spare tills. Because, what can you do if the till breaks down and you've got 300 people who need serving? You just throw the old till out, plug another one in and off you fuckin' go. It's got to be done, hasn't it? And you've got to have eyes in your arse in this business.'

Before she died, what role did your wife play in what you do?

'Just being in the background, saying "The show you did last night was marvellous . . . I heard ladies in the toilet say you were wonderful." And she's . . . she was a wonderful cooook. Marvellous. Very few and far between, that kind of woman. I was very lucky. I was very much in love with my wife. I would never get married again, because no one could replace her. I'd only start complaining, "Veronica wouldn't have done that." It would be persecution for anybody else I started knocking about with.' (He pauses for several seconds now.)

'But I've still got me mother, you see. "*What time will you be in, son?*" She's 88 years old, full of beans. She's a lovely cooook. She's absolutely marvellous.'

And you have a *son*?

'Yes, yes, Bernard junior. He's no comedian, but he's never been a hap'orth of trouble to me.'

(I glance at Manning's stage.) Will you still be doing this in another three decades?

'If I'm still around. If I haven't taken a dive like Tommy Cooper. If I have to go I want it to be on stage. But what about George Burns, eh? A hundred and ten or something isn't he? He's still strolling on to the stage, still smoking the cigars, still coming up with the quips, throwing the wise-cracks. Lovely.'

JACKIE MASON aka JACOB MAZA: *'All the best of times for me and you.'*
Photograph courtesy of Jyll Rosenfeld

JACKIE MASON

A Sick Individual

What is wrong with the world today?
Why is it in the condition it's in?
How did it come about? What caused it?
What is the nature of it, and how can we retrieve it?
. . . Mister?

In ten minutes, before a large London auditorium, Jackie Mason – New York's finest stand-up comedian – will be unfolding and re-honing several hundred celebrated witticisms built on comic irony, tendentiousness, devil's advocacy and analogy, all imbued with elegant Yiddish flavour. Mason is a brilliant patter man and *comic* technician who has shaped his thought processes perfectly to fit the stage. There he will be in ten minutes. Meanwhile, he is seated in front of a mirror in his star dressing-room, having returned from strolling through the theatre bar to make his presence felt. Now he is speaking 'transatlantic chat' on the telephone to another comedian 'back home'. He is announcing 'I am a great success here – they love me' and receiving reports of celebrity success and failure in other quarters – asking of the caller at one point, 'So he didn't sound too good on the Academy Awards, right?' In the dressing-room, too, are myself, a female acquaintance of Mason and an unspecified male to whom the blonde woman begins talking. The additional conversation means that Mason is *not* now being listened to by everyone present, and his demeanour shifts somewhat, so that he is more dramatic in his conversation, more disparaging, more abrasive in keeping the attention of those around him – his eyes flashing between our eyes, the mirror and the woman's legs. Into the telephone he requests information as to the popularity of his new restaurant in Manhattan. The caller, it seems, has walked past once, seen it far from packed to capacity and not chosen to pass the threshold. Mason notes that, since he has done this, reviews about the establishment's decor and cuisine have appeared in New York publications; as such the eaterie is probably now 'doing fine'. When Mason puts the phone down at the end of the call he has three words to sum up the caller: '*WHAT A SCHMUCK!*'

Jackie Mason is, in fact, a gentle, hospitable, charitable, philosophical man, who has only one other criticism to offer about a specific individual during the several times we shared company, that being against 'a complete jerk-off, a schmuck with short sleeves who thinks he's an international playboy', who comes up to Mason in a coffee-shop and 'pretends he knows who I am.' Those specific derogatory exclamations aside, Mason seems generally relaxed and satisfied with himself, his comic fame, with the 'big stardom' which in 1987 arrived on his shoulders as a result of his all-talking, all-shrugging ('Oy-oy-oy!') year-long one-man Broadway show *The World According to Me* (previously performed on the West Coast). This was an extremely lyrically woven two hours of build-ups and knock-downs of Jews, gentiles, politicians, blacks, Catholics, Italians, psychiatrists, Puerto Ricans, wives, husbands, the residents of Beverly Hills and assorted other 'types', including himself and individual members of his audience. *The World According to Me* was the life and light at the end of Mason's lengthy tunnel-journey through 'small-time and medium stardom'. He had been honing his critical observational jokes for almost a quarter of a century. Only now he had thousands per evening laughing with – and for – him, not hundreds. Finally his glorious poetic humour was recognised. Nowadays, he daily receives, in his own words, '. . . ten offers to make a film, 300 offers to go to a dance, 50 to go for a walk, 500 to send me money for nothing.' In a fashion he has finally grasped, through virtue of all this attention, 'the trick of human happiness – which is not to live for the goals of life, but for the *trip* of life.' The 55-year-old Mason is *finally* reasonably gratified, enjoying the scale of laughter resulting from his own existence, and thus enjoying his existence. 'It appears I am a big star' he offers. He signs my copy of his book *Jackie, Oy!* with a flourish, making sure as many people as possible see him do it. 'All the best of times for *me* and you,' he writes.

Jackie Mason is a short man who walks somewhat in the manner of one who has spent the previous six hours on a horse. He dresses smartly but nevertheless casually. His eyes, accentuated with engaging bags, are warm, thoughtful, amusing. His hands offer all kinds of texture and elaboration as he talks. Communicating is his thirst, his major talent, his 'genius'.

How outrageous could you theoretically be on stage? One of your lines, for instance, claims that you go out with Jewish boys.

'That is obviously a joke on racial segregation, on Jewish parents' attitudes; I'm turning the codes around . . . But people love gay jokes. As soon as you refer to *anything* remotely gay, people laugh straightaway. It's a kind of sick release for the laughers; that they're not gay – they look down on gays. It makes them feel superior – "Look how normal I am, look how that sick person lives." Maybe they fear unconsciously that *they* could be gay but like to prove to themselves that they never could be. Maybe even I fear that. I like to set the audience up, and set myself up – this is the main basis of my act, *twisting and turning*. I do this speech where I say "It's very sick to laugh at gay people. Personally, I don't laugh at them – I pity them . . . As a matter of fact I respect them, I do. Sometimes I take them home with me. But not for long – don't get nervous. A couple of kisses . . . *and out*." People love to laugh at gay jokes. Making a quick gay impersonation – it's a bit like saying a dirty word, hollering "Fuck you" on stage . . . *everybody* laughs.'

Jackie Mason was born Jacob Maza in 1934, the last of four sons spawned of a rabbi, 'a pious religious fanatic', derived from Eastern Poland who had not so long before adapted to the culture shock of settling on the shores of Lake Michigan (soon to relocate to Manhattan's Lower East Side). It was a 'given' assumption, a parental necessity, that all four sons of Eli Maza grew to become orthodox rabbis, his three young daughters to aspire to martyred housewifery. ('From the age of two I was told I'd be a rabbi. And you can't argue at two. You can't get an apartment.') For centuries members of the Jewish community had visited the males of the Maza household in pursuit of answers to questions concerning the minutiae of Talmudic knowledge and etiquette. But the shy Jacob Maza, who – incidentally – 'knew about sex at six years old', rebelled against his lineage and calling, against the strictures of orthodox Jewish faith and the Maza family itself. Instead he found solace, attention, and 'a profession' in humour.

'I was never religious, so I was a fake' notes Mason, of the period when he undertook five years of rabbinical training and then began holding services in synagogues. Previously he had acquired a degree in English and Sociology and had also begun first working as a social director (like Jerry Lewis, Buddy Hackett, Danny Kaye and Jan Murray) in the resorts of the Catskill Mountains, before swiftly becoming a regular 'Borscht Belt' comedian.

Sometime in the 1950s Jacob Maza became Jackie Mason. Throughout that decade he lived a life of duplicity, comeding during the summer months and working as a 'fake' Jewish scholar between times. His father, whose demands for his 'last son' to study religion ('He'd shout "Learn!", looking like he was going to have a heart-attack') had sometimes turned to violence, did not get to know of the thousand dollars in wages Mason brought home with him (and subsequently 'hid' by squandering) in the autumn of 1958. Eli Maza was told, but never believed, that his son's stage-persona was a discreet sideline. There was always a lot of aggression (if delivered subtly) in that stage-persona; indeed Jackie's postures and expressions have always reflected the demeanour of a boxer. Mason is a boxing fan and on stage borrows from their defensive and aggressive movements – the jabs, skips, retreats and sudden mighty blows. He is quick to point out that comedians, post-performance, often exclaim 'I killed them . . . I knocked them out/dead,' and it might then be fair to wonder whether his own stage 'aggression' is the result of feelings towards his father and brothers and the traditions they followed and against which he rebelled.

'As a child I never seemed to mean much. I felt left out of the family. I was the *oldest* of four brothers, I mean, the *youngest*. My father was very forbidding. My oldest brother was a genius and my second brother was a bigger genius. The brother above me (Bernie) was a *real* genius – because of him I developed a complex that I wasn't bright. If I got 99 in a test, he never got less than 100. I couldn't catch up with the son of a bitch! I felt he came on this earth just to show me up and I developed a complex because my father was always idolising him. I felt stupid, rejected, left out, never respected intellectually.'

Do you have a theory on what shuffles a person in the direction of being a comedian, what conceives that thirst for laughter?

'Like other forms of success he needs to overcompensate for something lacking in his life – he desperately needs the roar of the crowds to make up for love lacking in his childhood. It's about inner tension, discomfort, insecurity, longing . . .'

Did you have a strong sense of humour as a child?

'Not as a child. I was more introverted.'

What of your father's?

'He had a strong sense of humour. He liked to tell jokes from Hebrew literature, the great Yiddish writers of humour like Sholom Aleichem from Russia.'

Did he make witticisms while you went on your weekly walks with him – those times, mentioned in your book, in which you shared his company exclusively?

'In his own inimitable way. He used to make comments about people, about life, often humorous. My father had a great understanding of human characteristics. He saw the phoneyness, the pomposity,the pretensions; he knew how to make a joke out of the difference between a guy's reality and his pretence. I inherited that basic observational, critical approach to comedy. But if my father told a joke it wasn't in the way *I* tell a joke. I refined my comedy into one-liners, I became a technician to acquire the best professional approach. A technician in the sense of building jokes one upon the other, getting as many laughs as possible from a situation. I'm never happy unless I know one laugh builds on another, that I've achieved an *avalanche*. I want to believe absolutely that no one can be as funny as me.'

When did this process get going?

'I suppose I became funny at eighteen, 20 maybe, when I stopped being shy and started to look for attention. And the more and more I became a character among my friends, and in college and Hebrew school – I found humour was the best way to attract attention towards myself. I certainly didn't get much at home.'

On what did the divergence between you and your father hinge?

'The schism between us was over only one basic thought – that *I* didn't believe, that I didn't want to live a religious life. It's something that came early to me. I didn't want to sacrifice my feelings and comforts to its rituals and restrictions, because first of all I don't even know whether I believe in God. In fact I don't. There you are. And my father could not tolerate my avoiding it.

There was a moral obligation to become a rabbi, and to not do this – in his eyes – was tantamount to becoming a Nazi.'

Yet still in many ways you could say you are very similar. He was a rabbi, you're a comedian – you both took to reciting and honing speeches with similar undertones?

'I don't know if I'd give credit to myself for helping people spiritually, although it depends what is meant by the spiritual. But in a philosophical sense you could say there's a great similarity – making comments that have a moral point and purpose which is valid. My comedy makes fun of hypocrisy, double standards, certainly – the meaningless virtues that people live for. It makes a schmuck out of a guy who thinks life is all material things, meaningless goals that achieve absolutely nothing. Where do you go with 300 rooms in your house? And, yes, this kind of moralistic approach to comedy and my broad social philosophy are with little doubt a result of my rabbinical training – a training which directly contradicts materialistic society.'

I wonder, during your teens, how much effect mixing with anarchists and communists, on local street corners, had on your character?

'I would say little effect, although I enjoyed their company and trying to amuse them. Nevertheless, it's true that those types of people say a lot of the same things as orthodox Jews. It's for different reasons, but it comes out somewhat the same. Living for money is a sickness. You should live for spiritual values, for people. Giving of yourself to help others. I certainly became interested in politics . . . I can remember seeing Bertrand Russell [the atheist philosopher] give a lecture once and I enjoyed that immensely.'

Years before that, when you were thirteen, and made an impassioned, ad-libbed speech at your bar mitzvah, and your father hugged you warmly, *enthusiastically*, do you think that was a point in which your father realised, however briefly, that you were very similar?

'He appreciated my speech, but that did not stop his questioning the degree of my conviction and commitment to religion.'

If you had the chance to tell him, now, what you have said about the similarities in the philosophies behind his craft and yours . . .

'It would mean *nothing*. Absolutely nothing. It was important to me to know about life, but to him the urgency was to observe every dogma, every Jewish ritual. To him, if you made a phone-call on the Sabbath you were violating every orthodox principle of Judaism and first of all you deserved to *die!* . . . Hahaa-ha.'

Your father was so uncompromisingly orthodox that he couldn't get a prominent rabbinical posting; similarly you, for instance, got fired from six Catskills hotels during the summer of 1958.

'But *I'm* uncompromising about *comfort*. If someone wants me to get up early to work, I don't want that job. Isn't the right to sleep late more important? I'm doing a TV sit-com now on the condition that I don't, under any circumstances, have to be there before 10.30 in the morning, no more than four days a week – and this is unheard of. The point is, I didn't spend two decades becoming a star to suffer for it. I'm finished with suffering. Stardom is not something you suffer for, like suffering for children. You become a star to enjoy.'

What has success done for your equilibrium?

'Well, ask a guy who's been chasing a girl and got her, "How do you feel?" – he'll just say *"Thank God!"* After decades of emotional conflicts, guilts, masochistic drives, after all that time working on my self image . . . success was like buying my sanity back. Because you had to wonder if you were nuts sometime, having tried so hard and got nowhere for so long. The doubts are: Do you have a true measure of yourself? Are you unbalanced? Do you have a sense of perspective about your relationship to the world? Is your confidence misplaced?'

You make it sound as if your shows were never, or barely, appreciated until a couple of years ago.

'There are *degrees* of stardom. Before, I was a comedian's star, I was able to draw 200 or 300 into a theatre and make them laugh; maybe 400 if I was lucky. Now it's 6,000 . . . 10,000, for two years on Broadway.'

So you've now acquired what you always wanted?

'*This* was always my dream – to become this much of a star. I always troubled for this. I *wasted* all my money, I didn't save a quarter in 25 years, because I invested everything in my own productions, to make me a star. I would make a million dollars, invest it in a movie, it stank, I'd go back to work, make a half a million dollars a year for two years, do it again and all my pictures stank. It was just sweating and suffering, sweating and suffering. And I know it's a little sick to be such an ego-driven person that you spend every penny you got trying to make yourself a star. Not a little. If I had to be honest with myself, looking at myself in a mirror, I would say "This guy's nuts." If I saw someone else do what I did I would think "He is *insane*."'

Were people telling you that?

'They were, but it didn't affect me at all. It's like an alcoholic or coke addict who ignores your drawing attention to the fact.'

You criticise gambling several times in your book.

'Gambling to me is the most insane preoccupation in the history of the world. I never gambled a nickel in all my 25 years in show business.'

But you gambled financially with success and you gamble with the audience's affections.

'But real gambling has no real ambition. I felt mine at least was a solid, intelligent ambition. Maybe all those productions could just as well have worked for me. It's just that I stank as a producer. H-haaha.'

After each failure, how did you feel?

'Not too good, not too good. Periodic self-doubts. For about an hour. Then I got back to work on it.'

But did it make you more motivated, more *funny?*

'That's an interesting question . . . but one to which I'd have to say I didn't feel more or less motivated. The drive stayed the same, I never got discouraged. I never once felt there was something lacking in my material. I thought there was something lacking in my marketing. I knew I was a sensation because every time I got on stage I brought the house down. I don't want to sound like I'm showing off – it's not in my nature, I don't know if you noticed that? [an ironic wink] – but if I did a show with ten big stars I always got the biggest ovation and the biggest laughs. But the other guys would be big shots, big stars making $100,000 a week, and I'd only be making $5,000.'

The money is very important?

'No, no. I was just nauseous inside that I wasn't *a star*. I never cared about the money. I was practically broke all my life – however much money I made – and it never bothered me. At the moment I'm *saving* money for the first time in my life. I never *cared* about the money – just the ego trip and stardom.'

OK, then. Is rivalry amongst comedians intense?

'It's *very* intense. Everybody's self-conscious about such feelings and pretends they're not jealous, but you can see the bitterness in their eyes. When someone goes ahead in their career they get sick to their stomach. That's not much different from any other profession. But a comedian wants to be the very best at his trade, not just successful. He has to prove he's the biggest – the funniest. So if someone else gets ahead of you you believe "He just got a break – he's just a phoney bastard . . . *He stinks, the world stinks, my mother stinks, they all stink* . . ." H-hahaa. That's what happens.'

Are you secure now?

'I'm very secure and comfortable inside now. I feel like a guy who ran a race for 25 years and won. Like I'm sitting on top of a mountain and 5,000 girls are feeding me a piece of cake. Look at the expression on a Jewish girl's face at her wedding, or even her engagement party – it is the pleasure and relief of succeeding in the most important aspect of her life. Because that was her preoccupation, that was her aphrodisiac and that was her madness. H-hahaa.'

But, on a day to day basis, you still have to win over an audience in live performance. After the ubiquitous morning coffee, newspaper, bagel and cream cheese, how do you cope with the build-up to each evening?

'I don't have that many highs and lows. There's not that much volatility in me. I take life as it comes. I don't get nervous going to a show. A second before a show I'm still drinking coffee. I just enjoy being the beau of the ball, I enjoy being reminded I'm such a big star. I like seeing the audience look as if they can't live, can't smile, without me. I try to convince myself that the whole world stops because Jackie Mason is talking. I know it's just one big sickness, but I'm enjoying it. I know I'm sick from top to bottom, but *I don't care!'*

You handle your sickness with humour and . . . a certain aura of dignity?

'Yes. If you know how sick you are, you've got half the battle won. It's sick to be that sick, but it's sicker if you don't yet know the difference. If you think your behaviour makes complete sense you walk around like a complete jerk-off – like most of the big comedians walking around with their pompous airs. I know I'd *like* the world to revolve around me, but ultimately I know it doesn't. It's a sad thing that it doesn't . . . but I'm making the most of it . . . H-hha-ha-ha.'

Is there anything left unresolved. Your parents aren't alive now, but how do your brothers look on you?

'They were never as narrow-minded as my father, and mother. Even though they're strictly religious, they're tolerant enough of the idea that I have a right to my own life. And now I buy their cars, their homes, their vacations . . . It's hard to hate a person who takes care of everything you want. A child of theirs is getting married, I pay for the wedding. If they get a little nauseous, I pay for the medic. They cross the street, I buy a car. So they start rationalising that what I do is not so terrible. Ha-hhha-a. "He's on God's side, even though he's not so godly. He wants to be at the temple, Bernie – he just forgot the address."'

Sigmund Freud's Oedipus-complex theory explained how male offspring have a wish to depose the father. Freud further explained, in *Totem and Taboo,* the father-centred nature of religion and, in *Moses and Monotheism,* he traced – with the aid of his own Oedipus-complex – the psychosexual foundations of monotheism (One God, God the Father) and the Jewish tradition. When Eli Maza had beaten Jacob with the aim of encouraging him to study the *Old Testament* with more conviction ('Sit down and learn'), Jacob returned feelings – dreamings – of 'vengeance', a word Jackie Mason uses two or three times whilst talking about his comedy.

In 1958 Jackie/Jacob was ordained as a rabbi. His father's health had been failing for some time and Jackie/Jacob endeavoured, unsuccessfully, to keep the depth of his professional comic leanings from him. In the summer of 1959 Jackie 'conquered' the Borscht Belt, then found his own apartments in New York, but he left his possessions, and the illusion of his presence, at the parental home. In the winter of 1959 father Eli died, after which Jackie locked himself in his room for a remorseful, painful week. He then moved through two brief rabbinical postings (during which he incorporated ever more humour) before taking up comedy 'fulltime'. From that point, until 1987, he strove for the degree of comedic attention and stardom which he felt was his need, due, and madness.

Jacob/Jackie deposed his father, of sorts. Placing aside the father-centred religion of his family, he took on his father at his father's secondary talent – humour; humour being the more satisfactory and 'free' preoccupation. Mason's humour toys with much the same philosophy as traditional Talmudic teaching, but does so through the self-awareness and self-improvement required, acquired and anguished over since the dawn of Darwinism. Mason's autobiography, *Jackie, Oy!* – which has at its centre his ultimate success with *The World According to Me* – contains no photograph of his father (although there is a photo taken after his death which is headed 'The entire family'), and yet the book is dedicated 'To my father'. Meanwhile Mason now supports the family financially, becoming the Father. He has never started a family of his own. He ended the first of such potential relationships at the age of 32 in favour of giving his career full attention, and there have been many lapsed romances since.

Mason, we may note, believes he is 'blessed with the ability to forget almost anything'. Such ability held him in good stead during years of professional 'failure', but his father is not forgotten – merely adopted and reworked in his own form. Freud declared, whilst dissecting an array of jokes (many Jewish) in *Jokes and Their Relationship to the Unconscious,* that jokes are releases of tension and humorists are 'displaced personalities predisposed to neurotic disorders'. Elsewhere he proposed the equally important theory of 'small differences', a reflection on the evidence that people seem to reserve much, or even most, of their dislike and tension for people similar, but *slightly at odds,* with them and their beliefs.

Jackie declares his own atheism but utilises the lines 'Thank God' and 'God Bless' frequently; his droll humorous response to the question 'Are you a Jew?' from others in his profession is '. . .*Not necessarily!*' At one point during our rendezvous in a coffee shop, he begins to sing a Jewish hymn, adopting the tones of his father and his tradition. He directs this at a woman present at the table. He wants to know whether it is 'beautiful' or 'embarrassing'. He never thinks, on stage, about whether he is desiring specifically male or female attention, but he has always enjoyed the latter in its offstage form. Accompanying Bernie Maza to 'Young Israel' dances in his youth, and seeing Bernie acquire greater attention from 'dark-eyed beauties', Jacob adopted humour as a challenge to his brother's more 'serious' success. Asked if women in general desire him for his humour or his celebrity, Mason says he often finds it hard to decide. This indeed appears to echo shifts in the attentions and concerns of his mother, perhaps even his sisters, towards him in earlier days. When he describes his mother it is of 'a nice, gentle beleaguered woman' who sometimes seems to have been concerned 'only for my happiness' (asking 'Did you eat?' or saying 'Eat now, study *later*'), whilst at *other* times concerned 'that I should please my father' and 'follow in his footsteps'. His more earthed and pragmatic parent, his mother, was '*always* trying to be the diplomat'. Mason, as noted earlier, has never married and has no offspring. Several of his jokes decry the supposedly domineering nature of Jewish wives. Bearing these ingredients in mind, it is interesting, if not amusing, to wonder whether he could ever find a woman to replace his mother; further, to ponder how his humour would grow, shift, suffer or dissolve as a result of such a satisfactory, or multi-faceted, relationship. It may be relevant to add that, 'According to paradoxical Talmudic thinking', Mason notes, 'love cannot be disclaimed *or* proven.'

Where do your politics lie now?

'I'm a very liberal, crusading Democrat. Whether times are good or bad I can't be a conservative – because that means you have no time or compassion for the underdog. Conservatives fought against every piece of funding and legislation which ever served a purpose for the poor. Help an old lady get a plate of soup in America and they think you're a communist, already.'

Have you ever had a violent temper like your father?

'He didn't have a *particularly* violent temper.'

You've said he beat you rather a lot.

'Yes – because that's what he thought he *should* do. Not so much because of a temper. Hha-h-ha!'

Do you think much about the future?

'I really don't think about the future, because I know life has no future. Even orthodox Jews leave that as an open question. In my opinion, you have a number of years on this earth and if you fantasise that it means much, you're really more nuts than I am. You're here to enjoy yourself and do the best you can. People romanticise life and invent worlds they'll never see. It merely serves to avoid life here and now. If you can help a few people along the way and have a good laugh and a good time, then *that's it*. There's nothing else but bullshit.'

What is your function?

'To entertain . . . and tease . . .'

How important are your first few minutes on stage, in terms of setting the flavour of a performance's audience-response?

'It's an almost instinctual process – like studying a person you meet on the street. You don't want to say the wrong type of things to the wrong type, or mood, of person. You sort of say "Hello, how are you" – you work out what the person's character is, what makes him smile and listen. If they're laughing right away, you go into a faster pace; if they don't laugh you say a few ingratiating things to win them over. There's no specific system – you just sense the initial mood and work on it.'

So how much pre-thought do you now give to the structure of a performance, before each evening's show?

'Practically no thought at all, because the atmosphere and environment are ultimately so predictable – you don't have to vary it much. I repace material, change odd words, but people know what they're coming for – they know me and know what they want of me. Where it used to shift was in performing solely to students, gay people, steelworkers or a convention of doctors . . . To a doctor, you have to realise, sex is just not interesting – he wants the accent on politics. But throughout the long run of *The World According to Me* it's been a similar mix of Jews and gentiles, middle-aged and young folk, men and women . . . So, before you know it, you're talking to exactly the same audience every night. Ha-h-hha.'

Do you think humour can change opinions, or does it just briefly relieve tensions? Do you believe your style of satire can change people?

'I don't think I have that much effect on people. I don't think it works as easily as that. Maybe once in a while they might be shocked into realisation of how stupid a part of their behaviour is. But if you've been like that for years, are you going to change because someone told you a joke?'

A case in point is, for example, your jokes at the expense of Jewish people's ownership of video-machines – which they can't operate. Your audiences laugh *heartily* in individual and collective recognition, but one wonders if it would change them.

'I wonder that way sometimes too. H-hh-hhha.'

Do you think broadly speaking there is an inability and lack of desire in the Jewish consciousness to change, despite a great and noble propensity for self-analysis?

'The word is *stratified*. Because they work very hard to make money, because that's the most important thing to strive for – because they always think they never had a chance and work harder for it – when Jewish people achieve wealth they always announce ''I was always working with my brain to become a doctor or businessman, I never did anything physical.'''

Make money mit your brains not your hands?

'Exactly. When they buy a video they don't have the time or patience or interest to learn how it works. It's so incidental to the success-drive, which can overwhelm everything. And I don't think they'll ever change, for the same reason that *I* don't want to be bothered fixing a car. Listen, I figure I've worked so hard that I don't *have* to fix a car! . . . H-ha-ha.'

How do you estimate how rude, or cynical, you can be towards an audience?

'How much can I attack? That's another thing I can't sum up. Particular jokes, or phrasing of jokes, pass the line between good-natured humour and insult that can be taken personally. How far can a joke go? The key is *sensitivity*.'

When you are offensive to a specific member of the audience ('Do you remember *anything*, lady? . . . I'm sure you know it's a joke – well, *not you*, but any *normal* person'), *is* he/she specific or just imaginary?

'They are specific, I see a person there. But I only pick on people whom I sense are enjoying it. Anyway, ''This is for intelligent people – not for you'', is such a preposterous thing to say, they know I'm joking. Maybe I'm just sending myself up. Sometimes, if the lights are too strong, I occasionally can't see that the seat I'm talking to is empty. I once talked to an empty seat for an hour.'

Have you ever gone on and done a show which had a completely flat reaction?

'It sometimes happens if I'm having a rough day, but it's *very* rare. Maybe once a year for me. Although, I've been put on at a bar mitzvah party where nobody's listening, with no spotlight on me and I died. Maybe everybody was so fascinated by their chopped liver they didn't notice a comic showed up. But face a theatre of seats in my direction and I always know I'll win them over.'

Yet can that audience's love, and laughter, be fickle? Have you seen the scene, in Martin Scorsese's film *The King of Comedy,* in which a woman fan suddenly shifts from affection for Jerry Lewis to telling him 'You should get cancer, already!'?

'I've got that kind of reaction *many* times, and it's almost only from Jews. Haha-ha. One moment they're saying "Do you remember me, crossing the road in the green jacket, ten years ago, and I *waved* to you?"; the next moment it's "You're full of shit, and you always *were* full of shit!" In a cafeteria in Miami Beach recently someone said "Jackie Mason? I took a picture of you 23 years ago in Brooklyn, do you remember that?" I replied "Sweetheart, why don't you have a little compassion, I meet 100 people a day." "So what?" she replied, "I meet 1,000 people a day – does that mean I forget them? *Who the hell are you?* Some big shot? Fuck *you*! My sister-in-law found you funny – I *never* did. Because you're a comedian, *so what?* Drop dead, you son of a bitch!" . . . Hahaha. What do these people want from me?'

Are there many times when you don't want to play 'the comedian'?

'Oh well, a person who's funny always is an idiot, because it means he can't identify with reality. What kind of an idiot is *always* funny? A normal person should be able to feel the significance of life on *every* level, not just see the humour. There's tragedy in life that requires commiseration, that requires awareness, concern, compassion. I'm not always funny, and *I hope to God* I never live to be so stupid that I'm always funny.'

JOHN CLEESE

Professional Logician

'"Fuck supper!", I now invariably conclude, throwing logic somewhat joyously to the four winds. And so, we thrash about on our milk-stained floor, transported by animal passion, until we sink back exhausted on to the cartons of yoghurt.'
(From the Album of the Trailer of the Sound Track of the Film of Monty Python and the Holy Grail*)*

What does one conjure up in the mind on hearing the name John Cleese? The vision of a ludicrous head-scarfed lady in a launderette discussing Jean-Paul Sartre and the karmic return of 'huge flocks of soiled budgerigars' one has previously flushed down the lavatory? A mischievous soldier with 'an outrageous French accent' on the battlements of an English castle, circa the Middle Ages, threatening those below that he will make castanets out of their testicles? Or perhaps a depressed seaside hotel proprietor verbally accosting the world (and his wife) with the sentence, 'I would find it easier to cope with some of the *cretins* we get in here, my little nest of vipers, if I received a *smidgen* of co-operation from *you*'? It is always peculiar to meet a person popularised by, and yet shrouded within, years and years of notoriety, and one *so* tall, who has made his name through creasing up audiences' bodies, is perhaps going to be very peculiar indeed. Will he be a shadow of himself, a let-down, a confusion . . . a revelation? A few days before our first meeting I had spoken to a woman who had met Cleese on a few social occasions and 'fallen in love. . . He's *very* charming,' she said. In slight contrast there are the occasional rather derogatory comments made over the years by members of his ex-comic partnership 'Monty Python', as to Cleese's 'tall ego'; of his 'fondness' for 'money', 'structure' and 'authority'.

Cleese lives in a large Victorian house in West London, and sometimes works – just around the corner – in the small, low-ceilinged, windowless cellar of an unmarked building *pretending* to be an art gallery. Cleese's secretary adheres to this pretence, which involves occasionally offering for sale one or two vastly over-priced paintings, because of the local council refusing permission for the building's function to be altered. So the person whom Steve Martin (and many others) call 'The Funniest Man in the World' works from a fake art gallery. Is this funny?

(Top) JOHN CLEESE in thoughtful but gentle mood, 1988. Photograph by Gino Sprio. (Inset) Young JOHN and father. Photograph by Mrs Cleese

The semi-private Mr Cleese, the real John Cleese, appears before me besuited, imposingly lofty, 'slightly wiped' (from too little sleep), yet hospitable and intellectually chatty and relaxed about discussing the workings of the comic mind. He carries and fondles a flexible plaything (a substitute for his childhood toy rabbit, Reggie) and is, to all intents and purposes, extremely mellow.

Brandishing his book of scripts, *The Complete Fawlty Towers*, I open up the first meeting by begging an autographic scribble therein. 'Oh, certainly,' Cleese responds. 'What do you want me to write?' I propose something he once said, which rather took my fancy – that being: 'Personally, I rather adhere to the Bergsonian idea of laughter as a social sanction against inflexible behaviour.' 'Aaaah yes,' he confirms. But when I notify him that he first made this comment not – as he's thinking – only a few years ago in an interview, but seventeen or so years ago during a period he's 'almost entirely forgotten', he looks slightly surprised. What is so beautiful about this quotation is that it first surfaced as a six-second segment within the confines (or explosions?) of a Monty Python montage which included a nude organ-playing Terry Jones, surrounded by the media with microphones, who pompously declared 'I think the nude man symbolises the essential nudity of man.' This was self-reflection, mock self-importance, nonsense, piss-taking, comic philosophy and television-subversion all rolled into one.

Cleese pauses to peruse two small press clippings I have inserted within the first autographable leaf of the book. The headline to one is 'Cleese: I'm not funny', and the other – with a caption beginning 'John Cleese reckons he's lost his sense of humour' – shows the comic in question laughing, next to some stairs, in the company of fellow 'ex-humorist' Jonathan Miller. Cleese, for reasons hard to surmise, turns on a few leaves and deposits his quotation and autograph on page eleven.

'What Henri Bergson was getting at with that idea,' he expatiates, 'is that, the moment you get into the Seven Deadly Sins you're trapped by emotion. I think most people have habitual emotion, and almost anything that happens to them they interpret in order to feel that habitual emotion. So some people, for instance, feel *permanently* put upon, and others go around feeling that life is *immensely tragic* and this makes them feel enormously important because they can look down on anyone who's happy. . . Basil Fawlty is an excellent case in point. But we *all* interpret things around us in order to feel an emotion. And that's rigidity, And *that's funny*.'

Others suggest instead that humour is specifically centred in aggression. What of Stephen Leacock's proposal that laughter began with early *homo sapiens* battering each other over the head and exclaiming 'Ah-haa!!'?

'Ah-ha! I've never heard that one,' Cleese giggles, 'But yes, there's no doubt humour is critical. I don't think you can think of many jokes – except puns – which don't have some critical quality. Bergson did say that humour requires a momentary aesthesia of the heart.

In other words, just for a moment, to laugh at someone you have to withdraw sympathy from them. And then there's the theory of the Smile being a sublimated snarl. But I must admit *that* idea makes me feel *rather uncomfortable*.'

The Bergson ideas which Cleese holds in high regard are contained in the philosopher's book *Laughter: An Essay on the Meaning of the Comic*, published in 1911. The book is a strange one indeed, postulating elasticity and adaptability as the *raison d'être* of comedy. Bergson believed, quite simply, that something or anything inelastic is funny. In the course of the book Bergson says that a puppet on a string, a hunchback and even clothes are funny because they are mechanical. The idea is that we laugh at something to criticise it, to hopefully wake it (a person at least) out of its rigidity; this is an idea which fits in neatly with Bergson's broader philosophy concerning humanity. The theory suits John Cleese because he is a man who since the 1970s has tried to escape rigid emotions, to at least blunt the edges of his passions, his fixations, his anger, in favour of a more gentle scholarly philosophical personality. A half century present on earth, does Cleese still feel anger, the anger which first fuelled his comedy towards greatness?

'I've always had most difficulties, most confusions, with that emotion,' he replies, '. . . for reasons I couldn't begin to explain – for reasons of confidentiality. I would, for example, be in a restaurant, receive a cold meal from a waiter and be *completely* unable to say something so simple, so lightly assertive, as "Oh waiter, I'm sorry, but this isn't well cooked." Instead I'd become *very* tight-lipped, *very* angry inside, I'd literally go pale and carry it with me through the day – to take it out on someone else, or the world.'

There are questions and seeming contradictions raised by Cleese's espousal of Bergson. Perhaps, firstly, it is worth considering whether someone like him, who now tries *so hard* not to be rigid, *is* being rigid. Cleese is well noted for the great lengths of time he spends on drafting and structuring his comedy with great precision, believing everything has its rightful place, but is this not rigidity? Cleese says that his Basil Fawlty is funny because of its rigidity of character, because Fawlty gets locked into emotions. But maybe another reason Fawlty is enjoyed is because audiences somehow identify with his anger and situation and relish his bad treatment of others. In a sense, Fawlty is locked in a rigid predicament (work, his wife and the world), but is let loose only when he can insult, be sarcastic and explode. Watching the *Fawlty Towers* episode 'The Germans', seeing Fawlty wave his fist in the air and howl, 'Oh thank you God! Thank you so bloody much!', do audiences laugh because Fawlty is being paranoid and rigid (as Cleese now seems to be suggesting), or rather because they know exactly how he feels?

Cleese, perchance, is a changed man? In the late 1980s he talked of 'my life being far more important now than my work' (it is interesting that he could so precisely separate the truth), and desired

'. . . no more of that work-ethic *any more*'. 'I feel more flexible . . . more relaxed,' he notes, although flexibility and relaxation do not necessarily always go well together. He espouses the middle-ground in politics and is critical of other forms. At the same time he has said he feels 'no longer funny', adding that he thinks 'the rules of comedy have changed' outside himself. He is – as quoted earlier – critical of people who take a tragic view of life, but does not explain into the bargain why he thinks such a world-view entirely illogical.

Mr Cleese smokes one (and only one) Senior Service un-tipped cigarette and lies across a settee – he is long, hospitable and relaxed. Meanwhile, I ask him why he has a reputation for being so obsessed by structure.

'The *moment* you get into anything other than a gag,' he offers, 'you have to get structure right if it's going to work, and it becomes harder and harder the longer the piece becomes. Moving from a three minute sketch to a seven to eight minutes is much harder, half an hour is very difficult, and 110 minutes is an absolute bugger. I certainly don't know how to do it yet, but I've just bought some books about the Three-Act Structure and I'm about to get to grips with them.'

How did the material for *A Fish Called Wanda* evolve?

'Very lengthily and elaborately, and I realise in a way that *does* come from a work ethic. We produced 20 to 25 drafts. It started with the idea of someone with a terrible stutter trying to impart a very important piece of information, then a steam-roller came up, a gang-boss was proposed, a girlfriend for the gang-boss, that she would perhaps have an accent . . . From sheets and sheets of ideas there was structured a framework, ideas were brought in from all directions and made to fit . . . I like to be very methodical. It's all immensely time-consuming and the whole *Wanda* project really took a good two or three years out of my life.'

You're a disciple of the Marty Feldman theory of 'Internal Logic'?

'Yes. I think I was almost there myself, but he pointed out that however crazy a sketch or whatever is, you establish certain rules at the beginning. If everybody's standing in dustbins that's fine, but then if someone appears who's not in a dustbin you have to explain *why* . . . I recall, in Chicago in 1965, going to a café where a Polish guy, for five dollars, read my palm and said that "Your logical side is as developed as your creative side!" And I think that balance was always my strength. What I lack in characterisation I make up for in "shape", by dint of spending more time on it. And I think there's a natural progression, whether you trace Pythons or Woody Allen, in moving from sketches through to movies. You get instinctively drawn to longer stories, because it's more of a challenge. I can tell you a story about the experience we had making (the "best Python skits" movie) *And Now For Something Completely Different*. We were perfectly happy with it, but the first audience laughed for 55 minutes and then, until 70 minutes, stopped laughing. So we got the sketches that didn't work and moved them earlier, and it still only worked up to 55. It knocked away all our understanding of what comedy was about. So, over an hour, you've got to *really* start getting the structure exactly right.'

Adults and teachers seem to place structure on children progressively as they grow up. People tell children not to do enjoyable, instinctual things (like painting or playing) for their own sake. Is that healthy? Is perhaps *your* 'logical humour' a result of that authority?

'I think that's a complete misunderstanding of what "art" is. That it's something that just flows out without structure or thought is a complete misunderstanding. All the best creative people are fascinated by structure. It's absolutely right that the *key* to creativity is play, but you have to frequently and consistently *stand back* from that in reflection and criticism. There was a very interesting Berkeley survey which showed that highly-creative people have an ability for play, "doing something for its own sake" as you say, but they are also the ones who can tolerate longest the anxiety of not resolving something. They achieve better solutions by being mentally equipped to stick at the problems longest.'

Which may mean they are the sort of people who in the past had *had* to stick at them longest?

'Perhaps.'

But why do you think you chose to move away from seemingly free-form, and perversely-montaged, surrealist sketches?

'It just seems more important, as an older person, to develop on from that.'

Python member Michael Palin sounded a little ominous a few years ago when he said that – apart from Terry Gilliam – all the ex-Python team members would be doing 'more conventional things' from now on.

'Did he? That's interesting. But the point is, you can do very unconventional things within a conventional framework, and – on the other hand – lots of people end up doing *incredibly corny* things within an unconventional framework. So you have to look carefully at the framework *and* the content before deciding how conventional something is.'

You wrote a brief half-page introduction to your book of old sketches, *Golden Skits of Muriel Volestrangler, F.R.H.S. and Bar,* which was concise, almost throwaway, but extremely bizarre and funny, pretending that you were a woman Wing Commander who was once 'Chaplain to the Society of Rear-Gunners Against Dadaism', having retired after being poisoned by a kipper in Glastonbury.

(Cleese laughs with the sound of a quiet vacuum-cleaner sucking on a damp cloth.) 'Ha! yes – all that *rubbish*.' (He scowls.)

Do you still take satisfaction in shooting small bits of nonsense, like that, straight from the hip on to a typewriter?

'Just for fun? Yes, but you'd be surprised how long I took to write those 200 words. Rough draft, second, third, joke changes . . . so it has a shape to it, a whole rhythm. It's nonsense, a flow of consciousness in a way, yes, but there's great structure there. And it *is* true, actually, that I was once poisoned by a bad kipper in Glastonbury.'

You chose to play a stern headmaster in the film *Clockwise* (1985, written by Michael Frayn) which structurally comprised a very long graceful build-up to the wonderful material contained within his final momentous cathartic speech, to a headteachers' convention, about a spacecraft: '. . . endlessly interrupted by late-comers and flapping doors, *l-i-f-ting* itself off the launch-pad and *s-c-r-e-a-m-i-n-g* off into the depths of the universe never to be seen again until the end of time.'

(Cleese laughs heartily again.) 'Yes, he finally lost control, dear old Stimpson,' he offers, relaxing to his full six-and-a-half foot across the settee. 'He's a man who is desperately trying to control everything in life and finally breaks loose on *the* most important day of his life. The thing I most like about that script is that it all happened in one day. In fact we even considered naming it after that *lovely* Vivien Ellis song "This Is My *Lov-e-ly* Day". '

Was the headmaster funny because of excessive rigidity, or funny because of the embarrassment and confusion caused by his release from rigidity?

'Ummmm. Hold on a minute. I'll have to think about this one.'

It still seems peculiar that, in 1973, you gave up being part of such a cohesive TV unit as Monty Python – a group which perhaps could have adjusted to anything.

'That assumption is wrong. It could adjust to very little actually!'

But you had the opportunity, thirteen shows a year, to make philosophical, subversive and yet humorous points, and have eight million people talking about them the next day.

'We did the shows, books, tours, records . . . squeezing all but two drops out of it! And, besides I think Python material was far less interesting after the first series. Anyway, *I was bored*. And since Graham Chapman [his ex-writing-partner, deceased since this interview] has talked about it, I can say that the strain of working with an alcoholic was certainly a factor . . . But the point is, extroverts feel that if they're still getting applause and money that's a good enough reason to go on doing something. But introverts feel when they're not interested anymore it's time to move on. I certainly have a great problem with boredom though – I began to realise recently that I've been bored for most of my life. In fact it's very clear to me now that what I've been doing for the last few years (*A Fish Called Wanda*, namely) is not satisfying. I know I have the skills to make films, from script right through to publicity, but I get very little out of the process – I get *terribly bored*!'

Bored *rigid*?

'Exactly.'

What does interest you, on a day to day basis?

'Well, getting to grips with my inner self, if you'll pardon the phrase, and thinking why people do things. I read a lot; books are good companions. I enjoy reading about psychology, psychiatry, history, religion.'

Do you enjoy being alone?

'I've always had the capacity to enjoy my own company. It's never bothered me. The only problem is if you're with people who don't have that capacity. Sometimes I've been on my own, drinking a glass of beer in a restaurant, having a wonderful time with a fine book, and people have come up and said "You look so low, John." Well, clearly it is *they* who have the problem, *not me*. As it happens, the very next thing I intend to do is get in a car and drive up the North West coast of America. *Entirely alone*. Maybe for six weeks. I don't want to go with *anyone* else. If I was with anyone I'd have to say, "Do you want to stop here for the night?" '

Are you travelling with the possibility, or aim, in mind that you may chance upon a future project . . . acquire some comic inspiration?

'Oh Good Lord no! Quite the opposite . . . I want to get away from all that entirely. The bottom line is that, psychologically, I really may not be able, or want, to do comedy – or much else at all – in years to come. In five years I may not have the slightest inclination. But that doesn't bother me. At least, I don't think it will.'

It perhaps should be noted here that when Cleese later took this solo trek around North West America he did take time out to appear at a Hollywood Award Ceremony and deliver an Academy acceptance speech (from a *tiny* piece of paper) which comprised uproariously funny thank-yous to 60 or 70 people – Menachem Begin and God amongst them – who had played absolutely no part in *A Fish Called Wanda*. This undoubtedly fits Bergson's theory; Cleese comically adopted the inflexible behaviour of a celebrity locked into the expectations of his industry. On a more aggressive level, it can be seen as a piece of extreme and ungrateful sarcasm, Cleese relishing the idea of accepting a prize and at the same time placing himself way beyond it. Conversely, the speech was also funny because it was childlike, a piece of flow-of-consciousness 'silly name'-dropping which could be enjoyed almost entirely for its own sake. Whatever its source – rigidity, teasing, aggression or phonetic enjoyment – it was extremely encouraging to see Cleese on such comic form after a period of solitude and Pacific air.

You were born in the latter part of 1939 (27 October) – and you seem to have a vague obsession with Hitler.

'Indeed, I've played a few Nazis and I combed my hair in *Fawlty* with the covert suggestion intended! And I remembered once, under light hypnosis, being bombed, in Weston-super-Mare. They used to bomb Bristol, but if they had any left over afterwards they'd dump them on Weston. My joke on that is "I thought Hitler had no sense of humour." But Weston was a fair place, there was quite a bit going on, being a seaside resort. I don't think I felt too bored then . . . A bit later we moved to a nice little farmhouse further into Somerset, which is where I grew up. I was an only child.'

Very middle-class?

'Archetypally lower-middle-class, not that well-off . . . My father worked hard partly to put me through private school.'

How would you describe your parents?

'My father was 46 when I was born. He didn't fight in the war – he'd done his bit in the First. He drove an Austin 10 and sold insurance. He was hard-working, perhaps shy, and somewhat reserved inside.'

Is it fair to wonder whether Fawlty was like your father?

'No, I wouldn't really say that – except perhaps for a touch of the snobbery! Although I did buy a book on Transactional Analysis after the first series, and its lists of the things people say and do, and the faces they pull, while being "parental", fit Basil very closely . . . But my father was never firm with me. He was perhaps *too* kind . . . that's certainly how I look back on him.'

What of your relationship with your mother?

'That's not something I can completely go on public record about, because she's still alive. She's living at my house at the moment, in fact!'

You've been 'through' two marriages. What do you think of the theory that it's never quite possible to find someone as loving as your mother?

(Cleese laughs hard.) 'It depends what your mother is like! I think I've often got into relationships, over my years, with versions of my mother. These patterns beckon us all. So I'm inclined to think that, if your mother was tremendously healthy, bouncy, cheerful and interesting then you should marry someone like her. But if your mother was miserable, depressed and martyred, then find a miserable, depressed and martyred girl who has possibilities!' (He laughs again, a long, sucking laugh through a practically closed mouth.) '. . . I'm more or less resigned to being attracted to a particular type, and my best chances are to find an optimistic version of it!'

Can we talk about mothers' roles in the scheme of comedy?

'Well, I understand that mother-centred families are more likely to produce neurosis, and neurosis definitely seems to be the vehicle for creativity. Research seems to show that the *healthiest* families instead have power which is equally divided between man and woman. If one parent has to be dominant, somewhat, it's supposed to be better if it's the father . . . I felt that all of the Python team came from mother-dominated families in one way or another – whether manipulative mothers or very protective ones. It seems to be the case that comedians in the main have a depressed side to their personalities, and I would assume that the major cause of depression is having a somewhat uncomfortable relationship very early with your mother.'

Other male comedians have tended to suggest to me that comedy is related somehow to uncertain feelings towards the father.

'Animosity and rebellion are certainly in there somewhere, yes. Most humorous writers tend to be left-of-centre and anti-authoritarian certainly, with Kingsley Amis being one of the few exceptions. I think if boys don't have an uncertain relationship with their father they tend therefore not to be rebellious. I mean, more and more now, I think one's attitude to authority needs to be *absolutely neutral* – you should criticise it if it's badly used and more or less approve of it if it's being exercised well, rather than be a compulsive rebel, or overly obedient or in awe of authority.'

Was your father very amusing?

'He *could* be. He would be acting very straight in a restaurant and yet throw in a droll or bizarre comment – I remember once how he couldn't get served in Torquay and so got the order speeded up by announcing he was a doctor and that he had an operation in fifteen minutes. Once he was driving mum and me down a country lane, we screeched suddenly to a halt and another driver started being very rude to him. And father just slipped into a foreign accent and said "Ahhh, you are a fine old English gentleman, no?" Ha-haa. The other guy did a double-take with his eyes and then walked back to his car.'

A person's stunned or bemused reaction seems important in comedy.

'Oh yes, very much so – it doubles or trebles the laughs.'

What was your sense of humour as a child?

'A *bit* cheeky perhaps, but I largely kept to myself.'

Did you fit in well at school?

'Not really, I was a bit of a loner, I didn't fit in or mix well especially as my height soared. I was six-foot by the time I was twelve – taller than all my teachers at (St Peter's) Prep School in fact. I don't think I was particularly happy at school. I was always an outsider. At Clifton College, at fourteen, I was approaching six-and-a-half foot, I was very gangly. In a sense I stood out like a sore thumb and was bullied a bit, but I also knew that I could make people laugh and in that way make some form of contact.'

What form did the humour take?

'It wasn't being naughty or outrageous, not squirting people with water-pistols, or firing match-stick guns. It was verbal humour really, often directed at the teachers whom actually I mostly *liked*. Stuff based, I think, on my father's humour. It was quite clever wit really, a *bit* subversive. Probably funnier than what I do now!'

What humorists did you enjoy?

'I used to listen to radio shows like *Up the Pole* at eight or nine with Dad. Television didn't make an impression on me until about fourteen – I saw *Bilko, Amos and Andy* and George Burns and various others. But the biggest impressions came from discovering the Goons on radio, and the Marx Brothers films. I don't think there was anything remarkable about my comic tastes then, but I did enjoy – although rather nervously – doing the odd stage performance at the end of term.'

What did your parents expect of you – expectations which perhaps were exacerbated by your only-child status?

'Well, they sort of gave me the impression an accountancy office would be a good place for me . . . but then I *was* good at Maths after all. I subsequently did Maths, Chemistry and Physics A-Levels at Clifton, but I *never* really knew what I was aiming for. I taught for two years afterwards, at my old prep. school, before going to Cambridge, [Downing College] to study – as it happens – Law.'

The obvious point to make here is that Python spent a lot of time mocking the 'roles' its members in a sense were reared for.

'Well, certainly it makes it easier to play people whose worlds you have inhabited, experienced early.'

Did you choose Law because it offered order of a kind?

'Ummmm . . . *Possibly*.'

A few terms into residence at Downing College, Cleese made contact with the Footlights Society, very nervously at first, then began 're-working or rather stealing' pieces of other comics' style and material. Soon he felt his extraordinary physiognomy moving across comedy stages (looking like 'a hovercraft with flapping arms'), was chosen for the Floodlights show *A Clump of Plinths* and then *Cambridge Circus*, and the rest – after a fashion – is comic history. After six years of involvement (writing or performing) with assorted revues and sketch-type television shows, Cleese became one strong sixth of a group which was to revolutionise and regenerate (at least the possibilities within) TV comedy, granting him roles as endearingly ludicrous as Mrs Beulah Premise, Ann Elk, Tim the Enchanter and The Grim Reaper, which required 'a lot of lying-down in between takes'. Quite simply Monty Python stood out 'like a shaft of gold while all around is dark', in whatever medium they chose to exercise their advanced satire and surrealism ('I mean, *be fair!* I don't eat squirrels, do I?'). An extremely lucky collaboration of determined humorists with individual tastes and literary, facial and bodily skills, who joined to become more that the sum of their parts, it is interesting to ponder exactly what – beyond their common love of laughter – was at the centre of the Pythons' working relationship. One theory to ponder is that the group embodied the fabric – and thus the range of emotions – of 'The Family Unit'; with Cleese (of course) playing introvert father-figure, Jones as romantic nurturing mother, Palin as cheery mummy's boy, Idle as cheeky loner son, Chapman as decadent son and Gilliam as, perhaps, American cousin. Within those strictures, they took on the world (from the man on the TV to the man in the corner shop) . . . and they took on each other. But then, as they acquired families of their own, their relationship waned.

Is it not interesting the way members of the Python group are still rude about each other? They've often said rather cutting things about you, and a while ago *you* quipped: 'I left them behind. I said, *I can't stand you!*'

'It's just to amuse oneself. On American TV a while back I was asked about the others and I said that three of them are dead now, and that Gilliam was in a home and had only weeks to live. The station immediately received floods of complaints about how amused I was in my time of grief . . . But it's in a tradition that people who like, and are like, each other tend to put each other down all the time.'

That's about small differences really then. It almost seems to suggest that humour contains a degree of self-criticism, self hatred almost.

'Yes, people do ''deny'' things in themselves and ''project'' them on to other people. Denial and projection enter into humour. I think people often do joke about and attack what is in them, what they fear is *almost* them.'

Is it noteworthy that at the time you were doing *Fawlty Towers* you were in the process of breaking up with Connie Booth [Cleese's first wife and *Fawlty Towers* co-writer]?

'Well . . . we wrote one show together, five when separated and six when divorced. But the working relationship was always remarkably easy . . . Let's explore this further.'

Do you *have* to feel animosity towards people you're working with?

'I don't believe it so much now, but I used to view a writing partnership as a bit of a marriage. I can remember Connie complaining that I spent more time with Graham Chapman than her – but that's true of all working relationships surely?'

I'm surprised to see you smoke, because I once heard you hid Chapman's pipe out of distaste.

'It wasn't to stop him smoking! It was just to fill in time during incredibly *boring* filming on location in the Yorkshire Moors. I was just teasing, but I've never seen anyone get *so anxious, so rapidly*. I suddenly realised that it had a symbolic value for him that I'd never even guessed at. So I swiftly said ''Here it is'' and he kneed me hard in the groin. Fortunately he marginally missed what he'd been aiming at, but it was a *very* alarming experience. And when he retold the story months later he got it completely garbled and claimed he'd chased me across the floor of a studio, rugby-tackled me and sat on my head. Which was some *very* strange public-school fantasy.'

Was perhaps Terry Jones your alter-ego in the Python team; your wife? (Jones said more recently, 'I always felt John was rather more embarrassed than the rest of us in Python by what he calls ''silliness'' . . . but I just wish he'd be silly *more often*.')

'Good lord. It's true to say Terry and I were temperamentally very different. He was everything I wasn't. I was very logical, cold, tight, and he was flamboyant, noisy, emotional . . . and Welsh. That's why we used to lock horns so much. And I think it's true to say we two cared the most about Python. But, for whatever reasons, *he* got most upset when I left TV Python in 1973. But there's also Terry Gilliam, of course – *we've* always had a rather competitive relationship. What you have to bear in mind is that in those days, the Python team never showed any mutual respect for each other at all . . . [Pause] . . . On another level, though, I do simply find names like "Terry" incredibly funny.'

Are you much happier nowadays?

'Yes, without a doubt. I had a very bad time in the 1970s – a lot of changes. I'd wanted to leave Python but didn't know what I wanted to do. And, at the end of 1974, the first marriage was going wrong – always extremely unpleasant – the end of an emotional investment that creates a very sad feeling. After that you get over some primeval fear that's symbolised within a first marriage. And when Connie and I finally split in 1976 I was depressed for a year. Not, however, "a basket-case", as the press reported. You have to remember that the popular press are so psychologically pig-ignorant that they don't understand *anything*. I was never not functioning – but at weekends I tended to sit around and just feel rather melancholic. There's a depressive side to me, which is still in there, but – largely thanks to therapy and sorting out my ideas on things – it's far more understanding now.'

You looked pretty rough in the first series of *Fawlty Towers*, compared with the second – thinner, eyes very dark . . .

'Shall I tell you what it was? It was *make-up*! An attempt to look older and more haunted, with crow's feet . . . which, for some reason, I didn't use in the second. I was terribly amused though, because after the first series I went to Weston-super-Mare and my mother said "Oh, you're looking so much better than on television!" As it happens, I found the second series (1979) a lot harder to do physically. In 1975 I could rehearse Basil for seven hours at a trot without feeling anything untoward, but between 1975 and 1979 I'd obviously relaxed considerably, because I felt incredible muscular pain after doing the same thing.' (Cleese leaps to his feet.) 'You had to get sooo tense around the shoulders, round here, and here and here in the lower back.'

Did whatever anxiety you had at that time fuel the larger-than-life monster that is Basil Fawlty?

'I should imagine so. If I was to play something like that now it would be more from *memory*.'

If neuroses date back to childhood, can I ask whether you feel more reconciled with your parents nowadays?

'Yes, yes – much more. Dad's dead, but certainly with my mother [Muriel]. I have a really good relationship with her now, better than I've ever had – and she's in her late 80s. That situation, in fact, has changed a lot recently.'

Do you still feel a pressure on you to be *always funny*?

'Well, it now feels to me onerous that I have to put on a face in public places. I do feel this big expectation to be amusing. On the other hand, if I'm somewhere I'm expected to talk seriously – about my psychology book, for instance – I go feeling totally relaxed. Most other places I feel the expectation as I move around. And the expectation normally surfaces at the times I *least* want to be funny.'

Does your track-record haunt you?

'Well, that's why I've not really done anything after *Fawlty Towers* of a similar nature. It's partly because I haven't felt like it, but also because the question raises its head, ''Can I do something better or even as funny as that?'' And the answer is, I probably can't.'

There are intriguing contradictions in John Marwood Cleese, at least (or especially) between the *recent* and *past* Cleese. He says he doesn't like working in a group situation because it gives him less power over the operation, yet for years (starting in 1973) he was involved in making videos teaching workers and middle-management how to work, co-operate and get on with customers, and politically he is a great espouser of 'balanced' collective government. He believes, he says, 'totally in compromise', that 'the idea of purity beyond which there shouldn't be compromise operates in the simply paranoid schizoid mode.' What is uncertain is whether Cleese accepts that 'good' as well as 'bad' can result from aspects of the *full* range of emotions, and – indeed – whether he even now thinks some of the humour he had been involved with in the past was simply paranoid and schizoid. He says that he 'deliberately encourages my little girl [his youngest daughter, whom he enjoys jokingly introducing as his son] not to indulge in negative emotions', yet within a chapter titled 'Parental Firmness' in his book written with his ex-therapist Robin Skynner (*Families and How To Survive Them*) he mentions times he smacked his daughter into line with the effect that she seems to love him more for it. Also, he has recently become noticeably interested in 'exploring religion' despite his humour's past condemnation and teasing of religious concepts and realities.

'Let me just say that when you get interested in religion as I have – through Gurdjieff [the Russian Teacher and philosopher] partly – you get a *completely* different view of it than in churches run like public-schools. The idea of keeping order so that the headmaster upstairs will reward you is *entirely* ludicrous, and absolutely misses what religion's about.'

When you say that you're 'interested in religion now', what does that mean?

'It means that I've had one or two experiences, which I don't want to talk about, which suggest to me there is some spiritual dimension to the universe. And I simply say that it was a surprise when I came to believe it, because at seventeen I'd given up the C of E as being too unintelligent to be of interest. Churches are pretty unintelligent – the services they give you – but within them you can find terrific people. But I'm certainly not interested in dogma – you can't verbalise religion, it's a sense of experience. To try to say ''Believe this, believe that'' is *so* insane.' (He chortles now, hard.) 'The problem with religion is that it falls into the hands of all the people it shouldn't.'

And there lies an interesting paradox?

'Oh dear, yes.'

How do you rate Laurel and Hardy?

'They're a constant joy – health-giving, really. Hardy was *so* funny. Norman Cousins, incidentally, who I did a seminar with once, claimed to have cured himself simply with Vitamin C and Laurel and Hardy!'

It's interesting perhaps that Stalin and Mussolini were immense fans of the duo.

'Are you serious? They were? *That's* interesting. It's something I never realised – rather weird really. But you would think they would touch everyone. What I think it may relate to is paranoia and projection. That if you deny something in yourself you project it unknowingly on to someone else, you see it in them. So, in effect, the *healthiest* people are those who deny the least in themselves.'

Well, it depends what they're denying!

'Ummm. The point, though, I suppose, is that it was obviously much healthier for Stalin to be watching Laurel and Hardy than what he was getting up to the rest of the time.'

Do you think people identified with Basil Fawlty? Despite being anxious, short-tempered and moody, audiences seemed to almost love him.

'Yes, and this is rather bizarre, don't you think? I've never quite worked it out.'

When do they most like Basil – when he's going completely over board?

'I would say the single moment people like the best in all shows is when he attacks the car with the branch. That seems to me a non-paranoid joke because everyone says "*I've* felt like doing that," but it's so obviously a ludicrous thing to do, to punish a vehicle. However, when people laugh at Basil abusing the German guests (in "The Germans") I'm always a bit confused. Some people interpret it as a racist laugh, but I see it very much in the opposite direction – it's aimed at Basil *I* think. Because the Germans in the programme are all below the age of responsibility for the 1940s; they're nice, polite, they behave well, like most of the Towers guests. So really, Basil is just caught in this ridiculous nonsense he's got from . . . well, "Colditz" really.' (Cleese laughs more heartily at this thought than at any other point during our meetings.) '. . . My aim wasn't to make fun of Germans, it was just about Basil being concussed. It was experimenting with him going *completely* over the top. From thereon embarrassment lies. Because I do like to go into areas of taboo and embarrassment.'

Is comedy bitter?

'Humour, I think, can be used across a wide spectrum of psychological motives, from – at one end – the nastiest type of humour, which is trying to make one feel superior to someone else, to – at the other end – humour which says "Isn't it funny what *we humans* are like," which I think is the best type of humour in the world. The latter humour increases intimacy by being less paranoid in intent. So when you look at humour you have to look at the whole spectrum – the way some jokes reinforce perceptions of an individual or group, and others are broader, healthier.'

But earlier you explained how people project their feelings back and forth. Does it really matter what the initial intent is, so long as there's a laugh at the end?

'Ummm. But, just as we cry for different reasons and the tears actually chemically taste different, depending on the emotional type, there are definitely different intents and styles of humour or laughter.'

But one joke *can* be taken a different way by two different people?

'Right. A classic example of this is a joke I heard and then told Jamie Lee Curtis. I thought it was the worst paranoid sex joke I'd ever heard – *Why do women have vaginas?* . . . Answer: *So that men will talk to them*. But it made Jamie cry tears of laughter, because she saw not that the joke was funny but that the attitude *behind it* was, that anyone who was capable of making that joke was sooo insane that it became funny. So any analysis of comedy has to be incredibly subtle. Sometimes one laughs simply because something is just so outrageous. As an example I remember when we went to record a Python show in Germany and, the moment we arrived there, were told by the people who invited us that we had five minutes to wash and brush-up before being taken to visit a German concentration camp. ''Hurry up'' they said. They drove us straight to the camp, and we felt rather breathless, we couldn't really take it. When we got there, at the gate, there was some arguing going on – and we realised it was too late to get in. Graham Chapman shouted out, *''Tell them we're Jews!''*. It's one of the funniest things I've *ever* heard, but I still can't figure out why. It was something to do with liberation from the tense embarrassment of the situation. But it's a joke which still leaves a nasty taste in the mouth.'

You once said that you couldn't understand why people laugh at 'fart and wee-wee jokes'; and that *you* don't. But Jim Davidson (the Cockney comedian) says that a fart-noise is the one thing guaranteed to make people laugh.

'You've got to bear in mind the kind of audience Jim Davidson appeals to. My mother laughs at big bosoms and arses, actually . . . and Benny Hill and that kind of humour. I suppose it's a moment's liberation from things that cause anxiety.'

Toilet-training is the very first time a child really has to perform well for its parents.

'That's interesting. But when I'm in a room with a friend and feel like farting I simply say ''Excuse me'' and then fart. The friend does not then fall around laughing, and neither do I. There's no anxiety there . . . Although I should think I'd certainly be able to sit down and *write* something I found funny on the topic of farting. Maybe about a man with a bad case in the same room as the Queen to lend it a flavour of social (adult) convention. I do find people in authority, with airs and graces, very funny. The Queen, Thatcher and lots of MPs I find incredibly funny to watch.'

People, on the other hand, sometimes laugh at words and sounds of words that have no apparent meaning at all.

'Definitely. Sometimes you laugh out of delight at the shape of words. Similarly, perhaps, I often laugh out loud at the strange things conjurers and jugglers do. From disbelief or tension you find yourself absolutely delighted. And one form of that is ingenuity of excuse.'

Ahhh. Cybil Fawlty discovering Basil in the wardrobe of a lady guest's bedroom and him saying 'Just checking the hinges'?

'Exactly. It's the smoothness of his excuse. Why would a man be in a wardrobe? . . . To check how well the doors are screwed on, of course! Haa! If Cybil had said "What *are* you doing?" and he'd taken his time over it, it wouldn't have been funny – certainly not to me.'

Have you ever felt the attitude of not *caring* whether people laugh at a joke of yours? Python often exuded that flavour of rebelliousness.

'Well, sometimes you get your tail up and think "To hell with it, or them. We'll do it anyway!" It's good that that happens every so often, because you shouldn't *crave* laughter. There are, of course, lame jokes and also those that can be thrown away or slipped through, and as a comedian you learn how to put certain jokes on the off-beat. I agree you must have *some* cockiness, but posturing can go too far – into self-righteousness. If you really want to persuade someone to your point of view, it's not very effective to over-confront that person.'

W.C. Fields set out once to make a blind man funny.

'And succeeded! By making the blind man a threat – he was built up very cleverly over 20 minutes so that audiences perceived him as a threat to Fields' property and person. Fields' character, of course, was completely paranoid – he hated everybody – animals and small children were only the beginning of it. And in real life I think Fields was probably a very strange, very paranoid man.'

What does being rich mean?

'Last week in New York [flushed with the success of *Wanda*] I bought champagne three times, which I'd *never* done before. I thought, at my age, with a movie on my hands which is a genuine success, I'm *bloody well* entitled to it. And I rather enjoyed those three bottles. But I'll tell you my attitude towards profession . . . I mean, possession . . .' (Cleese then unfolds a long graceful parable about Gurdjieff testing the altruistic sincerity of his house-guests, and he summarises:) 'In other words, it's OK to have possessions if they don't matter too much.'

Graham Chapman was once asked what he'd do if he won a million pounds at Bingo, and he said 'I'd give it to John Cleese so he wouldn't have to work tomorrow'. How close to the truth of your acquisitive desires is that?

'Well, it isn't anymore. I only have one question for my accountant – "Do I have to work?" But there's a petit bourgeois part of me which is very cautious. I've never paid a tax man late . . . I think there was only one time in my life when I was short of money. I told a marvellous guy, a health instructor, that if he ever wanted to open up his own health club I'd put money into it. He set up the place very quickly, in Brighton, but three months later he was dead, from cancer. I lost a lot of money, and the degree of anxiety that provoked was almost continual for a year.'

What's your recipe now for a happy life?

'I think it has to involve a fair degree of self-discipline, but without self-righteousness. It involves acquiring or developing inner-security, and security within the world, which makes one less envious and paranoid. One of the characteristics of exceptionally healthy people, and this has been proven by research, is that they have a remarkable ability to tolerate ambivalent feelings; they can take criticism and don't feel the need to control other people. That involves compromise. Many people believe determination and clarity and definition of good and bad are a sign of health in a person; but *I* don't. I think they're a sign of weakness.'

Yet those ingredients are there, presumably, to protect us as individuals.

'Nevertheless, on any form of spiritual quest we *surely* have to strip them away. Because egotistical emotions send us down tunnels where we have no flexibility at all. But at least when I hear laughter I can believe that something other than pure egotism and inflexibility is at play.'

Is there any topic you wouldn't now make a joke about?

'Well, I have two or three friends who I could make jokes to about anything, including cancer. I have one friend who has cancer, and I tease her and she loves it. She feels that I don't think she's going to die, and it makes her feel better. But do you remember the jokes the morning after the shuttle disaster – *What does NASA stand for? . . . Need Another Seven Astronauts* – I still couldn't do anything like that *in public*. Jokes can be misconstrued. But I would certainly hope that, in an ideal world, there wouldn't be *any* topic you couldn't construct a joke around.'

But maybe in an ideal world there wouldn't *have* to be jokes?

'Oh good lord . . . I hope not.'

EMO PHILIPS

A Good Wheeze

Comedy is a trough.
And all of us pigs can have a sip.

'I don't really remember my dreams as a teenager, although I remember washing the sheets afterwards. I got teased a lot. All the kids shouted abuse into our garden, like "neo-Calvinist!", and I'd chase after them. But they'd always escape, because the chain would *snap* my neck back.'

Emo is standing in the corridor of an underground train, bemusing passengers (cub-scouts, builders and old folk) by undertaking strenuous, face-contorting pull-ups on two of the hanging handles which commuters normally utilise to remain steady. He continues conversing while exercising. 'In high school sex was all I thought about. You know, you're never satisfied with your appearance . . . Once I saw this real *hot* mama and followed her down the street, trying to think of something to say. After a few blocks she turned around and bawled "Get away from me or I'll scream!" I replied, "Listen baby, you've got a pretty big ego thinking people are following you just because they are heading in the same direction." . . . Then I turned around and walked *right* out of her house.'

Emo Philips, a comic who has been described as some sort of bastard offspring of Peter Pan, a plucked chicken and a question-mark, as well as 'a Protestant Woody Allen', is always 'On' (playing the jester). Almost always. One or two sentences, often just two-thirds, comprise the normal threshold after which he sees fit to unleash another surrealist metaphor, absurdist aphorism, epileptic twist of logic, ludicrous homonym, cheap or expensive pun or unsentimental tale of semi-imaginary personal misfortune.

'See, they all look at me,' he announces, during our three-hour, 207-joke stroll around London, part of the time lugging the bag and baggage which accompany Philips on his 48-weeks-a-year 'comedy trail'. He is a thin, 140lb, doe-eyed, slouched, six-foot-two-inches travelling man bedecked permanently in mis-fitting vaudevillian-like clothes and sporting a self-cut pageboy mop of hair (in the last year or two white hairs of severe adulthood have begun to flourish, yet it seems to matter not a jot). On stage his contortions become more pronounced, he brushes his hand more regularly through his hair,

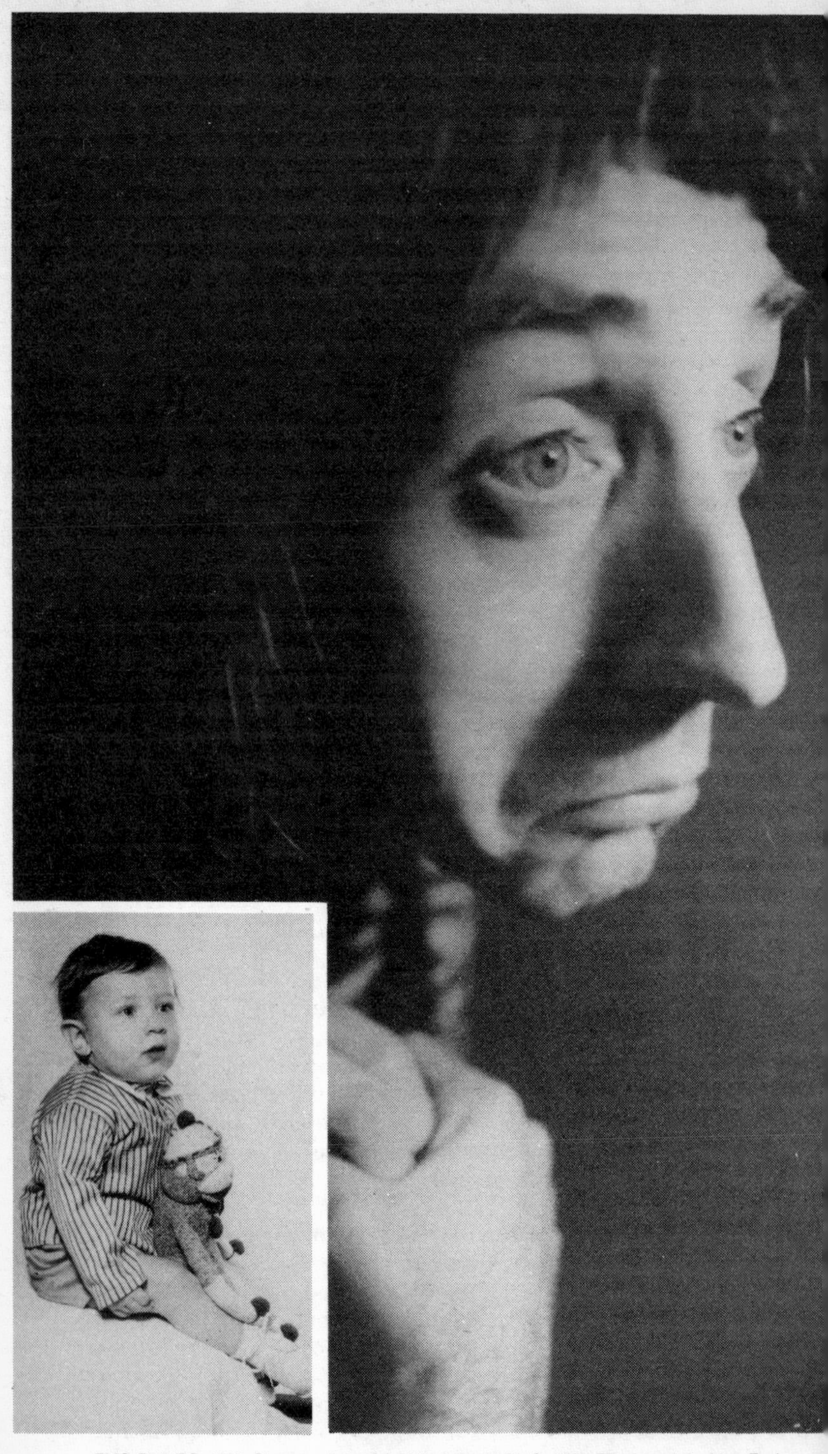

EMO PHILIPS, 1989. Photograph by John Hind. (Inset) EMO, 1958. Photograph by Vera Zool he spins his arms from the elbow, he tucks his shirt into his trousers like a wide-eyed pre-adolescent and occasionally exposes his markedly concave chest. The latter is part and parcel of his chest ailments, of his asthma, the sound of which surfaces in between his sentences, adding a mildly exasperated or bemused inflection to his bizarre jokes. 'I was a sickly child' he says, 'Everybody got sick of me.' Thanks both to his name (he was christened in memory of a Finnish friend of his parents) and his wheeze, Emo received more than his fair share of 'constant teasing' during school-days; but he actually says he liked such attention, that 'it taught me to take a punch'. This said, he coughs.

Emo was born in the city of Chicago in 1956. He moved to the suburbs of Downers Grove (which has 'no apostrophe, and no public rest-rooms either') at ten years of age. His joke on this topic is: 'When I was ten my parents moved to Downers Grove; when I was twelve I found them.' He describes Downers Grove as 'old and new' in style; 'very conservative' in attitude. 'You know Grant Wood's *American Gothic*, the famous painting of the pitchfork-wielding farmer standing impassively next to his equally deadpan wife?' he considers, 'Well, people in Downers Grove think they're *Hippies*.' His family surroundings (very female – sisters, mother, grandmother and all) never travelled beyond the small-town Mid-Western environment after 1966, which is somewhat at odds with the perpetual travel which the 'adult' Emo feels is his professional 'calling', stages, hotels and streets being his homes now. 'I don't know where I'll be from one minute to the next,' he says.

The humour Emo perpetually creates, as an on-stage comedian and off-stage acquaintance, combines the light homely details of small-town existence with cerebral, sexual and often macabre imaginations – it is flow-of-consciousness writing which has then been fine tuned. It often borrows the self-deprecating/self-pitying flavour of Borscht Belt comedians who make frequent references to their sad childhood, like Rodney Dangerfield, but it is more concerned with the profoundly ridiculous, with nonsense and twists in sense. 'Something caught my eye,' Emo says, adding, '. . . and dragged it fifteen yards.' His jokes often begin by begging sympathy for his supposedly sad, repressed or imprisoned upbringing. ('My parents brought me up with the three magic words, total sensory deprivation'), and veer precariously into the morbid, but Emo denies in reality that his parents were much less than 'decent baptist folk' (adding later that he is still a believer).

Is your mother Anne amused by and supportive of what you do?

'She's like an older sister to me,' (Long pause.) 'Although we've never had sex.'

You've described your mother as 'a Stan Laurel type', 'chubby', and 'a giggler'. She's an amusing, cheerful woman?

'Oh, she's smashing' Emo notes, leaving a slightly asthmatic pause before adding, ' . . . smashing all my things while I'm gone. My mother is the nicest woman on earth . . . since the sex-change operation. But, I'll tell you – it's not easy being 33 and still living at home, my friend. The other day I caught mom snooping through my socks and underwear . . . and it tickled . . . But mom's fun, she's carefree.'

Was your father fun?

'He had a temper, he got wound up. He'd yell and scream and my mom would laugh at him being that way. That only got him more that way. But he was a fine man.'

Was he a joker himself?

'Sure, he had a sense of humour . . . Often, as punishment, he would bury me in the backyard. Only up to my waist, mind. But you still got dizzy with all that blood running to your skull.'

How do you take the idea that most male comics are at odds with their father and in love with their mother?

'Well, it was always the family dog that I was after . . . It's an old-fashioned family I come from. When I'm home we sit around each night, picking lice from each other's hair. A close-knit family . . . mainly leaning towards the polyester fabrics. I have a couple of sisters, Kiki and Susan.'

You've described your father, who worked in the post office's 'dead-letter department', as having the manner of Moe Howard of The Three Stooges, with a touch of Robert Mitchum. What were his expectations of you, *seriously*?

'Seriously? He never thought I would amount to much. He wanted me to go into accounting. But I had a hard time with Mathematics. In fact it's my lack of Maths ability which kept me from being a nerd . . . But my dad's a *cool* guy . . . he's kind of *laid back now*.'

Emo slides in the last two comments in an understated manner. They only evolve into jokes – and very black ones at that – on realisation that his father, Walter Philips, died in 1978 (a while after Emo started on 'the comedy trail'). It is at this point that one wonders whether it is Emo's humour that has morbid undertones, or his morbidity that has humorous overtones. He has *numerous* jokes which involve garish violence, death and morgues; a fair share of them tinged with sexual undertones. He tells me one about working as a morgue-assistant which I will not repeat here for fear of prosecution. It is part and parcel of what Emo does to flick back and forth, or lay a balance, between life and death instincts.

Do you really remember your childhood days?

'I have amnesia, I don't remember too far back. I used to play on the train-tracks, I played Army . . . Hmmm . . . Once we combined the two . . .' Emo pauses at length, then admits with a light frown that within his normal time-scale he has been unable to conjure up a joke combining armed forces and railway lines. He wheezes lightly and he is *fairly* serious now. 'I always got into trouble when I was a boy, that's all I remember. I remember getting into trouble with small-minded authority figures.'

Was there a morality to your trouble-causing, or were you doing it to make a point?

'Well, perhaps unconsciously, but I wasn't thinking of that at the time . . . Actually, I don't think there was *any* moral anything. I wasn't *trying* to get into trouble; it's just that the powers that be took everything I said the wrong way. At school once a teacher said, "Emo, if you could be an animal, what would it be?", and I replied "I'd like to be a 75-foot tape-worm in your colon." So I was always getting castigated by the school principal, or getting beaten up by other students. They were jealous I think, they saw me as the next stage of evolution. But they're small-minded individuals, John. And today I'm here, and they're . . . well, back in America probably – unless they're on vacation here. But *they* had to pay for it, *that's* my point.'

Were there people you developed your sense of humour with at school?

'You mean *chums*? Not really. I'm pretty much a loner and always have been. I like to keep my relationships nice and shallow.'

But who did you *play off* as a humorist?

'You've heard of people having an imaginary friend. Well, I was this other kid's imaginary friend . . . But I never hung out on the street corner – I was never one of those guys. I was gregarious, but introverted. I used to just stay in my room, and I read the great classics of literature – like Charles Dickens, Rabelais, Nietzsche. I like books. Nietzsche said "That which doesn't kill me makes me stronger." And I followed that for a while, but then I learnt his brain had been eaten up by syphilis. There's an old joke – a tramp came up to me on the street and said "I haven't had a bite in three days" . . . so I bit him. If that had been Nietzsche's joke he would have finished with the line, "Well, you're inferior and deserve to starve."'

Are you opposed to intellectualism and philosophy?

'Ummmmm. I took a debating course in college and from it I learnt that the more you study an issue the more you realise the two controversial sides have almost equally valid views, and you're left totally on the fence. I realised that you could achieve that exact same result through maintaining total ignorance. And then you have all that extra time to play Pac-Man.'

Or tell jokes?

'Yes. Go forth and multiply! . . . Actually, I wouldn't recommend that path to everyone. The last thing I need is more competition. There's *no* security in comedy.'

Did you enjoy college?

'Not really; I dropped out. I never thought it was for me. And once you have show-business in your blood . . . well, y'know, it makes your arms real lumpy.'

What humour did you most admire during your late teens?

'Well, when I was about 18, *Monty Python* was showing on American television and I took to it with open arms. For me intellectual British humour was an inspiration. That for me has been the epitome of comedy – to be able to make people think but also laugh. So, right now *I* make people *think* they laugh. But some day I'll get it right.'

Is the finest comedy perhaps a blend of the childish and the intellectual or profound?

'It's a *bland* of that.'

Where do you fit on the graph?

'I think I'm off, outside the Venn Diagram.'

In what direction

'I don't really like to analyse myself, to be honest. I'll leave that to the urologist . . . I just get on stage and try to amuse people for an hour. *What can you do?* You give it your best shot . . . as the doctor said after I came down with that disease.' (Coughs.)

Do you get ill often?

'I'm always picking up something. My pockets are usually stretched out of shape. But you can't let that stop you doing what you want to do, to keep moving.'

'Whenever I walked down the street, people would laugh at me. I was about to buy a machine-gun and kill them . . . which is legal in America, by the way.'

Does everybody own a gun in America?

'Now, now . . . people abroad think it's real easy to buy a hand-gun in America; it's just not true. You have to put tons of coins in those vending machines.'

What happened on the way to the vending machine?

'I saw a comedy club or bar in Chicago – it was 1976. And suddenly the clouds parted, and the sun came out, and I realised there and then a life on the stage would be the life for *me* . . . *hi-diddley-dee*.'

Emo's very first on-stage joke, performed live and unpaid, toyed with and twisted the notion of his childhood medical condition: 'I had an asthma attack on the way over here. Three asthmatics jumped me. I know, I know . . . I should have heard them hiding.'

Did the audiences soon take to you?

'The first couple of years didn't go too well, because I was facing the wrong way. Then it hit me – "I'm not creating the right atmosphere for comedy." So I started pumping nitrous-oxide through the air-vents. And from that point on, it's been . . . well . . . several more years.'

Did you climb on stage with confidence?

'Well, I thought that if I could make just one person smile then I'll have already, you know, surpassed network TV sitcom standards. But it took a while for me to get *hot*. It was a few years before I started to get consistent laughs . . . It was rough going, but I never minded. It wasn't easy, but I kept my nose to the grindstone and . . . I'm glad to say it saved me thousands of dollars on a rhinoplasty operation. *What can I say?* Show-business has been pretty good to me. Comedy is my woman. It was rough but I stuck with it. And even if I didn't have any money I didn't mind. I still wouldn't mind. I'll stick with it as long as I get fed free. A bed, some scenery, some girls passing by, a little to eat. I'm sure I'd work for ten bucks a week at the Monaco Hilton.'

You made it big in the clubs in the early 1980s, now it's theatres. What's the most interesting audience reaction you've had during your epic journey?

'At the Apollo in Harlem they go ''woof!'' in between jokes. I quite liked that.'

How important are roots to a comedian?

'Well, you try and sever them as quickly as possible, and move on. Because if you're rooted in a small-town mentality it gives you a parochial vision. You want to stretch, be a citizen of the world, a *demi-monde.* A comedian has to be a citizen of the galaxy, don't you think? Of course, no one pays you to stay at home. So I'm on the road about 94 metric weeks out of the year. I'm *always* travelling.'

Do you enjoy travelling?

'Oh yes . . . Of course, if I had a wife and child at home I suppose I would *really* enjoy it.'

(Later Emo asked 'Did I really say that stuff about ''parochial vision''? I must have been possessed . . . That doesn't sound like me.')

The hotel room you moved into today was about two metres by one and a half.

'I don't need much space, for reading or sleeping. And I walk a lot. I keep a room back at my mother's home and luggage in my manager's office on Broadway. He's useful in that respect, I grant him. My agent brings offers to my manager and charges ten percent and my manager brings those offers to me, and charges another 20 percent. So the manager is pretty much like, well . . . an extremely expensive phone-jack.'

What are the contents of your travelling bags?

'You know, just underwear. You find a lot of it as you walk around . . .' Emo coughs croakily for a few seconds. '. . . Socks, fruit. Have an apple. I always carry a lot of fruit.'

How much would your possessions be worth if you threw them all together in a pile?

'I think they *are* all thrown in a pile . . . To me money is not important. This whole fame thing – the money, the celebrity, the drugs, the worship – I've never wanted any of that. Just give me some cole-slaw, John, and that woman over there in the Nazi outfit, and I'll be happy.'

One of Emo's stage reflections is that he is 'quite handy with the ladies'. He clearly enjoys, indeed encourages, the attention and conversation of autograph-hunters and others surprised by his colourful bedraggled presence in the street. Serious attention he reserves for females most resembling cheer-leaders. He ogles and salivates lasciviously in female company, pronounces 'you're a saucy little bag of oestrogen', blows his nose, beckons she sit on his knee, and at once he is a compassionate older brother, a cheeky son and an eccentric jester and a lover all rolled into one. 'Oh boy, this career's paid for itself,' he will say, 'Ohh, I'm so horny. You smell sooo nice . . . for a woman.' In an untelevised (shelved) interview with American TV sex-therapist Dr Ruth, Emo once pondered 'I don't know if I have sexual magnetism or animal magnetism. Though sometimes I'll find a squirrel stuck to my forehead.'

How do you get into rhythm before going on stage?

'I use one of those ticking metronomes that organs come with. I set it on Conga Beat. But on-stage the rhythm depends on the audience. If you do a show in a theatre to 1,200 people, with a lot of them laughing straight away, you're able to relax. But do a show for 30 people in Vegas who've just lost their life-savings and you can slide through an hour's material in eleven minutes. Sex and comedy are a lot alike . . . because you become one with the audience; you move in and out with each other. It depends on them as much as you. Plus . . . it's just as hard to clean up afterwards. Do you have a handkerchief?'

Is it women that you're really performing to, and *for*?

'Now you've caught my secret. The purpose of my act is actually to find Woman. That's why I dress in these form-fitting outfits. I'm a tease. And women sense my sensitivity.'

The New York journal *Village Voice* once announced that your proportions and demeanour suggest 'a long limp penis'.

'Indeed. And I sent the writer a letter thanking her for a quote I could use to help sell-out every time I play Greenwich Village.'

Do you have a large gay following?

'I *once* had a large gay following. But I ducked into an alleyway and lost him.'

Is humour an aphrodisiac?

'Well, *mine* always seems to go *down* when a lady laughs at it. But at least I've started going out with girls who are conscious. And guess what, I've ventured into the mammal family – so that's good for my sex-life. Because then you can procreate at lower temperatures. Women? Ummm. A naked woman means almost as much to me as a good pun.'

Do you think you understand women?

'Oh yes, I know how to talk to a woman. I'll say, "I wouldn't mind swapping lice with you, hot mama." Recently I kissed a girl. The next day I called her up to complain. I said "You gave me a sore on my lip." She said "Put something on it". I replied "O.K. – ten bucks says it was you." '

Seriously . . .

'This is all serious.'

Emo sees two American women walking in his direction. They do not stop to speak this time. 'Oh dear,' he exclaims, 'I'm beginning to misread my groupies.'

You obviously relish sending people away with autographed messages ('Thanks for being my one friend', 'To Jenny, thanks for the exploding suppositories'); do you receive much celebrity mail?

'I've got at least five or six fans in every city of America whom I call real *Emo-philiacs*. And they write me over and over, and I return letters over and over. I think they look on me as a role-model.'

Is the role you play, or rather the person you are, a pessimist or an optimist?

'I'm not a fatalist. And even if I was . . . what could I do about it?' He shrugs. '. . . *Nothing*. Listen, I'm an optimist in a fatal world. Emo goes through the crucible and comes out stronger.'

What's your favourite Laurel and Hardy film?

'Phoooo. Now we're talking.' (Sniffle) 'That would probably be *A Perfect Day*, the one in which they're constantly departing, forever saying "Bye!" but never get *anywhere*.'

You've been climbing the tree of comedy for the thick end of thirteen years now, Emo.

'Yes. I'm near the top of the sludge-pile of humour. And it's been a wonderful thirteen years in the business. Although it seems more like a decade and a third. I'm at the apex, the pea-knuckle[?], of my comic career.'

Does Beverly Hills beckon?

'I wouldn't mind. I love the beach . . . I love the sound of the crashing surfers against the rocks . . . I tried body-surfing recently. I was on the beach and I thought, you know, "How often is it you find a stiff washed-up corpse?"'

What offers wouldn't you accept as a working comedian?

'Oh gee. American TV shows like *Star Search*, in which you have two contestants, two singers, two comedians, two spokes-models and three judges who vote on how you go over. I hate all that cheapening. I won't be degraded. You can't do comedy in two minutes, anyway – it's impossible. But give me a show called *Stud Search* and the time-limit would greatly work in my favour . . . There's a cable programme called *Diving for Excrement* – I turned *that* down.'

What would your cushion be if you were suddenly to stoop into comic obscurity?

'Phoooo. It's a very good question. I'll have to start being nice to people. There's a saying that goes "Be nice to people on the way up because you meet the same people on the way down." Although, in America, most of them probably change coasts – so that helps some . . . Let me just engage these Japanese girls in conversation. *Sianara! Bonjour!*'

Is the way you joke in the streets *now* similar to your escapades as a child?

'Well, I have the advantage now that people come up to *me*.' (He crescendoes.) 'Because it's the fans that make you a star, a great force to be reckoned with . . .' He pauses for a cough and a waft of a handkerchief around the infamous, glorious Philips nose. 'As Adolf Hitler once said.'

Do you produce stage material through conversational encounters and thoughts in the streets, or do you sit down and work out material?

'I jot down lines on napkins, tickets, scraps of paper as I move around. Whenever I sit down to write I usually come out with nothing but haemorrhoid humour. So I stroll around. Things hit you from different angles. Then you regain consciousness . . . It's the weirdest thing – writing comedy. You just can't predict it. It's like having a chest cold.' *Cough*. 'Sometimes you'll be trying really hard to get it up, but it doesn't come. Then one night you'll be at a party talking to a girl, and suddenly a whole bucket will come up. That said, the key to finding humour, I think, is to turn something upside down . . . Like a small child.'

In the time since you surfaced as 'a national cult comic' in 1986 your stage material seems to have developed towards telling longer stories, making you more than just a purveyor of one-liners.

'Because then all you need is one good joke at the end! Regular comedy means you do a good joke every 22 seconds. Whereas someone like Mark Twain went on for an hour, had one joke at the end, and people said "Oh, he was just *leading up to it*. Isn't it clever how he did that?" Someone once said that "a humorist" is a comedian who scratches his head before every joke. And for a while I subscribed to that idea. But then the subscription ran out, and I couldn't get the student rate anymore.'

How much *do* you theorise comedy?

'I always try to look at and analyse it from a mechanical point of view. Different words can make jokes come over better. Words with a "K" sound in them are funny – like "Cancer". Well, that's not too good an example. Changing words around can make a difference. Then there's the one, two, *three* approach. Like "A Scotsman, an Englishman and an Irishman" . . . You always know there's three parts, so during the second you can go to the bathroom, take a short shower. *My* method is the twist, although each joke can evolve, word by word, over a year of shows into something entirely different and funnier.'

Have you ever delved into the books of comic theorists?

'I tried reading Sigmund Freud. All he does is list a bunch of Jewish jokes which used to be funny in German. He has one cute joke – "There's no place like home for the Alcoholidays." Is this funny? I tried reading Henri Bergson's *Laughter* once. He tried to explain why a black man or someone with a big nose is funny. Well, you laugh at a black man nowadays and you'll get a big nose! . . . So I don't follow any of those books. You learn humour *in the streets*. Because as soon as you've stepped on some dog excreta – it really helps you look at life in a humorous way.'

You once said that all comedians seemed to want to reach a point where they *don't* have to be funny.

'Well, I didn't say *I* wanted to. My point is, it seems as soon as a comic gets successful he adopts some charity, like a disease, and goes on chat-shows and becomes very serious. As soon as they get rich and middle-aged they say, "I'm going to die fairly soon, I think I'll sponsor a charity so God will like me." And God is saying, "How come this guy isn't funny anymore? I don't want him in heaven with me!" Would *you*? If you had to spend an eternity with someone, would it be a person who renounces all pleasure, all humour?'

Do you think God's pretty keen on laughter?

'I think he has a sense of humour . . . Otherwise, ummm-mm . . . well, why would he have given us George Bush?'

Does your religious upbringing still stand fairly firm in you?

'I *was* very religious as a kid. I was brought up a strict Baptist . . . But now every night I pray an ecumenical prayer, a prayer that I think speaks to the heart of every religion, no matter what your faith. It goes, "Lord, please break the laws of the universe for my convenience. Amen." '

Do you believe there is humour that is universal or humour that never wears off?

(Long pause.) '. . . If you've ever shaken hands with someone wearing those ink-stained gloves. *That* practical joke doesn't rub off for days. But, certainly, I'd like my comedy to be universal. Male, female, old, young, animal, vegetable, alive, dead . . . I just want to be funny *per se.* I don't try to be too heavy-handed in what I say. All I'm telling people, really, is – you know – "Wake up and smell the coffin." '

Is it too twisted to propose Emo is dispatching jokes to his father?

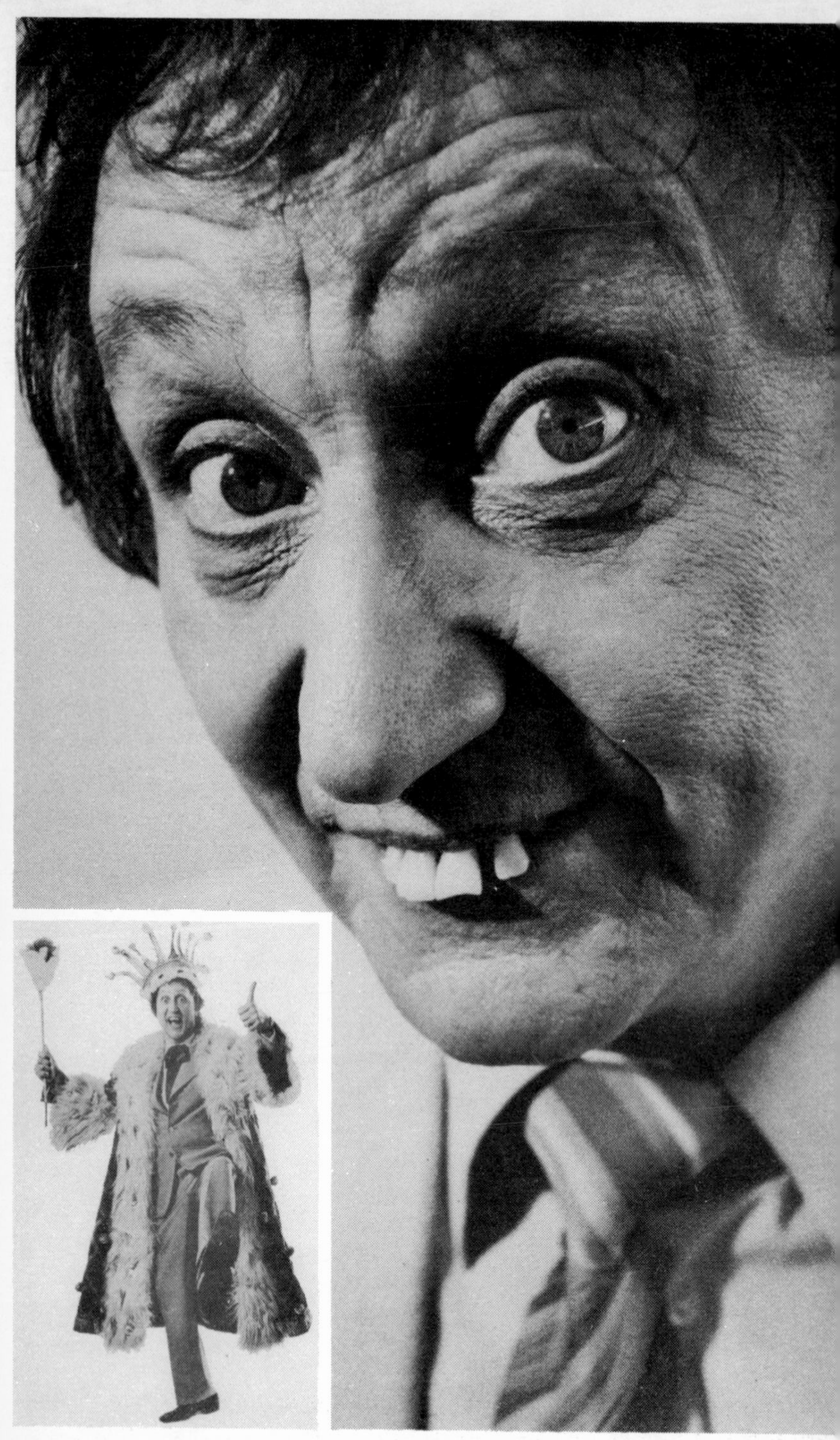

KEN DODD: '*Building a comic map of the mind*' Photograph by Steve Double (Inset) DODD in party mood
Photograph courtesy of George Barton

KEN DODD

Overwhelmed

I thank the lord that I've been blessed;
with more than my share of 'appiness.

By Jove missus, what a lovely day for . . . perhaps, tip-toeing up to Ken Dodd, OBE, tapping him thrice firmly on the cranium with a blooded pig's bladder on a stick, and bellowing – in a whimsical but determined voice – 'Kenneth, Kenneth . . . Can humour save the world?'

'Oh crikey' exclaims Dodd, 'Humour is a wonderful gift bestowed on us by our creator! . . . Because we've got to admit we were created.'

Can you elaborate?

'Our creator gave us this wonderful safety-valve for when we're frustrated. Humour, you see, is a beautiful balm to a hurt, stressed mind – to a psyche that has been battered and bruised, because sometimes *only* laughing at your troubles can save you. Humour's a tremendous relief from assorted repressions and ideal for occasions when you feel like murdering someone. Laughter, I think, is probably a more potent weapon, and certainly a healthier one, than violence.'

Dodd has read the Bible, obviously, but he had also perused and pondered on all the major works 'on comedy'. An almost fanatically obsessed humorist, Dodd is, at home, a serious scholar who has researched with a vengeance, and collected avid notebooks on, 'all there is to know' about 'das Komische', 'witzig', wit, humour, harlequinade, quiddity, quips, cracks, japes, jests, 'jokey-poohs' and the working of 'the chuckle muscle'.

'The more you go into this wonderful adventure' he says, still wide-eyed with enthusiasm despite his perennial research, '. . . the more you seek and find reasons in the human mind for what appear on the surface to be fancies, flipperies and little pieces of nonsense, the more you realise that the human mind is such an unbelievably complex instrument, sometimes it *completely* overwhelms you. It overwhelms you with the sheer immenseness of trying to build a comic map of the mind.'

The outward manifestations of that comic mind, at least on stage, are almost continual salvoes of jokes (up to ten a minute) and the extraordinary appearance, movements and expressions of Dodd's face and arms. His teeth, 'Thank God', are insured (or are they really?). This facial opening – the source of his barrages – contains what can only, in comic terms, be described as dental perfection, protruding as the result of a bitterly painful, but fortunate, dare-turned-bicycle-accident when he was only knee-high to a surrealist. 'I cried for days,' he remembers. Dodd is now into his 60s; at times he certainly looks it, but to all effects it seems as if ageing does not mean a jot to him. He still has at least half the spirit of a child, and despite assorted adult concerns and the learned way he records and analyses his jokes, he makes every effort to hone his life down to the bare essentials of structure so that the comic in him will daily prevail. He once told *Woman's Realm* magazine, of all people, 'Rigidity – it's death! . . . That's why I'm unpunctual.' His unpunctuality is certainly an escape from and a challenge to rigidity, but there also seem to be other reasons for this behaviour. Perhaps Dodd is tempting fate, relishing the adrenalin of perpetually arriving late; or maybe he can't bear to be at a theatre early because that in itself is worrying. Or *maybe* this lifestyle is his way of saying that the show can't go on without him – that *he* is the laughter-bringer around whom the world revolves merrily. This is because, however late he is, he can still seduce every weary soul in his presence. Notoriously late for appointments, rehearsals and performances, Dodd is nevertheless a journey-man comic – travelling 50–75,000 miles a year – who takes no holidays and works theatres day in, day out, as if his life depends on it. (His dramatic court case concerning tax in 1989 was the first time he cut off performances for a decade. Since then he has worked again constantly, save for a curious sojourn in Africa.) Living on the edge of his wits he evades illness, 'makes the theatre' by a hair's breadth, never fails to rouse an audience to its peak, and speeds along on a thirst for laughter which certainly exists in his public but which really is a craving emanating from the centre of his own soul.

'I'm a creature of excess' Dodd announces, rather proudly. He is speaking at eight minutes past two in the morning during a heady phone-call from his home in Liverpool, 'I try to put a quart into a pint pot and make every day last 28 hours.' Tonight, he explains, he'll be getting to bed 'around 3am, or 4am' and that a television film-crew are expecting to interview him in Nottingham (140 miles away) at around llam. It's more than possible he'll be a *little* late. Thereafter, come 3pm he is due to take the stage for a matinee performance.

Do you ever get . . .

'knackered?'

. . . Too tired to be funny?

'Oh no, no, no. Because once you hear your ''Five minutes, Mr Dodd'', you become a different person. It's like a horse at a starting gate. I was stage-struck in 1954 and I still am now . . .

perhaps more so. Once a ham, luckily, always a ham. You see, I just *can't* do without it.'

They call Ken Dodd 'The Comedian's Comedian', although who 'they' are and what 'The Comedian's Comedian' means is not clearly defined. Certainly he is a fine stand-up and perhaps the last of the Music Hall Greats. *Certainly* he is instantly amusing or entertaining to meet. Kneeling on the floor of his dressing-room in Shepherd's Bush, London, 20 minutes before literally storming on to television to uplift an otherwise lightweight chat-show, Dodd looks very funny indeed. His hair is combed into unusually straight clusters. He is wearing old brown trousers, a white vest and lashings of foundation cream, and is kneeling over a cue-card on which he is compiling, on the spot, the vague structure (which later he barely adheres to) of another 'show-stopping performance'. He was very late arriving at the studio, of course, and a nervous young BBC researcher is wanting to talk at least a few things over in advance (he never gets to) and is huffing nervously at colleagues in the corridor outdoor. Dodd has brought his pet poodle, Boodle, and it is making an almighty racket. Dodd explains that someone will have to look after Boodle when he is 'on'. By 'on' he means on television, for – in a sense – Dodd is always 'on' (playing the jester), at least in any outsider's or acquaintance's company. Show-time is in just three minutes. He has now donned a suit, one which – intentionally or otherwise – manages to satirise show-business joviality inside out. He clears his throat, something he does a lot – even mid-sentence or mid-joke – and it sounds remarkably like laughter – *Hha-h-hha*. His coughs are as semi-consciously inspired, and as perfectly timed, as his banter. 'Show-time!' Dodd makes a nervous smile as he walks out of the dressing room and to the studio floor. His make-up cannot hide the wear and tear of three and a half decades of comedy; his face has thick creases, not all laughter-lines. He admits to being self-conscious about his facial profile, but his side-on teeth, 'hooter' and lager-jowl ('I have a liking for lager . . . it's very important after the show') suggest that there is no place for aesthetically-minded plastic surgery in show-business. 'You have to admit,' he says again, 'you really have to admit . . . that the world is sometimes all the better for eccentrics.' With this comment he is blowing his trumpet disguised within humility. He needs audiences, certainly, but the world *really* needs his laughter-making. He is their 'trouper'. After only five hours sleep last night, the workaholic's eyes are blood-shot and heavily ringed. But, alert and alerting, there is still a vibrant sparkle within them which speaks of childhood, freedom and mischievousness. And at the same time they are also disturbingly intense.

On the studio-floor Dodd sings 'When a Child Is Born', his Christmas record, which has religious *and* parental connotations (he desires a child). Then he is interviewed on camera and, roughly a third of the way in, becomes noticeably irritated and restrained by the TV set-up and cameras ('a load of scrap-iron') and spontaneously slides into the wild-eyed comic character he cannot resist playing. He scoops his hair up into the air, his fingers take on the shape of mal-formed claws and he unleashes 35 joke ideas, many of them sexual – at least at their core. This is the man who once owned a car with 'The Comedian Who Is Different' painted along one side (the word different, it should be noted, was inscribed upside down). This is the man who once, out loud, proclaimed himself 'The Happiest Human in the Human Race'. Indeed he still occasionally toys with the latter slogan today, which is immensely encouraging, yet perhaps bizarre, because the woman who was 'engaged' to him for 22 years (and helped compile his comic notebooks) died of a brain tumour in the late 1970s. He said that 'her bravery' during her months in hospital, when he still devotedly performed, before finally giving up for a short while around her tragic death, was 'an inspiration'.

A religious confusion seems quite typical among comedians. Have you always been a religious man?

'My mother was rather religious, and I was brought up that way,' Dodd notes. 'Religion has been a very steady, important part in my life. But certainly my belief in God has been tested on occasions. And at those times I'm left with just comedy to carry me along . . . which is rather good at doing a similar job.'

Is humour the best thing humans have?

'Ummm . . . Well, it's certainly the icing on the cake. We have five recognised senses, plus a sixth sense – which women have more of than men and which enables them to know whether men are lying when they say "I haven't got any money". But we *also* have a seventh sense – that of humour. Humour is the sense of perceiving the incongruities of, and in, life . . . the long and the short, the thin and the fat. That's why so many double acts have such a polarity.'

Did you grow up liking Laurel and Hardy?

'Oh, I didn't like them as a child – I found them a bit *threatening*, despite their gentle sides. It's probably because I was a bit of a mummy's boy, which I wasn't proud of then but am now. Back then I didn't enjoy Hardy picking on Laurel. But I've since realised that Laurel and Hardy formed the perfect symmetry of comic incongruity. Where a lot of our double-acts have gone wrong in later years is that the two hemispheres of comicality remain undefined. To mesh with another comic the combination must be perfect. The straight man, for instance, may represent the world as bureaucracy would want it to be, and the outwardly comedic character supplies the world as it is. Sometimes the comic world flies off into the idealistic fantasy of how we would *like* the world to be, but the straight-man – with suitable cynicism – shows us that it is impossible. The point about Laurel and Hardy is that they were *more* than the sum of their parts; they were somehow completely attuned to each other. Growing older I've realised how *perfect* they really were.'

You're very much an individual though?

'Well, I've performed with foils on radio, some beautiful *feeds*, and played Malvolio in theatre (Shakespeare's *Twelfth Night*) which made me realise, in a heart-warming way, just how much we *do* all rely on other people. But I'm a loner for the most part on stage – I really always have been. Yet, in a sense, I *am* part of a double-act, because my straight-man is the audience. Usually the people I speak and refer to, out there in the stalls, are *completely* mythical people. When I say "missus" there isn't exactly someone there; nor when I say "I'll talk to you sir – *you* look sensible." So I use the audience as an imaginary entity.' (He clears his throat: '*Hhha-hh-a*'.)

Could you do without them?

'I need the feed-back, the sound of laughter – I can't imagine ever wanting to be without that. It's the finest sound in the world.'

You've lived your entire life in the house where you were born.

'Yes indeed.'

That's sweet, but rather unusual?

'Yes it is sweet. But it also gives me a strong sense of perspective. To live, or be "based", in a place where you've *always* been – that is very important in humour.'

You put the semi-mythical village of Knotty Ash on the map.

'Knotty Ash is a *real* place and not, as some people think, a fig-leaf of my imagination. Its a village six miles east of Liverpool. The people of Knotty Ash are a cross between Liverpudlians and Lancastrians. Knotty Ash has two churches, so there's no waiting. It also has, umm . . . four pubs, a chiropodist . . .' (a cough) '. . . a post office and a newsagent called Bobby Basket. We used to have a milkman but he's gone now. Down the road, where there's a garage, there used to be a smithy. I live in this old Georgian farmhouse, which is over 200 years old but which I've rebuilt a bit and refurbished. I have a big garden. I have no desire to move to London – although people frequently tell me that I should – partly because I don't like being in slow traffic. It all fits in with my philosophy, you see. Knotty Ash is my home, my base . . . my roots.'

Kenneth Arthur Dodd was born on 8 November 1927, second son (Dodd also has a sister) of Arthur and Sarah Dodd. These parents were, he says 'Peter Pan and Wendy – they gave me a wonderful childhood.' Mother, a small woman, was strong, protective and encouraging. She ran the house frugally to suit the times. Father Arthur – who was prone to serious gambling sessions – worked long and hard (often until midnight) in the coal and haulage business, running a firm that Ken's elder brother Bill is now in charge of. Arthur Dodd, Ken says, 'believed in originality in all things . . . that you should never be a *second* anyone.' The hard-working Dodd Senior was '. . . the funniest man I've ever known, far funnier than I'll ever be'. Whenever Ken was ill his father would offer eccentric, and yet caring, words like 'I shall have to call Doctor Chuckabutty'

– 'he played around with names a lot.' Dodd's childhood was spent playing amongst assorted pets in the garden at the back of the family home (originally bought by his grandfather), singing in the church choir, play-acting, 'daring to be different', 'running free in the field', getting into trouble for tomfoolery at school, all at the same time as being 'rather shy in company'.

'From four years old I was a regular reader of comics like the *Rover*, *Wizard* and *Hotspur* and I remember sending away for itching powder and stink-bombs, things to cause a bit of fun, nuisance, havoc. I also got a Punch and Judy set, for my eighth birthday. Then one day, when I was about ten, I saw an advert in the *Wizard* I think, which said "Fool your teachers, amaze your friends – send 6d in stamps – become a ventriloquist." For that I just got a little booklet, and that encouraged me to pester my parents for a ventriloquist's figure. I called it Charlie Brown. Which was a very bad idea, incidentally, because "vents" should always avoid saying "B". Anyway, I subsequently spent a lot of time talking to Charlie – or rather talking to myself.'

Did theatre mean anything to you at that time?

'When I was fairly young, the Dodd Family Five [Arthur, Sarah, Bill, Ken and younger sister Sarah] attended a lot of shows at regional theatres. Father took us to see every good variety bill that appeared in the North West. So I got an early and regular taste of the lovely fruity pit-orchestra, of the smell of cigar smoke and orange peel. The lovely magical world of live variety theatre. A huge illustrious world. In the early days every comedian had his own style. There were parson comedians, railway porter comedians, you name it – shy, brash and long-suffering husbands, husband-and-wife duos . . . *Everyone* had a uniqueness, unlike today – I must add – when everyone wears a mohair suit and trots out the latest one-liners that some scriptwriter has worked on. They're just raconteurs now – speakers of other people's thoughts.'

When did you first perform?

'With my Punch and Judy kit I suppose – I charged friends and local kids a copper or two to sit on orange crates and watch. My very first real show was at St Edward's Orphanage on a Christmas Day. My dad wrote the script, and very good it was too. I performed for a parents/teachers association, in the village hall . . . small but memorable beginnings.'

When did you first start researching comedy as a subject?

'I started really *thinking* about humour at twelve or thirteen, when school felt unexciting. I didn't dream of being a train-driver; I wanted to be a comedian. Dad had been a sort of part-time musician and encouraged me to be a singer. I'd wanted to sing myself. But comedy sort of came more into play. But I had no real idea how to comede. So I started thinking, "What *is* this peculiar thing that makes people laugh?" *What is a laugh?* Why these short explosions from the mouth? Anywhere else, by the way, and you'd be in dead trouble. So I started by visiting the library. I remember, at about fourteen, looking up all the words to do with humour in the dictionary – starting with laugh, L-A-double F, then laughter, humour, comedy, joke. . . . Gradually I started exploring what people had written about comedy, and the more I delved into it the more I realised it was all relatively uncharted country. Reading books, I'd *already* experienced journeys like going to the Moon, with H.G. Wells and Jules Verne . . . but here at last was an uncharted land that I could really get into, and explore completely in my *own* imagination. And humour, of course plays an enormous part in mental health. If one is able to dream, to day-dream, create crazy notions, whimsy or nonsense or surrealism . . . it's like discovering little diamonds.'

Ken left High Holt Grammar School at fourteen, and for many years delivered coal with his father (often bronchially ill) and brother, 'humping hundred-weight sacks' and 'cracking lots of jokes', while performing occasionally in off-hours. By 21 he was quite frequently singing and ventriloquising, and 'occasionally' joking, in front of audiences (as Professor Yaffle Chuckabutty, Operatic Tenor and Sausage-Knotter), but had also set himself up in earnest with a mobile shop – a day-time career involving driving around Liverpool housing-estates encouraging folk to buy pots, pans and polishes which he'd labelled with his own 'KayDee' brand-name. A road-side and door-mat salesman, he found that jokes kept the sales flowing, especially with the older female folk (the same 'missuses' he'd encountered hauling coal with the family). It was not until he was 27 years old that the 'still rather shy' Dodd made the full break from salesman to professional performer – under the combined pressure of the long-standing influence and encouragement of his mother and his girlfriend. 'I went the full-hog at last', Dodd says, but explains that 'I didn't approach it that differently anyway – I am, in a sense, a salesman of jokes.' He chose a specific manager, he says, 'because he looked like my Dad', and his first *professional* engagement was a successful spot at the Nottingham Empire in September 1954. But he remembers more vividly a sour performance shortly afterwards, at the Glasgow Empire. His opening line was 'I suppose you're all wondering why I sent for you!' ('I have to admit I stole that off an American comic'). He knew that Scottish audiences were notoriously tough on English comics, but the manager had told him, 'Tell no football jokes and you'll get the bird on Friday,' and he was determined to be applauded. 'On Friday, first house,' he reminisces, 'I staggered on to the stage with me hair all over the place, me teeth sticking out of me face, me eyes popping out . . . I sort of *jerked* myself across the stage, and the thought shot through my mind – "I *deserve* the bird for this." I can still see that aggressive lot in front of me now . . . And as soon as I'd thrown them "I suppose you're all wondering . . .", a man in the third row, with half a bottle of whisky, stood up, slowly uncoiled himself and shouted, "Christ! What a 'orrible sight!". And that was my first laugh, or sort of . . . So I galloped through my act as fast as I could and sprinted off, and out.'

From the outset Dodd kept notes on his performances and logged them away in a manner which some would label extremely workmanlike, others anally-fixated. Taking elaborate notes *during* performances was the job (which she enjoyed) of Dodd's girlfriend, Anita, who had given up being a nurse to be his 'aid'. Much was made of their eccentric relationship, which involved Dodd seeing her but living with his parents, and Anita sitting at the back of the theatre, or off stage, each night, jotting ratings on each of Dodd's jokes or routines in black books. The system involved codes such as V G (for very good audience reaction), X (for bad reaction), a box shape (for a real audience roar), S-L-O-W (for slow response), and jottings took in details like location, time, weather outside and much besides. Correlating and elaborating on these notes Dodd devised what he calls 'A Giggle Map of Great Britain'.

> 'It just seems common sense,' he says, 'that – as I travelled around – I should compile charts and maps of how jokes go down in different areas and places at different times. To know what brand goes best in what place. And gradually I built up a grand piece of intelligence; about where irony is most liked, where to do one-liners, when to be more aggressive, when or where to be zanier, more friendly or more lovable . . . all sorts of information, special anecdotes. It's my treasure trove really.'

As a system, does it work?

> 'It's very complex. Time of the year, material, region, weather . . . and especially "sense of occasion", which is really what it all hangs on.'

So is there a 'very worst audience' you could identify, in time or space?

> 'My generalisation, which is half a joke but also rather true, is that "The worst audience in the world is one that hasn't paid to see you." '

You mean, it's about money?

> 'Or rather, I think, the exercising of choice. That way I know people have *chosen* to see me. The point is, while some folk might say Ken Dodd is not bad on a good night, other folk might say they would like to see him strangled.'

Dodd's career, spanning 35 years now, has covered television, radio, the West End, pantomime, million-selling records, but most consistently and enthusiastically, live theatres nation-wide – large, small and tiny. He long ago set himself the task of playing them all, 'there's thousands of them', and still hopes to succeed. In all this time he has acquired no real status-symbols, lived a frugal homely life, and has retained the simple individual lifestyle of being a freelance, with only a home (with three rooms full of books), a booking-manager, a Volvo estate car, a girlfriend, a carrier-bag or two and assorted notebooks to contend with. His love is live theatre, to leap centre-stage and startle an audience into laughter (he calls himself 'a fireworks comic') and then carry them along – appreciatively – into his ludicrous but likeable world of strange names, eccentric but localised twists of common and uncommon themes, elaborately disguised sexual innuendo and joyful flights of fancy; all in the aid of '. . . rich human belly laughs, cascading cacophonies of chuckles, great *giggling* guffaws'.

What part do the love-songs play in your act?

'They're a moment's rest from exercise of the chuckle muscle. I sing romantic ballads, I suppose, to change the pace, to break up the show . . . to give it more heart, really. I often like to finish a show with one. To leave the crowd with *a tear-ful ear-ful*.'

Do you still get stage-fright after all these years?

'Oh yes – to this day. I'm a very nervous man, but that's part of the fascination.'

How do you feel, during heady laughter, as you stand on stage?

'Ten foot tall.'

Carefree?

'You certainly forget any or all troubles you have off-stage.'

Is humour driven by aggression?

'Certainly it can be; but I'd like to think my comedy brought people together as much as possible.'

What are the more theoretical ideas you've explored concerning comedy?

'I couldn't really understand it at first, but I gradually got the hang. Josh Billings, for instance, said that laughter is feeling good all over. Aristotle was one of the first – he said that the essence of comedy is "a buckled mill-wheel", which I think is rather profound. It's normality with a twist. Steven Leacock disagreed and said that laughter goes right back to the earliest man and woman, who used to bop each other over the head with a log and shout the triumphant cry, "Hah-hah!" '

And a suitable 'what a lovely day for . . .'?

'Oh . . . Oh yes, by jove – what a lovely day for, for . . . for getting some ice-cubes, dropping them down the front of your wife's nightie and saying "How's *that* for the chest-freezer you've always wanted?" This is the superiority theory of comedy. One of the oldest forms of humour in the world is that in which one village laughs at another, one city at another, one country at another, or jokes about pecking orders. Creating those jokes is about finding common denominators . . . I do all types of jokes, really, and amidst it all I stand as this little resilient character who's never really cruel, and . . .' (Dodd falters in this summary of his on-stage persona pauses and then coughs.)

Is humour too big a subject ever to understand fully?

'Well, it's a big journey. But humour ought to be studied in much greater depth, *I* think. It affects everyday life as much as anything else I can think of. There ought to be a Chair of Humour in various universities to study this phenomenon! It plays a part in communication, in negotiation, in business, in politics, in religion.

How many times have you heard a businessman, or whatever, who is highly skilled but whose jokes are truly pathetic? They just don't know what humour is and it's letting them down. Humour could work to everyone's advantage. A lot of politicians are quite witty, I suppose – which is not quite the same thing as being a *humorist*. "Humorous" is having a sense of fun; "wit" is more barbed and usually scores directly off an opponent. I don't think wit's really the cleverest way of negotiating. You shouldn't be scoring off your opponent – you should be putting your whole argument into perspective with the use of judicious clever humour. Abe Lincoln, Churchill, Mark Twain – for example – all had that.'

Talking of the personal intentions behind humour, what of Sigmund Freud's theories?

'Freud said that humour was psychic economy – the conservation of psychic energy. A release of pressure. He categorised and explored hundreds of jokes . . . But he had an unhappy knack of explaining himself in convoluted phrases. Perhaps his writings just lost something in the translation, but my little joke at his expense is, "The trouble with Freud is that he never played second house, Friday night, at the Glasgow Empire!" '

Dodd's humour, of course, often lies on the borderline of coyness and obscenity, of sexuality and the perverse. His language is a sensual one – concerned with 'cucumber operators . . . bottoms . . . kippers . . . Diddy ladies, tattiphilarious diddilation . . . nikky-nokky-noo . . .' and the finer points of 'discumknockerating' behaviour. He speaks of comedy in terms of human-contact, trust, joy, nourishment ('a tonic'), fertility ('making and seeing the audience blossom like a flower'), and admits that being a comic performer derives from 'a colossal desire to be loved'.

His early professional appearances involved him walking on stage with a euphonium, phallic in appearance, which he then flaunted but never played. 'Tickling Sticks' have long been his trade-marked prop, and he brandishes them (he has a variety of sizes) whilst ejecting a stream of comic lines containing bizarre innuendo. When Dodd says – to an semi-imaginary female within the audience – 'Have you ever been tickled under the circumstances?' or 'Have you ever been tickled by goodwill missus? Good old Willie', it almost seems as if he is directly equating comedy with sexuality. The author of this book well remembers a time in the 1960s when, in a schoolyard, young boys would sing a song based on Dodd's hit record: 'A pe-nis, a pe-nis, the greatest gift that I possess. I thank the lord that I've been blessed, with more than my share of a pe-nis.' Either the bulk of the male attendances of this particular school were pathologically exceptional, or Dodd is a comic subversive. A subversive *to all intents*, perhaps, or *in all innocence*. As a man so technical in his research of jokes, and yet so seemingly instinctual in throwing them out of his mouth, it's hard to understand exactly how much Dodd *does* understand the causes of what he's saying.

Certainly he admits he's '*very* interested in psychology'. Then what psychological force, for instance, lies behind Dodd's vision of a semi-imaginary Knotty Ash, the perpetual childhood home? (While Dodd took lie-ins, mother ironed for, organised things for and enthused over him until her death in 1970. She was his first bookkeeper, storing his wages in shoe-boxes. After 1970 Ken then lived with his father until the latter's demise.) On stage Dodd's jokes frequently touch on the topics of matrimony, childhood, oedipal and inferiority complexes, family conversations and occasions of humiliation therein, and moments of physical and mental release from authority – all wrapped within 'the familiarly fantastic'.

If there is a personal purpose, what lies behind the creation of Diddy Men? Are they Dodd's child substitutes? 'Certainly they're an identification point for children,' he says; 'my way into their minds'. Dodd has his jolly and supportive Diddy Men whenever he calls for them, on stage; off stage he had Boodle the poodle. Dodd has never produced any children although he says this is 'certainly not for lack of trying'. 'Chaplin' he notes, 'had his first child *very* late . . . so there's still hope!' 'I like children,' he offers, 'and I hope *I'm* one, at least most of the time.' At one point, while talking about his comic research, he stumbles and says: 'I collect my kids . . . I mean, I collect humour, like other kids collect railway numbers or stamps.'

What – might we wonder – does Kenneth Arthur Dodd's hair mean? What does it stand, or stand-up, for? Stan Laurel, for instance, made much of an erratic plumage.

'In the olden days everyone used to wear their hair slicked back, like Air Force pilots. But I always secretly wanted curly hair. It's the one thing in my life I've always wanted! I was terrified during my early days on stage – I still am, it's all part of the process – and I had this habit of ruffling my hair up anyway. But you just instinctively know that part of the comedian's persona is *anarchy*. So I deliberately went on stage in a broken-down suit, Army boots, and my shirt hanging out the back. That was my gesture of defiance.'

But the high hair – is it not also related to the peacock syndrome? Does, perchance, the comedian attract sexually?

'Well, there's a lot of love in laughter, and that's the sexiest kind of love you can get. Humour is sexy, yes. And the two are often interconnected. I like the fact that over 50 per cent of my audiences are usually female. Some theorists believe humour is all to do with sexual tension.'

Is the tickling stick a phallic symbol?

'Oh, I think it's *slightly* phallic, yes . . . Some people say so . . . But others call this a fallacy.' (With this gag Dodd emits a harsh cough – a perfect punctuation point that derives from childhood bronchitis and emphysema, illnesses his coal-merchant father also suffered from.)

What was your reason for carrying it on stage?

'I first picked up the stick because I noticed that the jester in olden days always carried some kind of prop in his hand – like a pole with a head on, or an inflated bladder on a stick. That was the fool's licence – he provided the safety-valve within the strictures of the court, whether it was before royalty or before a squire. Pecking orders obviously irked people, and their fool was allowed to do and say whatever he liked. He was the social safety-valve. He could make fun of the most pompous and the most powerful of people.'

But you've aligned yourself with Margaret Thatcher – is this the Jester and the Authority Figure or something more supportive?

'Well . . .' (He falters slightly.) 'Well, politics is a very personal thing . . . Harold Wilson, of course adopted me as a comedian in the 1960s. I played for Ted Heath and Jim Callaghan when they were Prime Minister, and Thatcher's been to see me three times. I'm *very* honoured. And yet I don't think I agree with any one party . . . Um, I'm just a private person, the same as everyone else . . .' (He pauses at length.) 'I would never want to get deeply involved in politics, although I have strong ideas about individualism and working hard, knuckling down.'

What sort of ambitions or aims do you still have?

'Ahhh. Now, my big ambition is to somehow create a cross between *Hellzapoppin* [the Hollywood 'surrealist' film] and music-hall – Fred Karno's Company and "The Crazy Gang". To create a real British comedy theatre company, a family which could perform every kind of comedy the British people love – sketches, songs, farces and visual and verbal humour. To create a real *family* of comics . . . To appear in those hundreds of little theatres out there run very professionally by enthusiasts, with lots of different comics gathered around me.'

Dodd, on and off stage, seems such a strange combination of elements, many of them seemingly contradictory: he is an 'individualist' who wants a family; an anarchist and a proud parents' boy; an adult and a child; an adult whose parents are dead and now wants a child but also wants to remain childlike; a gut-level flight-of-fancy 'funster' and yet a serious academic theorist ('. . . Kant . . . Schopenhauer . . .'); a man who analyses comedy daily and yet says it can feel like 'pulling the wings off a butterfly'; a performer who arrives late and over-runs shows, and yet '*never' misses* a show; a man concerned with money and yet few of its trappings; a rebel *and* a religious man; a freedom-fighter ('What a lovely day for . . .') and yet a man locked into assorted show-business and mystical superstitions (his mother crossed his palm with silver as a baby). He is a frequent charity-worker with a reputation nevertheless for 'austerity' or even 'meanness'. (He reportedly once handed a taxi-driver a tea-bag as a tip. Whether this was a piece of meanness or not, it is nevertheless certainly A Good Joke.)

Shortly after meeting and speaking to Dodd, as above, his professional *and* private lives were suddenly exposed to public and legal scrutiny in a court case in which he was 'stripped naked' and gave perhaps the performance of his life to successfully evade charges of 'deliberate non-payment of tax'. In court he told: how 'for 40 years I have read every possible book, and I hope I *have* every possible book, on humour and the psychology of humour'; how he took no holidays until he was 51, and how he had lived a very frugal life while amassing hundreds of thousands of pounds in his house (before finally moving lumps into banks from 1979 onwards). Of the latter eccentricity he said he did this for several reasons – because he liked having a lot of cash 'to hand' (even though he rarely spent it), as a nest-egg, as a measurement of his achievements, because his family had always avoided bankers, and because it was proof to his parents that he was a success. Showing the court a short film of his home, the modest and rather dilapidated Knotty Ash house, he told how 'I *never* throw anything away, because you never know when you'll need it.' He noted that 'I'm nervous of having (money) and nervous of not having it'; further that 'I'm only as rich as my last show.' Recorded as potentially dangerously ill at the beginning of the trial (with ventricular tachycardia, or irregular and speedy heart-beats), he left the court in triumph, sending the jury God's best wishes and – immediately on encountering the outdoor air – sliding schizophrenically into his buck-toothed, peacock-haired, 'I'm the happiest human in the human race' persona. He was suddenly the japester and workaholic inquiring almost unbelievably of those assembled, 'Does anyone know where I can get a gig tonight?!' All Dodd's pieces fell together in those few vivid moments, strange though the resulting jigsaw is. This was Dodd as clown (happy and sad), as anti-bureaucrat, as japester, as trooper and workaholic, as 'the winner', as religious man, and as surrealist.

Dodd – a 'surrealist'? There is one last question I had asked Ken during our conversations: *Above all,* what is your very favourite '*What a lovely day for . . .*'?

'Oh, good Lord, I have hundreds . . . What a wonderful . . . Oh . . . Ummm.' (He pondered hard.) 'Ummm, by jove . . . what . . . what . . .' And finally: 'Oh, what a wonderful day for *s-h-o*-ving a cucumber through the vicar's letter box and howling, "Look out! The Martians are coming!!" '

It is hard to imagine that a man so obsessed by studying comedy would not realise this, his very favourite idea, has the connotations of imposing extra-terrestrial sexuality on a mortified Knotty Ash cleric.

'I'm not going to explain it, spell it all out' he offers on inquiry, '. . . I suppose . . .' (he coughs) 'I suppose it has a *wealth* of meaning.'

Hold your duster up for the camera, Ken.

'Duster? *Duster*? Fuckin' 'ell! It's a *tickling-stick*; a tickling stick!'

LAUREL AND HARDY: '*The puzzle, of course, is Life.*' (Top photo)
Photograph courtesy of Hal Roach Studios, Hollywood

LAUREL, aged 13, with mother (Bottom left)
Photograph by brother Gordon Jefferson

Young HARDY, aged 8 (Bottom right)
Photographer unknown

'. . . SADDER, WISER AND DIZZIER?'

Never, for God's sake, ask me what makes people laugh. I just don't know!
– Stanley Laurel (mid-career, while making half the globe do exactly that)

Laurel and Hardy are, it seems, the most loved comedians in the world, if not by critics then at least by me, by many comedians (as we have seen in this book), and, most importantly, by a large bulk of 'the international masses' – many of their short films were performed in five different languages. True cinematic angels of the kind there may never (for assorted reasons) be again, this duo still – 50 years on from their hey-day – remain, at their best, timeless and near-faultless humorists. (While writing this book, I met clown Vyasheslav Polunin – 'Russia's Robin Williams' – who had a carrier-bag full of Laurel and Hardy videos, bought in London. 'For inspiration, of course!' he explained.)

The Stan Laurel of the screen was, to a large extent, a pure clown, Oliver Hardy a more subtle pantomimist, perhaps, and an almost effortless actor. Whatever or whichever they were *individually*, it seems ridiculous to mull over which was actually the funnier, because they were such a cohesive comic unit, such a monumental fusion of characteristics, that many viewers today still do not know, or perhaps even *want* to know, the name of one from the other. Laurel was the thin fellow, Hardy the fat, although the ludicrous grinning and scowling butler character in their film *The Laurel and Hardy Murder Case* simply referred to them as 'the two shabby gentlemen'. Like a fiddle and a bow they made music together of a simple but profound nature; all of their films (at least the ones they were allowed to control) were glorious exercises in human observation and tragi-comedy. But how on earth to *possibly* sum up their work? Within the nineteen minutes of their outing *Helpmates*, for instance – eighteen and a half minutes of which are concentrated entirely on themselves (without interruptions by others) – here are just some of the events that occur:

> Hardy makes *twelve* facial double-takes and Laurel nine; Hardy makes nine squints of appeal or bemusement to the camera, and Laurel six; Hardy bangs his head three times and Laurel once; Hardy sits on a soda-syphon, slaps one man to the floor and incapacitates another by hurling a plant-pot at him; three of Hardy's suits are rendered unwearable; two tables and hundreds of pieces of crockery are destroyed; Laurel pokes a telephone in his eye and the savage end of a plunger in Hardy's eye

(accidentally); Hardy's doorbell comes off the wall; Hardy falls through his own floorboards; Laurel breaks one window and Hardy breaks two; there is a glass explosion; Hardy trips on a floorsweeper twice; Hardy has a chimney-load of soot projected into his face; Hardy is soaked by water four times and covered by flour once; Hardy returns 'sadder, wiser and dizzier' with a black eye from his wife; and Laurel burns his fingers and then burns Hardy's house to the ground.

But not necessarily in that order. And that list, of course, excludes all the classically, finely tuned lines Laurel and Hardy rendered to each other mid-action ('Will we have mar-malade for breakfast?'). Ageless character comics who may well end up being immortalised, Laurel and Hardy's simple *raison d'être* was the perpetual way they confronted and suffered – with dignity and resilience and *in togetherness* – the absurdity of existence.

Surprisingly little is known of the early background of Oliver Hardy – but a few important personal details can be tracked down. In real life he was born on 18 January 1892 in Harlem, Georgia, and soon took his first name from his father, who died when he was only eleven months old, and his adopted middle name (the elegantly announced 'Norvell') from his loving but 'distant' mother. It seems that Oliver Norvell looked on the family maid, a spirited black woman, as his early mother figure – she lullabied him, cared for and nursed him, and he knew *her* as 'mama', not his real mother (whom he called, by contrast, 'Miss Emily'). Emily Hardy, now husbandless, was extremely busy running one hotel or another – the lounge and porch of the latter premises allowing the sapling Hardy much time to people-watch. Hardy doubtless obtained much of his gentleness, his proportions, his walk and his dance from his 'maid'/mama, as well as his glorious singing voice ('Yooou are the ideaal oooof my dreeeams'), which became his early intended career. He nevertheless acquired an interest in fortune-telling, numerology, religion and superstition (and possibly his later highly excessive gambling) from his real mother, but also from the fact that his father had died so early. He gained his delicate genteel deportment and niceties from his mother, his mother's sister and assorted passers-by, and theatrical hotel-guests helped inspire his interest in performance. Hardy was a rather introverted youngster – he had two brothers and two sisters, all older than him and all only *half*-siblings. In a sense, Hardy's whole life was a search for identity. He fought a constant mental battle with his weight and had to endure taunts of 'Fatty' and 'Fatso'. He was also for ever engaged in a more intricate battle to understand what his father had been like – he described his difficulty with this struggle as 'a feeling of being removed from oneself'.

Hardy became a 'theatre manager' in his late 20s and went on to perform mainly as 'heavies' – criminal types – in his early film parts, chiefly because of his sheer size (although he had a highly sensitive nature off screen and he was known professionally and socially as

'Babe'). Nevertheless, in that early work, he still brandished many of the unique flourishes and mannerisms (and delayed bullish run) that, with Laurel, helped create perhaps the finest film comedy ever made.

Stan Laurel, who in effect controlled – uncredited – most of the duo's writing, directing and editing (until their feature-film career was ruined by inept or authoritarian assembly-line film-companies), came from Lancashire in England. He was born, Arthur Stanley Jefferson – the Arthur being his father's name – on 16 June 1890. His father was a theatrical manager, producer and performer (mainly comic), working-class turned 'middle-class', who perpetually lived the show-business life. Much of the time, when young, Stan – generally energetic but fairly unhealthy – was moved around schools and lived, along with his older brother and 'baby' sister, at the home of his grandma Metcalfe and her alcoholic argumentative husband. Stan's father was usually away working while mother (too ill to take care of the children) generally had no choice but to travel with him. Father was a philanderer and maltreated his ailing wife, who was intermittently a singer and actress. It seems Stan loathed his father for his treatment of mother Madge but loved him for his big name in the Northern theatre world. When the shy but mischievous Arthur/Stan did attend the music halls of his father he eagerly began taking copious written notes on the workings and nuances of all comedians appearing on stage, then slowly he began evolving material of his own (before a mirror), without the knowledge of his father but with strong encouragement from his mother. He thought her simply 'saintly', but – his mother aside – comedy became Stan's true fixation in life; and he took to the stage with a vengeance at sixteen, with (as the story goes) a stunned father sitting in the audience, unbeknownst to Stan.

Comedy was now all. He joined the hard travelling world of underpaid entertainers (refusing to take any monetary aid from his father) but had to rush home, at seventeen, to witness his mother dying, making him inconsolable for months. Thereafter his meetings with his father were dutiful and reserved, and he joined the playfully violent Fred Karno comedy team and set off (twice) to America, thereafter to return very rarely (although significantly, he chose to make his first 'official' visit home just after winning an Academy award in 1932). He finally found his home in the California countryside, looking – as it did then – villagey, like the locales of his childhood and the nameless settings of most Laurel and Hardy films. Moving through stage eventually to film, it took Laurel years to find real success or a strong unique character. He toyed with many roles, the dandy amongst them, and indeed really felt his talents lay in writing and directing for others (notably the artistes of Hal Roach, whom he respected but argued with perpetually), something he was considered a maestro at.

Laurel took little seriously in life except comedy, yet he was a highly complex man. He apparently had a personality of almost complete guilelessness but gave several wives a very hard time (he thought, in return, they gave him a hard time); he was an internal egocentric who nevertheless treated friends, old and new, with great generosity (almost to recklessness); homes and apartments seemed tedious to him (he relished hotels and boarding houses); he had increasing bouts with the bottle; he worked all day and much of the night, constantly enjoying, but nervous about, 'gag'-creation; he had severe dark moods and depressions away from the film-set; he was never able to forget the disharmony he experienced in his parents' and grand-parents' homes; he was wilfully self-destructive when things were going best for him; he made sudden brooding departures from home, for days, with a small suitcase, to return with a silent ingratiating smile; he was an atheist who perversely believed in reincarnation (Hardy, meanwhile, read the Bible each morning).

Laurel's teaming with Oliver Norvell Hardy came about by accident – they were vaguely noticed as 'working well together' in a film or two they both happened to appear in. Stan was not initially keen on a teaming but everything suddenly gelled after their first few collaborations, and the Laurel-Hardy axis became indestructible within a matter of months, perfect within a year.

With the exception of Hardy, Laurel wanted complete filmic control on set (and thankfully got it most of the time), but he could never be bothered to spend much time playing the business and social game of Hollywood, therefore he became a powerful but underpaid film-figure. He had an eccentric attitude to money (like Hardy, who once threw a year's wages away on a bad bet). This philosophy (or foolishness) was splendidly encapsulated in almost all the duo's films, brilliantly easing and deflating the Western world's anxieties over the 1930s Depression, and – more universally – humanity's perpetual economic obsessions. 'What humiliation,' Hardy would say, 'Creditors *hounding me* at my very fireside;' to which Laurel – after proposing an intriguing but *ultimately* unsuccessful scheme to aid Hardy – would note, '. . . and then you wouldn't have any interest to pay, and you wouldn't have any hounds in your fireplace.' It is interesting to note that while Chaplin (who Laurel briefly understudied) lived out the latter part of his life in Switzerland, with his millions, Laurel spent his retirement on slender (but not, as is sometimes claimed, desperate) means . . . a tidy pensioner with his number still in the Hollywood phone-book and with a cup of tea on the boil for all who knocked on his door, comics and fans alike. It is also worth noting that Laurel continued to write (sadly redundant) dialogues for Hardy and himself after Hardy's death.

For many years Laurel and Hardy barely knew of the dimensions of their success around the world – their reputation as the only truly great film comics to transfer successfully from Silent to Sound. The latter medium – their true home – they took to almost *effortlessly*, adding joyful philosophical and 'nonsensical' conversations to their dogged activities. The duo's films were made, ultimately, by organically 'winging it' – by sitting around on set, talking over a thin rough-script, having a drink, suggesting and confirming sets, ideas and basic dialogue and then leaping into performance, creating mainly first-take classics to be topped up with brilliantly simple and powerful cut-in (second-camera) shots of their primally innocent faces, plus mould-breaking sound effects and editing style. This was mime, artifice . . . true *grande illusion* which returned its international audiences to a childlike state and yet nevertheless spoke poignantly of the real, harsh world – 'to mime' meaning, in essence, 'to imitate life'. Laurel and Hardy were vaudevillians, extra-realists, absurdists *and* unknowing surrealists (their horse-in-bed pre-dated Luis Buñuel's horse-in-a-bed). In each of their films, all in essence comic nightmares, they completely re-created their social, economic and domestic positions and yet stayed forever the same, battling on and on against semi-self-imposed troubles, heinous *scraping* car noises and strange karmic forces. They took each remorseless knock that came their way with great dignity ('I wonder if we could trouble you for a slice of but-tered toast?') while organising reciprocal destruction within 'the codes of the Gentleman'. Remaining largely considerate of others ('My friend and I are willing to sacrifice *Our All*'), practically the only times Laurel and Hardy actually laughed on screen, with menace or otherwise, were when they were accidentally drunk . . . or when suddenly, urgently united together in savaging someone who was trying it on too far with them. A tilt of the hat here, a baffled or dumb look, a squint . . . then into the fray for a good tar and feathering. Sometimes Laurel was too baffled or taken aback to aid Hardy ('Why don't you do something to hellllp me?') but close combat was another thing. 'Ummm,' Stan seemed to be pondering, as he changed from cherubic passivity to manly belligerence, 'Ummm . . . you can't get away with flicking or fisting my partner under the chin like that – here's the same in return, *plus* a twist.' 'Dooooh!' would reply James Finlayson, or one of their other regular actor protagonists, in return, 'Dooohhh!' Then, having momentarily stopped squabbling and confusing each other, Laurel and Hardy would move on to confidently 'grab the bull by the horns and put our best foot forward', only to stumble predictably (yet in their unique way) over each other, and the world, once more.

Recurring and intriguing themes and flavours have emerged within the introduction and main body of this book. Personal and 'professional' contradictions and ambiguities abound in humorists. They are people, or personalities, who are destructive and constructive, hostile and friendly, 'sensical' and nonsensical, egotistical and masochistic, foolish and intelligent, rebellious and conformative, honest and dishonest, shameless and guilty, precise and yet chaotic . . .

All these things seem to me to be intrinsically linked back to childhood and parental forces. From the first clear sight it makes of 'the world' a baby – now beginning to laugh – takes on board a battle with real life, as opposed to the intermittent bliss of a mother's presence, at least of breast or bottle. It hears and makes sounds, it sleeps and dreams frequently, it encounters scowls and smiles. Slowly it learns of possessions, of taboos, of measures of control;

here are the beginnings of proof-of-worth, of money, of good toilet-manners, of Art. It learns, too, of differences between 'the adult world' and 'the child world', and of distinctions between the sexes – of love, aggression and rivalry, both sibling and parental. The father has to be taken on board as a real presence, or at least as a mythical character that exists or existed somewhere in time and space. He is often 'the first intruder' but also an identification point – the 'well-spring' from whence the child came and a symbol of the (male) child's own future.

The child's sense of its self, and existence, is formed around parental flavours and forces. A strange picture of the source and meaning of life is presented to everyone in the shape of parental figures. Sex, in its broadest sense, is in effect the source of love, of aggression, of food, of guilt . . . In Woody Allen's comic reckoning, sex is also crime – 'We are all sentenced to die for a crime we didn't commit,' he observes. Each child creates sense out of the nonsense that results from this 'crime', but never – as throughout life – does 'it' ever quite fit together. There's always a piece from the jigsaw which goes missing. Life, for good or bad, goes on with generation after generation teaching and inflicting controls, pleasures, expectations, guilts and assorted characteristics on to the next. Each person, as he/she grows, has to strive to come to terms with his/her own ultimate selfishness, the pleasures and pressures of 'mother' and 'father', the realities of the world and survival, the knowledge of cruelty and death, the (non-) existence of a God or Gods, and thoughts and realisations of order, absurdity and infinity. All these mental requirements taken together make human beings unique animals, and humour fulfils a unique function in challenging and relieving these thoughts and forces.

Seeming hyper-sensitives, with sexual and philosophical backgrounds to boot, great humorists are those who adopt humour and laughter-making as a mission, a method, a need, a livelihood, a way of 'public' life. They fear, love and even hate audiences, often simultaneously. They want to show painful truth and yet 'disguise' it in laughter. They want to cook up nonsense, aggression, joy, anarchy and outrage, and yet have it all under their own control. All the time, if successful, they are exploring and relieving the tension of their sexual, social and philosophical characters, while giving and getting 'audience satisfaction'. That he/she works out these tensions on stage, not in real life, implicitly suggests that – if humour is rather aggressive – no *real* physical violence is intended.

Perhaps humorists, riddled with irony as they are, are therefore ultimately even lovers of the world. Certainly they seem to be constantly pining for something, or at least dreaming of 'a reconciliation'.

I cannot stop myself including here two thoughts reflecting a lack of, or quest for, reconciliation with one's parents, voiced recently by master comic wordsmith, Robin Williams. Of his mother Williams said, 'She used to read me this poem which went "I love you in blue, I love you in red, but most of all I love you in blue" . . . Well, thanks Mom – that shouldn't mess me up much.' Of his father he said the man had 'a drier sense of humour – which is basically "Shut up!" . . . that kind of *arid dry humour*. Ayatollah-style funny.'

Perhaps, though, we should go back, in spirit, to the first humorist 'interrogated' in this book, Barry Humphries. As we are near 'the end' it might be worth mentioning a couple of his latest thoughts, *in* comic character, and *out*. As Edna on television he stumbled erratically over what seemed to be a very personal line: 'I think it's true that we all disappe . . . er, disappoint our parents, and they, and they, in return disappoint us.' And in interview, as himself (not as 'caring, sharing' Edna), he has recently said, completely seriously, that he'd like to think what he did for a living was his way of showing his love of life and people. These thoughts, once again, point to birth and childhood.

I have left the iconic Laurel and Hardy until the end of this book because it seems to me, more and more, that they offer interesting thoughts and conclusions on the central forces of laughter and comic creation. As a coupling – or duo – I feel Laurel and Hardy stand as guards to the key to 'comic resolution' which all humorists and humour pine for. The question is: why *on earth* would two characters like Laurel and Hardy stick together, through thick, thin and thinner? And, indeed, why on earth would we so relish them doing so? Quite simply I believe it is because, both despite and because of their perpetual failings, they resolve great generational forces within us. The fiddle and the bow are mother and father, wife and husband, siblings, it often feels, but – most importantly and ultimately – parent and child. Hardy, the tackler, is the father-figure who believes he knows best and that his colleague – a dumb protégé – needs to be guided and sometimes bossed around. Laurel, the perpetual helpless hopeless 'sexless' son (but occasionally genius conjuror), nevertheless proves, and we recognise, that Hardy is not superior to him, and even – ultimately – perhaps slightly *more* hopeless and helpless ('I don't know how *anyone* could be so clumsy as you . . .' CRASH!).

Through Laurel and Hardy, father and son, Oedipal opponents (neither had sons in real life), are finally reconciled in time and space, bantering thoughts like 'She says I like you more than I do her,' '. . . Well, you *do* don't you?', 'Welllll . . . we won't go into that!'

Sexuality is truly an eccentric force in their world. In *Twice Two* they played themselves and each other's wives. In *Our Wife* they were accidentally married to one another. In *Brats* they played themselves and their own sons (to superb effect). In *Their First Mistake* they adopted a baby together and Oliver 'accidentally' fed Stan. The writer Molly Haskell once dismissed Laurel and Hardy as a 'two-man wrecking crew' of female – that is, civilised and bourgeois – society. She called them 'by metaphor, latently homosexual'. But then, she's never been a son.

It is said that after Hardy's death Laurel explained that Hardy (the golfer and free-mason) had never really shown vocal appreciation for Laurel's creativity – perhaps that is the very set-up and tension (a strange mirror-image of their on-screen pecking order) that held their professional relationship together. Whatever, they were both complete and utter martyrs to each other (and life) on screen. And in this perpetual push and pull, in this resolving and replaying and rebuilding of father and son relationships, in their momentary, unsentimental resolution of Oedipal forces and life's anxieties and misfortunes, audiences are driven near to 'the very nub of it all'. Here are 'rivals' genetically *and* spiritually united. They fight and exacerbate each other's misfortunes, but they can never be apart. They attract and escape death together. Human tensions are thus philosophically dispelled back over previous generations of (at least male) parent and offspring and parent and offspring. They are branded the same, relieved of guilt and tension and united, at least in theory, right back to the time – as history goes – of the primitive human hunter-gatherers of East Africa.

The primal building blocks of human neuroses – authoritarian and sexual forces – are, in the Stanley and Oliver scenario, blown momentarily apart. Which, I'm sure you'll agree, is a fairly *neat trick*.

To end then, or rather begin afresh, here Laurel and Hardy, the Comedic Champions, compose. Or rather they sing and yodel to their own tiny sons (played by themselves, Hardy without moustache) in their classic short film *Brats*. I will ask you to sing or hum the song slowly, phonetically, and correctly please, and perhaps to ask a partner to come in half-way through with a harmony.

Go to sleeeep my ba-a-bee, my ba-aa-bee, my baa-aa-aaaa-by.
Goo to sleep my ba-a-bee, my ba-a-bee, my baa-aaa-aa-ay-beeee . . .
Yoddle-eedle-eedle-eedle-ooo, yoodle-eedle-eedle-ooo, yodddle-ee-ee-ee-ee-yoddle-ee-ee-di-deddle-umm . . .
(Courtesy of Hal Roach Studios)

That'd make a soothing end to the day (and this book), don't you think? But nonetheless, perhaps the *very last* words should be a bit less comfortable . . .

FINAL WORDS

There is the story (does anyone know whether it is true or not?) about an old actor on his deathbed.

Leaning gently over the bed to hear the dying man's last poignant words, his colleague asks, 'Is dying hard?'

'No,' groans the actor. 'Dying is easy. *Comedy* is hard.'

Here's Woody Allen, speaking in 1987, shortly before becoming a father for the first time:

'Someone once asked me if my dream was to live on in the hearts of my people. And I said, "I would like to live on *in my apartment* forever!" You drop dead one day, and it means less than nothing if billions of people are singing your praises every day, all day long. You wouldn't *know* it. You'd be better off with a couple of years' extension.'

Stan Laurel's second to last sentence (spoken in real life, off-screen, moments before his demise) was 'I'd rather be skiing than doing this.'

'Do you ski, Mr Laurel?' asked his nurse.

'No,' said Laurel, 'but I'd rather be doing *that* than *this*.'

SELECT BIBLIOGRAPHY

Henri Bergson, *Laughter: An Essay on the Meaning of the Comic* (Macmillan, London, 1911)

André Breton, *Anthologie de l'Humour Noir* (Sagittaire, Paris, 1950)

Michele Brown and Ann O'Connor, *A Dictionary of Women's Wit and Humour* (J. M. Dent and Sons, London, 1984)

Graham Chapman, *A Liar's Autobiography* (Methuen, London, 1980)

John Cleese and Robin Skynner, *Families and How to Survive Them* (Methuen, London, 1983)

Paul Clements, *The Improvised Play: The Work of Mike Leigh* (Methuen, London, 1983)

John Durant and Jonathan Miller (editors), *Laughing Matters: A Serious Look at Humour* (Longman Group, London, 1988)

Martin Esslin, *The Theatre of the Absurd* (Eyre & Spottiswoode, London, 1962)

Dame Edna Everage, *My Gorgeous Life* (Macmillan, London, 1989)

Ronald J. Fields, *W. C. Fields by Himself* (Prentice Hall, New Jersey, 1973)

J. Y. T. Greig, *Psychology of Laughter and Comedy* (Allen & Unwin, London, 1923)

Fred Lawrence Guiles, *Stan: The Life of Stan Laurel* (Stein and Day, New York, 1980)

Freddie Hancock and David Nathan, *Hancock* (William Kimber & Co, London, 1969)

Richard Janko, *Aristotle on Comedy: Towards a Reconstruction of Poetics II* (Duckworth & Co, London, 1984)

Buster Keaton, *My Wonderful World of Slapstick* (Doubleday, New York, 1960)

Arthur Koestler, *Act of Creation* (Hutchinson & Co, London, 1964)

Stephen Leacock, *Nonsense Novels* (McClelland & Stewart, Toronto, 1945)

John McGabe, *Babe: The Life of Oliver Hardy* (Robson, London, 1989)

George Mikes, *Humour in Memoriam* (RKP/André Deutsch, London, 1970)

Monty Python Partnership, *Just the Words* (two volumes) (Methuen, London, 1989)

David Robinson, *Chaplin: His Life and Art* (Paladin, London, 1986)

Alexei Sayle, *Great Bus Journeys of the World* (Methuen, London, 1988)

Michael Sellers, *P.S. I Love You* (Collins, London, 1981)

Dawn Langley Simmons, *Margaret Rutherford: A Blithe Spirit* (Arthur Barker, London, 1983)

Ralph Steadman, *Sigmund Freud* (Penguin Books, London, 1982)

Victoria Wood, *Up to You, Porky*, and *Barmy* (Methuen, London, 1985 and 1987)